FAITHFUL
IN THE
MEANTIME

A Biblical View
of Final Things and
Present Responsibilities

Barry L. Callen

Evangel Publishing House
Nappanee, IN

ISBN: 0-916035-74-3

Library of Congress Card Number: 97-60625

Printed in the United States of America

5   4   3   2   1

DEDICATION

To the Christian saints of all centuries, most of whom already
rest in God, and many of whom yet remain in this life and
are being called to live in hope and be faithful in the
meantime. One who remains is Arlene, the wife
who shares my life and labors and desires
above all to be about the Lord's
business while time remains.

TABLE OF CONTENTS

Preface 9

CHAPTERS

1 The End Is the Beginning 15
　　—A Different Sense of Timing 17
　　—One Word and One Image 21
　　—Balancing Near and Here 24
　　—Asking the Right Questions 26

2 Weary of Speculation! 31
　　—Another Book on "End Things" 32
　　—False Timings of the End 36
　　—What Then Is "Prophecy"? 48
　　—God Will Be Faithful 52
　　—Glancing Ahead 56

3 What Influences Our Interpretation? 61
　　—Place and Tradition 64
　　—Time and History 69
　　—Revelation, Language, and Truth 73
　　—Once in Grace, Always in Grace? 77
　　—Jesus as the Focus .81
　　—The Spirit as the Teacher 83

4   Shifting Systems of Expectation **91**
    —Bankrupt Utopias 94
    —Millennial Models .100
        —Postmillennialism 102
        —Premillennialism 104
        —Dispensationalism 106
        —Amillennialism 108
    —The Role of Historical Context 111
    —The Bottom Line 115

5   Teachings and Significance of Jesus **123**
    —Teaching Discourses in Matthew 124
        —The "How" of the Kingdom 126
        —In the Meantime 128
        —The End and Beyond 131
    —Jesus Inaugurates a New Age 134
    —Did Jesus Predict A. D. 70 or 1948? 142
    —Christ the Resurrected King 147

6   Hope Within History **155**
    —A Distinctively Christian Humanism 157
    —Blessed Are the History-Makers 165
    —Living From and Toward a Vision 172
    —The Church As Eschatological Event 177
    —Will Our Faith Have Children? 183

7   Advent, Easter, Pentecost, and the End **187**
    —The Dark Side of Advent 189
    —God's Then Enables God's Now 197
    —A Theology of Hope 207
    —Downpayment on the Promise 211

8   Images of Christian Hope 217
  —The Past, Last, and Present 219
  —A Second Coming 222
  —A General Resurrection 224
  —A Separation: Hell 228
  —An Absence of the Sea: Heaven 240

9   Thy Tents Shall Be Our Home 245
  —Celebrating In Advance 248
  —Accountability and Mission 254
  —In the Wilderness with God 258
  —End of the Story 263

Select Bibliography 271

Index of Subjects and Persons 275

PREFACE

A Christian book about "final things" should be prefaced by an awareness of the crucial contexts of beginning things and present responsibilities. In the beginning, *God...*(Gen. 1:1). Likewise, the God who existed before the initiation of creation is the same God who will be when creation finally has run its full course and is consummated. This God who is the creator and destiny of all things is known best in Jesus Christ, God with us, the Alpha and Omega, the beginning and the ending. The future intentions of God are approached best in the context of God's defining past with us humans, especially in Israel and in Jesus, and in light of God's present with us, especially in the ministry of the Spirit of Jesus Christ.

Eschatology is a central concern of biblical writers and should be an essential perspective that permeates Christian truth as a whole. Rather than being "the tail end of a doctrinal system,"[1] it is of the essence of the life of faith. Leading representatives of the theology of hope (J. Moltmann, W. Pannenberg, etc.) properly stress both the reality of the consummation yet ahead and the present implications of such a hope. This interactive emphasis of future-present helps to overcome the false dichotomy often allowed to exist between this-worldly and other-worldly orientations of Christian vision and life.

In these pages about final things there is emphasis on the *presentness* of God, the One with us now. The central burden is on

---

[1] Clark Pinnock, in Pinnock and Delwin Brown, *Theological Crossfire* (Grand Rapids: Zondervan, 1990), 221.

current implications of what was and will be. The great challenge of what will be is to learn how to wait properly while God, whose future it is, remains present, active, and purposeful in the todays that lead to tomorrow and draw their perspective and strength from anticipation of the future of the coming God. Accordingly:

> We affirm that Jews and Christians are *partners in waiting*. Christians see in Christ the redemption not yet fully visible in the world, and Jews await the messianic redemption. Christians and Jews together await the final manifestation of God's promise of the peaceable kingdom.[2]

The hardest time is this present time of waiting. It is the time of responsibility when much about the future is still unknown. When one believes in a sure appointment with a future destiny that is to be unspeakably wonderful, all time before that final time demands patience and disciplined faithfulness.

There is danger in the waiting. Having been too long on a hard road, how easy it is to drift into dreaming about the comforts of home that hopefully are just around the next bend—a dreaming that can cause a sleepy sliding off of the road and the failure to ever reach home safely! As the New Testament concludes, it puts on the lips of persecution-weary Christians the prayer, "Come, Lord Jesus!" (Rev. 22:20b). But then the very last words are: "The grace of the Lord Jesus be with all the saints. Amen" (22:21). The "come" is the hope, the reaching for final things that some day will bring justice and joy for the faithful. The "be with" is the plea for the needed wisdom and strength for all believers who must wait and be on mission in the meantime. It is a prayer for the essential fortification of each disciple's commitment to present responsibilities in circumstances still far from ideal.

---

[2]Statement of the General Assembly of the Presbyterian Church (USA), June 1987, as found in *The Theology of the Churches and the Jewish People* (Geneva: WCC Publications, 1988), 118 (emphasis added).

Christian expectations of the future rest securely in the belief that Jesus will come again in glory and power, bringing with him all the joys of the eternal home of believers. Many of these believers, however, are still on the road, still waiting, still enduring the rigors of journeying with their Lord through this troubled world, still facing mission tasks yet incomplete. So the pressing issue of Christian "eschatology" (study of destiny and final things) is not speculating on details of God's coming future, but addressing how best to relate "final things" and "present responsibilities." How should the *then* of faith's expectations relate to the intended *now* of faith's mission?

Two recent publications set the present scene in which this vital question must be answered. First, in 1992 the International Theological Commission of the Roman Catholic Church released the official document *Questions in Eschatology*. Having reaffirmed the classic Christian hopes for resurrection from the dead and the certainty of future life with God for the faithful, it identifies three contemporary cultural and theological factors now threatening the classic hope of the Christian faith in life everlasting. These factors are (1) novel new interpretations of traditional Christian beliefs, (2) secularism with its autonomous vision of humanity and the world without God, and (3) "temporal messianism," the tendency of some Christian theologians to so emphasize political, economic, and gender liberations that they obscure if not deny salvation beyond this life and world.[3]

This present volume has no novel interpretations to offer, is sensitive to but does not join the forces of secularism, and agrees that there is real danger in reducing Christian hope to merely the process of gaining freedom from worldly oppressions. Even so, it will be argued that the Christian's hope for the future must not lead to an abandonment of present mission—which brings us to the sec-

---

[3]For elaboration and analysis of the document *Questions in Eschatology*, see Peter C. Phan, "Contemporary Contexts and Issues in Eschatology," *Theological Studies* 55:3 (September 1994), 507ff.

ond of the recent publications, Jürgen Moltmann's *The Coming of God: Christian Eschatology*. Here is a moving expression of vigorous concern that Christians will abandon the intended *now* of their faith, choosing instead a constant longing for and speculation about final things at the expense of actively engaging in present responsibilities. A believer certainly should not deny the reality and anticipated joy of the future of the faithful; but neither should an affirmation of the future be allowed to undercut the demands of mission today. Moltmann rightly insists:

> Eschatology is always thought to deal with the end, the last day, the last word, the last act: God has the last word. But if eschatology were that and only that, it would be better to turn one's back on it altogether; for "the last things" spoil one's taste for the penultimate ones, and the dreamed of, or hoped for, end of history robs us of our freedom among history's many possibilities, and our tolerance for all the things in history that are unfinished and provisional. We can no longer put up with earthly, limited and vulnerable life, and in our eschatological finality we destroy life's fragile beauty. The person who presses forward to the end of life misses life itself.[4]

Together these two publications lay the groundwork for this present volume. The Christian faith includes a robust hope in that which is yet to be, a glorious future made possible by God. The faith also recognizes the in-the-meantime experience of believers and has much to say about the present responsibilities in this world of those who know their final home to be elsewhere. Today we live in volatile and dangerous times, times often hostile to dedicated followers of Jesus Christ. This time, however, is the very time for which Christ died and to which he now sends his faithful disciples

---

[4]Jürgen Moltmann, *The Coming of God: Christian Eschatology* (Minneapolis: Fortress Press, 1996), x-xi.

who are yet waiting for his final appearing. Those who truly believe and sincerely hope in the soon-coming of God's glorious future are those very believers who are called to be faithful in the meantime.

To be overly preoccupied with the future at the expense of the present is to replace discipleship with dreaming. God, the source of all hope, also is the source of the commission for believers to go into all the world as redemptive forerunners of the future that already is breaking into the present, first through the life, death, and resurrection of Jesus, and now through the ministry of the Spirit of the Christ and the faithfulness of the people of the Christ, the church. To be with God *tomorrow* requires being about God's business *today*! In New Testament thought, serious discipleship takes priority over speculative dispensationalism; the significance of Pentecost far outweighs that of Christian ponderings about purgatory, premillennialism, and the perseverance of the saints. The call from the future of God and the foundation for participating in God's future focus on the present work of the Spirit in fashioning new creations fit for the tasks at hand and the future yet to be.

In the very beginning, the divine Spirit swept across formlessness and a beautiful creation came to be (Gen. 1). At the very end the same Spirit will invite a redeemed creation to come and take the water of eternal life as a gift (Rev. 22:17). Between this beginning and this ending, there is God's people called to be faithful in the meantime. In this crucial interim, new creation is still the work of the Spirit. In fact, the church is seen best as "a continuation of the Spirit-anointed event that was Jesus Christ," a community of the faithful created by the Spirit on the day of Pentecost "to carry on the kingdom ministry of Jesus and be firstfruits of the new humanity he represented."[5] John Wesley said it well:

---

[5]Clark Pinnock, *Flame of Love: A Theology of the Holy Spirit* (InterVarsity Press, 1996), 113.

No, it cannot be; none shall live with God, but he that now lives with God; none shall enjoy the glory of God in Heaven, but he that bears the image of God on earth; none that is not saved from sin here can be saved from hell hereafter; none can see the kingdom of God above, unless the kingdom of God be in him below. Whosoever will reign with Christ in heaven, must have Christ reigning in him on earth. He must have "that mind in him which was in Christ," enabling him "to walk as Christ also walked."[6]

To add to the usefulness of this book a series of questions follows each chapter. They are "Matters Worth Exploring" especially in group settings. Available separately is a *Study Guide* containing all these questions and concise answers to them. For readers of various interests, two search aids have been prepared and are found at the end. One is an *Index of Subjects and Persons* and the other a *Select Bibliography* of the books found most useful in the preparation of this work. With these the book can be useful to those who have strong scholarly interest in the subject of Christian eschatology, while also being accessible to others who may not have technical concern in the subject, but care deeply about being faithful disciples of Christ in these "last days." The author's central concern is that today's church be filled with a biblical hope that fires it for Christian service.

Barry L. Callen
Anderson University
May, 1997

---

[6]Thomas Jackson, ed., *The Works of Rev. John Wesley*, 14 vols. (London: Wesleyan Methodist Book Room, 1829-1831), 10: 364.

Chapter 1

THE END IS THE BEGINNING

※

See, I am making all things new. (Rev. 21:5)

※

This is how Dietrich Bonhoeffer took leave of his fellow prisoner, Payne Best, in Flossenbürg concentration camp as he went to his execution on April 9, 1945: "This is the end—for me the beginning of life."

※

The Christian vision of reality sweeps from creation to consummation, from God saying "Let there be!" to the final divine announcement that "It is enough!" The general biblical story line between this beginning and this end is that God's good creation chose to fall away into sin, that God then chose to intervene in order to redeem and restore, and that this restoration process was highlighted definitively in the first coming of Jesus Christ and will be fully accomplished by Christ's promised return to conclude time itself as we now know it. Many questions surround this simple salvation story, especially questions about what is yet to come. These questions often have divided Christians and sometimes have spawned diverse and even bizarre scenarios of the end times still ahead. In these pages we hope to sort through the most frequent of these questions and give some perspective to the issues.

One central concern is to avoid distracting speculation about details of the future and to focus instead on the intended faithfulness of God's people in the meantime. Embodying in the present the relevance of hope for the future is the burden of the New Testament's message and clearly is the church's mission. Today is hardly a time for more shallow promises and abstract witnesses that carry with them no life evidence of the *present* meaningfulness of *future* expectations.

The terrors faced by humanity in the twentieth century have put the ominous word "apocalypse" on many lips and into the titles of many books and movies. Especially during the decades of the Cold War, people everywhere feared a nuclear apocalypse that was being faced by all the world. The irretrievable annihilation of thousands of plant and animal species by the ruthless industrial exploitation of nature has been called the "ecological apocalypse." Ethnic genocides and dreaded new diseases now stalk the earth, threatening the very foundations of human civilization. What is the credible hope that can survive in all of this? What is the hope that points to an enduring reality beyond all of this—but without abandoning the need to face all current crises constructively in the meantime before hope realizes its final fulfillment beyond this world?

The new generation, now being called Baby Busters or Generation X, features people with a lack of hope. These millions of young adults tend to live only for the moment and often feel disconnected from others. They are pessimistic about the future and have learned not to trust anyone who offers absolute answers on major questions about life and the future.[1] If Christianity has the right answers, they often ask, why can it not keep its own house in order? Is not the world of Christians divided, scandal-ridden, and escapist, just more of the problem? They deserve an answer. The biblical answer centers in a right understanding of Christian eschatology—and then, of course, a putting of that understanding into beneficial practice in today's world. In the biblical view, a focus on

---

[1]See Todd Hahn and David Verhaagen, *Reckless Hope: Understanding and Reaching Baby Busters* (Grand Rapids: Baker Books, 1996).

final things is never to be disconnected from a commitment to present responsibilities in light of those final things.

A Different Sense of Timing

The Christian community was launched initially by a pattern of vigorous preaching, the content of which sometimes is called the "eschatological kerygma." The first Christian evangelists were sure that they knew what time it was in God's eyes. It was the beginning of the end, the bursting forth of a new age in the "last days." C. H. Dodd, in a book of far-reaching significance in the field of Christian eschatology,[2] summarized this early Christian preaching in six points.

1. The age of fulfillment has dawned (Acts 2:16, 3:18, 3:24). The messianic age envisioned by the Hebrew prophets was now present.

2. The arrival of this new age has taken place through the ministry, death, and resurrection of Jesus. All had taken place according to the plan and foreknowledge of God (Acts 2:23).

3. By virtue of the resurrection, Jesus has been exalted to the right hand of God as messianic head of the new Israel (Acts 2:33-36, 3:13).

4. The Holy Spirit, now present among believers in the Christ, is the sign of Christ's present power and glory. "Being therefore exalted at the right hand of God, and having received from the Father the promise of the Holy Spirit, he has poured out this which you see and hear" (Acts 2:33).

---

[2]C. H. Dodd, *The Apostolic Preaching and Its Development* (London: Hodder and Stoughton, 1936), 38-45.

5. The new messianic age will soon reach its consummation by the great event of the return of the Christ. "That he [God] may send the Messiah appointed for you, that is, Jesus, who must remain in heaven until the time of universal restoration that God announced long ago through his holy prophets" (Acts 3:21).

6. The immediate result of all the above was the urgent appeal for repentance, accompanied by the offer of forgiveness, the Holy Spirit, and the promise of salvation, the very life of the Age to Come for all who would choose by faith to enter the elect community of the Christ. "Repent, and be baptized every one of you in the name of Jesus Christ so that your sins may be forgiven; and you will receive the gift of the Holy Spirit" (Acts 2:38).

Therefore, the appropriate sense of timing among Christians informed by apostolic foundations involves direct awareness that, in Jesus Christ, the time is *now*. God's primary promises have been fulfilled. God's Son now reigns and is coming again. God's Spirit now is available as a gift of grace to form and empower the church for its mission in the world. The call is to repent, receive, and become part of the new creation that now functions through the ministry of the Spirit as an advance taste of the Age to Come, that Age of God already here in the crucified and risen Jesus and soon to come in the return of the victorious Jesus.

Given this historic core of gospel proclamation, what is the most important question for the church to answer today? What is of primary importance and what is only secondary, merely speculative, even distracting from the current challenges of Christian discipleship? We gladly join Irenaeus, one of the earliest Christian theologians, in insisting that the future is not a minor category or an optional addendum to the larger body of Christian teaching.[3] Instead, it is essential to all aspects of Christian faith and practice. As Thomas Oden says, careful inquiry into the coming consummation of God's design is a "cohesive" task which "highlights the final hope that frames and radically contextualizes all other temporal affirmations." This task recognizes that "all the vital energies of the prophets, apostles, and martyrs focus on events yet to come that will illumine all present life."[4] Therefore, a focus on the future is crucial and should not be a matter of mere curiosity for Christians, but a foundation on which responsible discipleship "in the meantime" can rest. Too often, however, what is crucial is allowed to become an obstacle to the very thing that it is meant to support— present discipleship. The timing most crucial is God's *now*—in light of God's past actions and with confidence in God's coming victory over all that fouls creation and resists the divine will.

All people are aware of the human calendar. What is categorized on this calendar as the second millennium A.D. (at least in the Western world) is about to end with the year 2,000. Much more important for Christians, however, is another "calendar," a completely different sense of timing, one related to the human calendar in a way little understood and often debated. Assuming that a truly sovereign God exists and has an overarching plan for the progress and final outcome of human history, the key timing question asks where we now are on this more elusive divine time-calendar. Given the teachings found in the New Testament, and particularly as the beginning of the twenty-first century dawns, what might it mean to claim that "the end is at hand!"? Jesus, after all, came two millennia ago announcing exactly that (Mark 1:15). Further, what does it mean to be faithful in the meantime?

Christians certainly do not agree about the details of what lies ahead—although all do have confidence in the God who is sover-

---

[3]As quoted in *Ante-Nicene Fathers* (1895-96, reprint, Grand Rapids: Eerdmans, 1979, I:5236-67).

[4]Thomas Oden, *Life in the Spirit* (San Francisco: Harper, 1992), 368-369.

eign over all tenses of time. A proper understanding of past, present, and future is crucial. Jesus at the last supper with his disciples instructed them to participate with each other, to *do* this in *remembrance* of him *until he comes* again (1 Cor. 11:26; cf. Lk. 22:19). For the Christian life, therefore, memory is central. Hope is to be pervasive. But the emphasis, the key to interrelating the three tenses of time is the present "do." In every present time faithful Christians are to be doing as Christ instructs, informed by the past of God's actions and assured by the expectation of what God yet will do. The proper posture for Christians is to be standing in the tension of the times. Carl Braaten has summarized this well:

> The kingdom of God is both the foundation of the church and the goal of the world. Therefore, we have and we hope; we give thanks and sigh for more. Living in the tension of such a posture, we cannot be religious dropouts with an idle faith and a passive hope. The hope of the kingdom is an invitation to work while it is day, to be active in love, to sow the seeds of the word and spread the flame of the Spirit.[5]

The many issues involved are almost all controversial and lie beyond the usual human ways of knowing. Therefore, as I write here, I share the sentiments of an earlier writer:

> In this work I am seeking to sort out the teachings of the Bible and the positive contributions they offer to our faith. It is not my intention to erect a system, to set dates, or to make spectacular identifications. Nor do I intend to hurl ridicule or invective on those Bible stu-

---

[5] Carl Braaten, *The Flaming Center: A Theology of Christian Mission* (Philadelphia: Fortress Press, 1977), 43. John 9:4 reports the instruction of Jesus: "We must work the works of him who sent me, while it is day...." The moving autobiography of David Elton Trueblood is titled *While It Is Day* (Harper & Row, 1974).

dents with whose methods I may differ and with whose conclusions I may disagree.[6]

I do not intend to attack and ridicule the impassioned pronouncements of others; but neither do I have any intention of being either neutral or ambiguous. Pure neutrality is hardly possible and ambiguity would be of little interest or help to anyone.

One Word and One Image

Allow me to introduce a word and then an image. I urge that the reader not be "turned off" prematurely either by the word or the image, even though both get much bad press and often are misunderstood. The word is *eschatology*. From the Greek *eschaton*, in its narrow sense it means a consideration of the end or end-related matters (signs of the times, second coming of Christ, judgment, millennium, heaven, hell, etc.). More broadly viewed, it has to do with the goal of history toward which the entire biblical story moves. This includes all in the past and present that relates to the achievement of the restoring goal that God intends, flowing together as an interrelated whole from creation to the new creation, by way of the divine renewing of fallen humanity. I trust that the frequent use of the word eschatology in this book will make its biblical meaning clearer and more significant for Christians seeking to live the life of faith in the present. The goal of God for the future is, in some real sense, to be a functioning reality even now.

Part of the complexity of the use of the word eschatology is that it can and often does have two meanings. The "end" can mean either "the ceasing to be of what was" or "the perfecting of what was once begun." Put another way, time as we know it will stop one day and/or what we now know in part and have become in Christ eventually will reach their fullness, their intended goal. To illustrate these two meanings of "eschatology" in relation to this

---

[6]William Sanford LaSor, *The Truth About Armageddon* (San Francisco: Harper & Row, 1982), 7.

book, by the time the reader has finished reading the book (come to the *last page*), I trust that my intent in writing it will have fully *matured* in the mind and present life of the reader.

Now for the image too often related to eschatology and its enthusiasts across the centuries. Cartoonists often have portrayed anyone absorbed with eschatological matters as wild-eyed and mindless alarmists carrying signs on their backs reading "The END Is Coming!" Ever since the time of Amos, prophets have cried in the streets, "Prepare to meet thy God!" (Amos 4:12). Today those carrying such sobering messages include non-eccentric scientists, philosophers, economists, politicians, and environmentalists. Future shock has set in as the twentieth century ends. We all stand aghast at the rapid changes all about us, changes that have both great possibilities and frightening potential.

Are we humans about to enter an unbelievably wonderful golden age or an indescribably terrible dark night—or neither? Or, as a critic like Karl Marx charged, is Christian eschatology just so much socially destructive superstition? Does it merely soothe troubled people with baseless future hopes, distracting them from the urgent task of transforming the present world? Do the promises of eschatology offer comforting hope for the distant future that gives up on the present and thus, by default, allows the terrible suffering of many people to go on and the outrageous luxury of others to remain passively unchallenged? For Christians, in other words, does the future expectation of the faith motivate and nurture present discipleship or does it encourage a socially irresponsible escapism?

Now even the utopian societies that sought to base themselves on the dream of Marx have fallen on hard times. Denial of God's future obviously does not guarantee a better present. Biblical faith persists and may not be as irrelevant to life now as Marx charged. A large segment of the American public still clings to the conviction that the Bible offers the key to understanding human history and its final end at the hand of God. This is true even—and maybe especially—in these times when the "secular" mindset of the general culture seems so alien to any such religious conviction.[7] This book, then, is about a Christian hope that should not and need not distract believers from transformed and transforming life in the present. It explores how a linking of history now and the ultimate end later is crucial to how a Christian should think, hope, and live.

The good news in Jesus Christ is that faith in him is not merely a thing of the present, nor a thing of the future. Rather, "it announces the future with the power to shape the present."[8] Christian eschatology, understood rightly in its wholeness and in the context of its own purpose, is essentially about God's intent to create all things new. It is, says Jürgen Moltmann, "the remembered hope of the raising of the crucified Christ, so it talks about beginning afresh in the deadly end." The end of Christ, the crucifixion, was actually the beginning of Christ, the resurrection. Therefore, Christian eschatology follows this christological pattern— "in the end is the beginning."[9]

In some sense the end surely is at hand! Human calendars are marking off the months left before a whole millennium gasps its last. What will the twenty-first century be like? Will there even be another century? May it be that God's timetable and patience are near *their* end? Before another human generation has grown to maturity, will history be interrupted by a tribulation, a rapture, a divinely-initiated millennium, and/or the second coming of Christ? Or are these not priority questions for present pondering?

The stakes are high. Some Christians open their Bibles, check the week's headlines, and proclaim with great confidence

---

[7]See, for example, Paul Boyer, *When Time Shall Be No More: Prophecy Belief in Modern American Culture* (Cambridge, Mass.: Belknap Press of Harvard University Press, 1992).

[8]Carl Braaten, *Eschatology and Ethics* (Minneapolis: Augsburg Publishing House, 1974), 70.

[9]Jürgen Moltmann, *The Coming of God: Christian Eschatology* (Minneapolis: Fortress Press, 1996), xi.

that they know what the human race soon will face at God's hand. Other Christians, also with their Bibles wide open, are far more modest in what they are able to find in its pages about the details of the immediate or distant future. One thing is quite clear. Some two thousand years ago, when Jesus first arrived in flesh among us, the burden of his preaching was that *in his own ministry* the Kingdom of God *already had come very near*. "The time has come," he announced in Galilee. "The Kingdom of God is near. Repent and believe the good news!" (Mark 1:15). Christian eschatology, therefore, is primarily about the *Last One*, the One whom the New Testament calls the beginning and the end (Rev. 22:13). Jesus Christ is the realization of God's creating, redeeming, and consummating purposes (Jn. 12:31; Heb. 1:2; 2 Tim. 1:10). To know Christ is to know that now is the time to be about God's business!

Balancing Near and Here

What, then, is an appropriate Christian view of "end things"? How should believers balance what is hoped to be *near* with what is known to be *already here*? How does that for which Christians hope relate to the mission of the church in the present evil age before the curtain of history finally falls? What should be made of biblical material like the Book of Revelation, sometimes called the "Apocalypse" of John? *Apocalypsis* (another key Greek word) has the root meaning of "taking off a covering, laying bare, making naked or plain." Such writing apparently was intended to reveal, to make the hidden more obvious. How do we deal with biblical material intending to clarify that nonetheless leaves so many modern readers sharply divided about its real meaning?

No one deals with such questions in a vacuum. This writer admits to being influenced by elements of the Pietist, Anabaptist, and Wesleyan theological traditions, and thus is weary of the constant speculation by many biblical interpreters about specific events and even timetables associated with the end of the world (see chapter 2). Surely the primary focus of the gospel of Jesus Christ is on the discipleship responsibilities of the here and now— and for the sake of the world's salvation now as well as at the time beyond time. If Christians would only recognize humbly the forces outside the faith itself that so easily shape biblical interpretation regarding these complex matters (chapter 3), be on guard against the shifting systems of expectation that frequently tempt believers to lose their way (chapter 4), and rightly link the birth, teachings, death, and resurrection of Jesus to the coming end (chapter 5), then disciples of the Master could again bring the power of their future hope to bear redemptively on the human history that yet remains (chapter 6).

We who would be about the Lord's business today always must relate properly the first advent of Jesus and our future expectations related to his coming again (chapter 7). We must have our hearts and heads filled with the transforming images of true Christian hope (chapter 8) and live productive lives of faith in the wilderness of this present evil world (chapter 9). The real challenge is to be faithful in the meantime.

Yes, the end, the Kingdom of God, in some real sense is at hand! This has been the case ever since the appearance of Jesus two millennia ago. Not only will Jesus Christ come again some day, but his birth long ago launched the "last days." The Holy Spirit was poured out in the last days (Acts 2:17) and even the very first Christians were living in the final time, the concluding phase of God's salvation plan still being played out in what is left of our human history. It is relatively unimportant whether some day there will be one or two resurrections or whether a pre-tribulation or post-tribulation position is preferable biblically. Of vital importance is being clear about the meaning of God in Jesus Christ and the significance of the ministry of the Spirit of God for both the present and the future.

After all, Jesus himself is the "Alpha and the Omega, the first and the last, the beginning and the end" (Rev. 22:13). The story of Jesus constitutes the heart of Christian belief about first and last things. It is the Christ who stands at the center of all authentic Christian eschatology. He fulfills God's redemptive goal "*for* us, especially during his earthly ministry; *in* us, in his work through the Holy Spirit; and *with* us, particularly at his second coming."[10] The Christian life is lived between being presently "in Christ" and eventually "with Christ" in the fullness of his victorious presence. The old age has been judged by Christ and already is passing away, but the new age has not yet been fully brought about. The tyranny of death has been crushed by the empty grave of Jesus, but mortality and depravity still remain active in the world. The powers antagonistic to God are disarmed and defeated, but they not yet destroyed. To be Christian is to live between evil's defeat and its destruction and to be a living sign of the victory of God already emerging.

The reader should understand that, as developed here, the general subject of eschatology is much more than reflections on things *yet to come*. Christian eschatology involves things *yet to be done* by those people inspired by hope and willing to be faithful in the meantime. Eschatology affirms God's coming consummation of all things by a faith already well informed by what (Who) already has come, Jesus Christ. A faithful focusing on Christ both nurtures confidence in tomorrow and commissions disciples for the urgent tasks of today. There is an anticipatory aspect to authentic Christian eschatology. In Christ's resurrection, the expected end has already occurred in proleptic fashion, meaning that the end has been realized in a significant way that impacts the present without precluding its final and universal realization in the future.

Asking the Right Questions

A key problem with much that parades itself as Christian eschatology is that interpreters frequently lead with the wrong

---

[10]Adrio König, *The Eclipse of Christian Eschatology* (Grand Rapids: Eerdmans, 1989), viii.

questions—and then proceed to answer them with great confidence. They tend to ask: When will Christ return? Exactly what will happen just before and after the second coming? Which millennial theory should excite us the most? Is the modern State of Israel the full and final fulfillment of the Old Testament promises? Which contemporary religious, political, or military figure likely will turn out to be the Antichrist? Is the "mark of the beast" your e-mail address or social security number?

I propose a different set of primary questions, a set that I judge will lead more dependably to the heart of the Christian gospel and undergird what the church is to be and do in the meantime, between what we know of Jesus from the New Testament and what we anticipate concerning Jesus when time is no more. Specifically: How can contemporary Christians acquire an adequate understanding of the Christian faith and then engage in its effective embodiment in this world? How can the substance of the faith become a driving force in the service of the church's mission until Jesus returns? How can believers live in the reality of *now*, with adequate faith roots in the church's *yesterday*, roots that are inspired by hope in the *coming tomorrow*, and out of that past and hope provide the proper vision for a *transformed today*?

That which *will be* is to make a difference *in the meantime* through the servant faithfulness of the church, the body of Christ yet on earth. The first Christian community did not experience the resurrection of Jesus only as the ground of hope for the future; they received it as the stimulus for spreading and representing the gospel in the present. The end is at hand! In our very midst is the presence of the Risen Christ who is Alpha and Omega. "But if it is by the Spirit of God that I cast out demons, then the Kingdom of God has come to you" (Jesus, Matt. 12:28). At this very moment, the Spirit of the Christ ministers to enable mission in this world—until the time of mission ends and a better world arrives. A proper looking forward toward God's *then* requires and helps equip for serving faithfully in the *now* of God's world.

The following pages are devoted to an extended exploration of this crucial then-now relationship and the responsibility it places on all who would be faithful in the meantime. We join gratefully in the prayer found in the final lines of the New Testament, "Amen. Come Lord Jesus!" (Rev. 22:20b). We also, however, resonate loudly with the very last words of the New Testament, "The grace of the Lord Jesus be with all the saints" (Rev. 22:21). Beyond the two "comings" of Jesus (once humbly in ancient Bethlehem and finally in great triumph before the eyes of all the world), it is crucial to join the New Testament in focusing on both the two "comings" and on the two "becomings." These are reported in John 1:14 and 1 Corinthians 15:45. "The Word *became* flesh." "The last Adam *became* a life-giving Spirit." God came in Jesus to bring life in the present of our fleshly lives. In our view, therefore, the hope of Jesus coming again should strengthen our present experience of life-giving divine grace so that, in the meantime, we can be faithful agents of God in this troubled world that he loves and for which Christ died.

Matters Worth Exploring

1. Does the subject of "eschatology" peak your interest or "turn you off"? Why?

2. What is the essential meaning of "eschatology" in the biblical context?

3. What are the right questions to ask in first approaching the whole arena of Christian eschatology?

4. The first Christian preachers had a core of truths that formed their constant message. As they understood things, what time was it in God's eyes and actions? Should this same core of truths and sense of God's timing be the center of Christian preaching today?

5. What is a good way to balance the "near" and "here" of Christian hope? How is such balancing crucial for Christian mission in our troubled times?

6. Is it true that most young adults of today ("Baby Busters" or "Generation X") have tended to lose hope for a better life now and for any hope in an ultimate future that will be real and good?

Chapter 2

WEARY OF SPECULATION!

✵

Jesus informed his curious and anxious disciples:
"No one knows about the day or the hour." (Matt. 25:36)

✵

Hope as the embracing theological category has to be
freed from the wreckage of Christian history.[1]

✵

While Trinitarian and Christological doctrines have received detailed attention and definition in the great councils and creeds of church history, eschatological teachings have been only broadly affirmed without ever being explicitly developed and sanctioned as "orthodox."[2] There has been a widespread reserve about anything that verges on mere speculation and has no consensus status in the larger Christian community.

Possibly the last thing Jesus said to his first disciples involved a caution about their already obvious tendency to speculate about the future because of their own curiosity or anxiety. At the time of his ascension, the disciples asked him when he would restore the Kingdom to Israel. His answer? "It is not for you to know times or

---

[1]Jürgen Moltmann, *The Coming of God: Christian Eschatology* (Minneapolis: Fortress Press, 1996), xv.

[2]The Apostles' Creed, for instance, affirms only that (1) Jesus will come to judge the living and the dead and (2) there will be a resurrection of the dead and eternal life.

seasons, which the Father has fixed by his own authority" (Acts 1:6-7). Having said this, Jesus shifted the intended focus of the lives of his disciples to their mission of bringing good news to the world in the meantime, in whatever time there turns out to be before time as it is now known will end.

The fact is that Christians over the centuries frequently have been curious and anxious about what lies ahead. They often have not hesitated to speculate about the future and even develop detailed schemes about what is yet to come. Clearly the resulting frequent cycle of anticipation followed by disappointment, a cycle that has plagued the church's hoping over the centuries, has been a negative to Christian witness in the world. If only Jesus could be taken seriously, both in his own reserve about detailed future knowledge and in his own preference for focus on the commission given to his church for life and ministry in the meantime. This is why Jürgen Moltmann insists that "hope as the embracing theological category has to be freed from the wreckage of Christian history."[3]

Another Book on "End Things"

Too much already has been said about the presumed details of the future that God surely and maybe soon will bring about. Why, then, bother? Why write yet another book on the subject of "end things"? Is it not the case that the truth about the future is virtually anyone's guess and that such guessing, so often turned into arrogant confidence by self-appointed "prophets," has been very divisive and distracting in Christian church history? Yes, this is the sad case. Even so, there are important reasons why another look is worthwhile—at least, a book of a certain kind.

First, another book is worth the effort because, over the centuries and in most if not all nations, someone's prophetic visions of the future have shaped public policy, justified wars, and either undergirded or exploded national morale. Often a preoccupation with prophecy has flourished among oppressed or merely bored

---

[3]Moltmann, op. cit., xv.

populations, taking people to another time and place that liberates them from the present and opens for them new doors of perceived possibility. A widespread valuing of prophecy persists today in part because the environment that breeds it also persists. One should not be ignorant of that which motivates so many people and governments. W. A. Visser't Hooft put it this way: "Tell me what your eschatology is and I will tell you what your attitude is in relation to church, state, and society."[4]

Second, in a specifically Christian context, surely something about this subject goes beyond insignificance and mere speculation. The Bible addresses various aspects of "eschatology" (study of "end things"). Death, for instance, is a subject of universal concern and lies at the very foundation of Christian theology (the death and resurrection of Jesus, e. g., with the subsequent call for believers to die to an old life and be newly alive in Christ—Galatians 2:20). The question of death's meaning is inextricably bound to the question of life's meaning. As often has been said, until one has come to terms with death, one is not yet prepared to really live. Everyone is involved directly with this subject. Can something helpful be said?

If one grants genuine authority to biblical revelation, a fresh look at this whole subject area surely is warranted, especially in a time of so much apocalyptic anxiety, "prophetic" proclamation, and public confusion. Without question, many attitudes that a Christian has about society, the church's mission, education, current events, and ultimate destiny are influenced deeply by that believer's perspective on eschatological matters. Numerous related questions inevitably arise. Will the Spirit through a faithful church succeed in bringing real renewal to our world? Or is the second coming of Jesus the only answer? What about the modern State of Israel? When will judgment and justice finally appear on the earth—or will it never? Is there a hell to be feared and a heaven to

---

[4]W. A. Visser't Hooft, *The Kingship of Christ* (N. Y.: Harper & Brothers, 1948), 83.

be gained? And what does all of this have to do with the real-life calling of every Christian?

The subject of eschatology may not be easy and is full of perversion potential, but it hardly can be ignored. When not ignoring it, however, discipline is required to not overreach what has been revealed biblically. We must recall that the prototypical human sin was the fateful attempt in the ancient garden to penetrate forbidden knowledge (Gen. 2:17). Faith is called to live by hope, a living hope that is prepared to trust the God of the future in the midst of human *unknowing* of much detail about that future. Balancing a hoping by faith with the much that is yet unknown tests the patience of many. A little story helps illustrate the point. A doctor was busy with a patient when his assistant burst into the room.

"Doctor!" she exclaimed. "You know that man to whom you just gave a clean bill of health? He was walking out of the office, and he dropped dead! What should I do?"

"Turn him around so it looks like he was walking in," answered the doctor.

Isn't that about the way so much of "biblical prophecy" gets handled in many of the popular books and by many of the more colorful preachers who confidently tell us so much about the future? First they make an attention-grabbing prediction, then all the hearers wait to see what actually happens. If it turns out that the prediction is the opposite of what finally does happen, the clever modern-day "prophet" just turns things around somehow and keeps the freshly revised predictions sounding dramatic, urgent, and still believable. The result lies somewhere between a mere media game pandering to a hungry religious consumerism and an honest but overzealous reading of the related biblical texts.

The point deserving to be made, of course, is not that believers ignore anything that the Bible actually teaches about the past, present, or future. Rather, the legitimate challenges as believers are (1) to be appropriately modest in human claims to divine knowledge and (2) to handle properly the biblical revelation in our hands.

We beleaguered humans seem so anxious to know God's future that we are prone to speculate, system build ("computer model" eschatology), see what may not be there, relate it to the headline in the day's newspaper, and make rash claims that often grab an anxious audience, then fall flat—or require subtle rearranging to keep them faced the right way and sounding up-to-date and still believable.

On the other hand, the proverbial baby of true prophecy must not accidentally get thrown out with the dirty bathwater of undisciplined biblical interpretation and future speculation based on the dubious results. "The mainline moderate-to-liberal pulpit," observes Thomas Long, "has been so embarrassed by the eyeball-rolling fanatics on the fundamentalist fringe and still so captivated by a present-tense, let's-get-real, demythologized gospel that eschatological language has either ceased altogether or become hopelessly vague."[5] Christians do indeed need and have a hope-giving vision of the future that is rightly found in the biblical revelation. The task is not to abort the hope, but to refine one's perspective on the hope.

Such refinement apparently has been going on from the church's very beginning. The New Testament writers themselves probably did not expect the second coming of Christ to be delayed by 2,000 years or more. Rather, the earliest expectation was that the finalization of the plan of God could happen at any time and likely would be relatively soon. The early Christians were right at least in the substance of their hope in the second coming of Jesus and in the urgency of its demand for immediate mission and serious discipleship. They set the pace for most believers to follow in being prone to think of their own times as the final times, chronologically speaking. Calendar misreadings of the timing of the Christian hope have been around from the church's beginning and show no evidence of ending in our present time.

---

[5]Thomas Long, "Preaching God's Future," in Barry Callen, ed., *Sharing Heaven's Music* (Nashville: Abingdon Press, 1995), 197.

False Timings of the End

You just had to have been there to have experienced the fear that spread temporarily. Herbert George Wells was responsible for a radio drama called "War of the Worlds," a striking scientific fantasy first written in 1898. The Halloween broadcast on October 30, 1938, sounded so shockingly real that many thousands of listeners literally panicked. The intent had not been to disrupt society with frightening unreality, but to alert the public to the dangers and opportunities that lay hidden in the technological world coming to birth in the twentieth century. Even so, the world of the late 1930s was arming for an awful war and people were desperately hoping for the best—and poised to believe the worst, including that a sudden invasion was possible by aggressive beings from Mars!

Numerous people in the "modern" twentieth century, rather than gullibly accepting as real what was not even intended to be such, have deliberately passed off as a sure scenario their own agnostic vision of the coming future. So many false claims about the future have been part of human history that skepticism is judged the best stance. There is an old Chinese proverb that says, "To prophesy is extremely difficult—especially with respect to the future!" There also is the warning in the Hebrew Scriptures (Deut. 18:20-22) anticipating failed prophecies made even with good intention in God's name.

There is, however, another stance, one that avoids skepticism about all faith visions of the future and also resists rash speculation related to such visions. Many Christian believers of all centuries have insisted that the Christian task is not to engage in fruitless speculation, but in Christ-like living. John Wesley, for example, refused to be caught up in the popular prophecies of his day. In one letter (1788) he comments on the prediction of a Bible scholar that a millennial reign of Christ on earth would begin in 1836: "I have no opinion at all upon the head: I can determine nothing at all about it. These calculations are far above, out of my sight. I have only one thing to do, to save my soul, and those that hear me."[6]

Wesley aside, many Christians today insist that belief in God's faithfulness, and thus the enduring hope of believers, is not enough. They see much more in the biblical account that gives them a virtual roadmap of the end-times. They also see current events reflecting what they understand the Bible to have predicted long ago. Here are a few examples of the presumed beginning-of-the-end events that often are highlighted today: the proliferation of chemical and nuclear weapons among terrorist groups (the "secret power of lawlessness" to be unleashed, 2 Thess. 2); the European Community is fast becoming a reality (the "revival" of the Roman Empire, the "ten toes/nations" in Daniel 7); world economies have become inextricably linked through the World Trade Organization and other international standardizations of law (the consolidation of "buying and selling," Rev. 13); and recent global networking in cyberspace that has thrust businesses worldwide into a crypto-graphic "brave new world" (the "increase of knowledge" spoken of in Dan. 12).

Regardless of how much all this linkage of ancient images and current events may be bad biblical interpretation (see chapter three), and may be more human anxiety and speculation than real biblical prophecy, it is nonetheless common and tempting. Hal Lindsey's *The Late Great Planet Earth*[7] sold over 15 million copies in the 1970s, and dozens of similar apocalyptic bestsellers cram the prophecy shelves of religious bookstores today. Their content is dramatic, urgent-sounding, and apparently even market driven. If the authors do not write mainly for profit, at least the Christian bookstores feature them for maximum sale when the topic is "hot"—like in the weeks during and right after the Gulf War in the early 1990s. Timothy George has referred to the dan-

---

[6]John Wesley, *The Works of John Wesley*, 3rd ed., 14 vols. (reprint of 1872 ed., Kansas City: Beacon Hill Press of Kansas City, 1978-79), 1:23.

[7]Hal Lindsey, *The Late Great Planet Earth* (Grand Rapids: Zondervan, 1970). See also his more recent *The 1980s: Countdown to Armageddon* and *Planet Earth—2000 A. D.* (Palos Verdes, CA: Western Front, Ltd., 1994).

ger of trivializing Christ's second coming into mere "fodder for fanatics" and an "eschatological itch" that occasionally has induced Christian escapism from responsible engagement with surrounding culture.[8] Surely the itch will get most enticing and almost intolerable as the end of the twentieth century now approaches—an obvious time for many to anticipate the end of all things.

Concerning the frequently sad result of unleashed speculation, Wendy Murray Zoba observes: "The eschatological titillation of some has caused the disaffection of others and the confusion of many."[9] Mark Noll warns that modern-day "prophets" often tend to be "blown about by every wind of apocalyptic speculation" and sometimes are even "enslaved to the cruder spirits of populist science."[10] Thomas Long sees a distortion of biblical prophecy when "every tremor in Israel, every leadership change in Russia, every currency crisis in the Common Market, every war rumor in the Middle East lets loose a riptide of Armageddon anxiety." This hair-trigger distortion, he rightly judges, betrays "both the historical naivetè and the essentially narcissistic assumptions that lie behind fundamentalist eschatology—namely, that the whole of God's hidden plan for the world...and the sum of all biblical prophecy have to do with me and my generation."[11]

Some of these ill-considered assumptions are imaginative but harmless, some curious and a little distracting, some potentially dangerous. Consider this, for instance:

One rather frightening by-product of this process of interpretation is that it is so easy to *create* the very sit-

[8]Timothy George, "The Lure of the Apocalypse," *Christianity Today* (June 19, 1995), 16-17.

[9]Wendy Murray Zoba, "Future Tense," *Christianity Today* (October 2, 1995), 19.

[10]Mark Noll, *The Scandal of the Evangelical Mind* (Grand Rapids: Eerdmans, 1994).

[11]Thomas Long, in Callen, op. cit., 196-197.

uation which is being described so that the interpretation given brings about its own fulfillment. Russia, for example, is to be destroyed by nuclear attack—and scripture must be fulfilled! It needs little imagination to understand the consequences of such a belief, especially if held with deep conviction by politicians and the military who have the power to press the button and to execute the judgment thus prophesied and foreordained.[12]

One can see the appearance of ill-considered assumptions and failed anticipations very early in the young life of the church (1 Thess. 4:13—5:11; 2 Thess. 2:1-11) and then early in church history (Montanism, latter half of the second century). Will the end be today and which hill should we climb to get the best view of the coming Christ? Who will speak for God in the last days—and might it just be me? Prophetic speculation has also been a part of various periods in the subsequent history of the church. Several examples will be sufficient to make the point. One happened in 999, the other in 1844.

The approaching turn of the millennium in 999 A. D. was widely believed by European Christians to be the moment at which Satan would be unleashed (Rev. 20:7-8) and the world would dissolve into ashes. One thousand years after the birth of Christ was to be the death of history. On that New Year's Eve in Rome, Pope Sylvester II celebrated what the faithful believed would be the last midnight mass of human history. Anxious and repenting crowds flooded the streets. Christians all across Europe donated their homes and lands to the poor as final acts of contrition. In Jerusalem that fateful night thousands of pilgrims milled about, some hysterical, all waiting for the End. Finally the moment came—*but there was no fire from heaven.* Amazingly, a new day soon dawned!

---

[12]D. S. Russell, *Apocalyptic: Ancient and Modern* (Philadelphia: Fortress, 1978), 64.

Rather than the end, disciples of Jesus found themselves still living in the waiting time.

The major theological work of John Wesley in the eighteenth century was focused primarily on issues of salvation, not eschatology. Regarding the latter, he expressed caution and lack of personal certainty about specific future expectations and especially date-setting.[13] Even so, in his *Notes* on the Book of Revelation he freely incorporated the speculative pattern of Johann Bengel concerning Revelation 4-20. The earlier German scholar had understood this portion of the Apocalypse to prophesy in detail the history of the church from the first century to the return of Christ (which Bengel predicted would be in 1836). The language of calamities was thought to be describing the Germanic invasions and fall of the Roman Empire, followed by the spread of Islam and the severe persecutions of true Christian believers before and after the Protestant Reformation of the sixteenth century. The Antichrist was said to be the Roman papacy of the Middle Ages.[14] While it all made sense as a coherent system of thought, Bengel nevertheless was clearly wrong, at least in his time assumption about the return of Christ (1836) and probably about some or all of his identifications of apocalyptic symbols and historical events.

Another such miscalculation occurred in nineteenth-century America. William Miller, a New England farmer and Baptist preacher, thought he had cracked the code for determining when Christ would return. The world would end between 1843 and 1844, the timing determined by use of the Jewish calendar and Daniel 8:14 ("Unto two thousand and three hundred days; then shall the

---

[13]See John Wesley, *The Works of John Wesley*, 3rd ed., 14 vols. (reprint of 1872 ed., Kansas City: Beacon Hill Press of Kansas City, 1978), 12:319.

[14]It was noted by various interpreters that the Latin title of the Pope, *Vicarius Filii Dei*, Vicar of the Son of God, had the numerical value of 666 (cf. Rev. 13:18). Many earlier Christians had believed the Antichrist to be Emperor Nero whose name *Neron Kesar* also had the 666 value. Similar observations have led to a range of other Antichrist identifications over the centuries.

sanctuary be cleansed").[15] When this time passed without incident, the whole prophetic affair became known as the "Great Disappointment." Miller is estimated to have had as many as 100,000 expectant followers, many of whom went back to their original church affiliations after the failed prophecy, while some formed "adventist" churches, the largest of which became the Seventh-day Adventist Church. Early Adventists thought of themselves as modern Israel wandering through a new wilderness toward the heavenly promised land. It was natural for them to theorize that the forty years of Israel's time in the desert would be duplicated in their own experience—thus focusing fresh expectation of Christ's second coming on the year 1884, another failed apocalyptic anticipation.[16] These failures of "millennium arithmetic" may have brought disappointment, but they did little to impede the rapid advance later in the nineteenth century of a different variation of futurist premillennialism now known as dispensationalism (see chapter four).

Although quite different in character, yet another misappropriation of apocalyptic symbolism also occurred later in the nineteenth century. In part it was in reaction to one prominent advocate of the general Adventist tradition. This example of misappropriation did not predict the exact year that Jesus would return and the world would end. Rather, it employed an apocalyptic vision to inspire Christians to seek major church renewal in the face of the expected soon-coming Christ. While this movemental environment was serious discipleship and not prophetic frenzy, it soon failed nonetheless as an assured prophetic validation of movement identity.

The movement in question this time was the Church of God (Anderson), inspired by the burden of Daniel Warner for the unity

---

[15]See William Miller, *Evidence from Scripture and History of the Second Coming of Christ, About the Year 1843* (published in 1836).

[16]See Jon Paulien, *What the Bible Says About the End-Time* (Hagerstown, MD: Review and Herald, 1994), 20-24.

and holiness of the whole church.[17] A significant development emerged in the self-understanding of key leaders of this young movement around the time that its publishing work, the Gospel Trumpet Publishing Company, moved to Grand Junction, Michigan, in 1886. In part it was the acquiring of a new way of establishing the movement's emerging identity, a way being drawn increasingly from biblical prophecy. Seventh-day Adventism was strong in this part of Michigan and soon Warner was well acquainted with the work of a leading Adventist editor and writer, Uriah Smith.[18] Smith had developed a complex system of interpretation that coordinated a reading of biblical prophecy with the emergence and historical role of Adventism.[19] Warner initially was repelled by this system and its presumed justification of Adventism; but then he became attracted to much of it—with key refinements.[20] For persons in Indiana, Ohio, and Michigan who were intrigued at the time by such eschatological issues, Adventists and Church of God movement pioneers clearly became competitors on the scene of prophetic interpretation. There was agreement, however, that these biblical materials in the Book of Revelation portray a map of the church's history from the first to the second coming of Christ.

Warner became absorbed in Uriah Smith's general system of interpretation. Soon, having altered key details, Warner was himself presenting this general plan of biblical prophecy as a prophetic framework and dramatic rationale for the young Church of God movement. This plan began appearing with the October 15, 1883,

---

[17]See Barry Callen, *It's God's Church! The Life and Legacy of Daniel Warner* (Anderson, Ind.: Warner Press, 1995).

[18]R. W. Schwarz, *Light Bearers to the Remnant* (Boise, Id: Pacific Press Publishing Assoc., 1979), 81, 185, 192.

[19]Uriah Smith, *Thoughts, Critical and Practical on the Books of Daniel and Revelation* (Battle Creek, Mich: Review and Herald Press, 1882).

[20]Daniel Warner's personal copy of Uriah Smith's 1882 book (more than 800 pages long) now is in the archives of Anderson University. It includes handwritten marginal notes by Warner, clear evidence of his extensive interaction with this material.

issue of the *Gospel Trumpet* when Warner identified the first "beast" of Revelation 13 as Roman Catholicism and the second as the Protestant "churches" that sprang from it. The one was a harlot, the other the harlot's daughters. A pivotal *Gospel Trumpet* article appeared under Warner's name in the June 1, 1887, issue. This was the first time Warner developed from biblical prophecy and published a chronological timetable for the reformation of the church. Now being seen was "an exact parallel" between the description in Nehemiah 2-6 and "the present work of cleansing the sanctuary, or restoring the complete walls of salvation." In the April 7, 1892, *Gospel Trumpet* is a large chart detailing the key dates of church history, with their prophetic references, all culminating in the "fall of sectism, A. D. 1880." In fact, sectism did not fall, although the vision of its expected soon demise inspired much healthy church renewal and was an early signal of the coming "ecumenical century," the twentieth. In 1942 Otto Linn, a Church of God New Testament scholar, published a commentary on the Book of Revelation that ended the dominance of this biblical source of movement self-understanding.[21]

Joining the Church of God (Anderson) movement as an outgrowth of the nineteenth century Wesleyan/Holiness Movement was Pentecostalism. This new movement found birth in the Azusa Street revival that began in Los Angeles in 1906. The central focus was the second coming of Christ, although many people today associate it primarily with the gift of "speaking in tongues." The earlier nineteenth-century "perfectionism" underwent a theological paradigm shift concerning how God would accomplish his purposes. The change was from "gradual within history" to "instanta-

---

[21]Otto Linn, *Studies in the New Testament*, vol. 3, Book of Revelation (Anderson, Ind.: Commercial Service Company—Warner Press, 1942). For fuller discussion, see Barry Callen, *Contours of a Cause: The Theological Vision of the Church of God Movement* (Anderson University School of Theology, 1995), 188ff., and John Stanley, "Unity Amid Diversity: Interpreting the Book of Revelation in the Church of God (Anderson)," *Wesleyan Theological Journal* 25:2 (Fall 1990), 74-98.

neous beyond history."[22] William Faupel has noted this significant change and shown that the resulting "imminent premillennial return of Christ proved to be the primary motivation for evangelization and world mission…. Their *real* concern was to engage in activity which would hasten the return of Christ."[23]

Pentecostals generally understood themselves to be a special people who were called do a special work related to the second coming of Jesus, a work to be authenticated by mighty signs and wonders. While the Church of God movement, focusing more on holiness than on special divine gifts, sometimes thought of itself as the "Last Reformation," Pentecostals were the "Latter Rain" intended to fall on the early twentieth century just before the "tribulation sun" came to ripen the grain for the final harvest. Such an understanding obviously has shifted in various ways in the decades since and has been analyzed often as the twentieth century now closes with the final harvest still waiting.

So, does this long pattern of failed prophesies discourage new tries? Hardly. World Wars I and II inspired numerous Antichrist identifications and pictures of the imminent return of Christ. Prominent was Leonard Sale-Harrison (c1875-1956), an Australian who spoke frequently in "prophetic" conferences across North America. His 1928 book *The Remarkable Jew* went through twelve editions, selling over two hundred thousand copies. Others of his books were reissued numerous times in revised forms, changed as necessary to keep abreast of current affairs. The 1939 edition of his *The Resurrection of the Old Roman Empire* identified Italian dictator Benito Mussolini as the one reviving the old Roman Empire, copying Julius Caesar, and, as judged to be predicted, trying to reestablish a state cult with himself at the center. Surely, Sale-Harrison concluded, this signaled the approach of the

---

[22]Donald Dayton, *Theological Roots of Pentecostalism*, Metuchen, NJ: The Scarecrow Press, 1987), 21-28.

[23]D. William Faupel, *The Everlasting Gospel: The Significance of Eschatology in the Development of Pentecostal Thought* (Sheffield, England: Sheffield Academic Press, 1996), 21.

end of the age in the late 1930s or at least in the early 1940s. Such prophetic preaching and virtual date-setting in light of dramatic current events "certainly can make for a literal interpretation of the Scriptures, and the Bible becomes as relevant as tomorrow's newspaper, and perhaps just as erroneous."[24]

When all these predictive schemes fell by the way as historically wrong, new visionaries like Hal Lindsey decided that the historical key to modern-day prophetic fulfillment had not come until 1948 with the founding of the modern nation of Israel. Israel, Lindsey claimed, is "the fuse of Armageddon."[25] In a more recent book Lindsey reports: "Jesus promised us that the generation that witnessed the restoration of the Jewish people to their homeland would not pass until 'all these things'—including His return to Earth—would be done."[26] Ever since 1948 there has been considerable "dispensationalist" attention given to the role modern Israel presumably is playing in the sequence of final world events.

Also in the 1947-48 period came the first reports of "flying saucer" sightings (later to be called Unidentified Flying Objects or UFOs). There was one case in New Mexico where there were dramatic but conflicting reports of such a saucer actually crashing and its craft and the remains of killed inhabitants having been recovered and analyzed. Some interpreters said that more advanced and peaceful "peoples" from elsewhere were coming to help this planet avoid nuclear disaster. Others argued that it was all a figment of human imaginations driven to near paranoia. Finally, the United States government officially reported that the New Mexico incident had been only a downed weather balloon. Increasingly, however, the public became suspicious, curious, fearful, open to the possibility of "space ships" and space beings suddenly arriving

---

[24]Robert Clouse, in Carl Armerding and Ward Gasque, eds., *Dreams, Visions and Oracles* (Grand Rapids: Baker Book House, 1977), 35-36.

[25]Hal Lindsey, *The Late Great Planet Earth* (Grand Rapids: Zondervan, 1970), 44.

[26]Hal Lindsey, *Planet Earth—2000 A. D.* (Palos Verdes, California: Western Front, Ltd., 1994), 3.

from outer space. Such openness also reached to many in the general public who now were believing in the possibility of God soon arriving to alter or end this present world (possibly through the madness of nations using atomic bombs on each other).

Followers of the militant Muslim Ayatollah Khamenei overthrew the Shah of Iran in 1979 and set off a flurry of fresh eschatological "announcements" by some Christian interpreters of the "signs of the times." Then the invasion of Kuwait by Iraq's Saddam Hussein in 1990 shifted the attention of many prophetic pronouncers from Teheran to Baghdad. Some Christian interpreters of biblical "prophecy," having seen on television the Iraqis set fire to hundreds of Kuwaiti oil wells, talked vigorously about the now obvious "Armageddon." In December, 1990, John Walvoord's publisher rushed to market an update of his *Armageddon, Oil, and the Middle East Crisis* (a million copies were in print in just a few weeks!). Then, with Iraq's rapid military defeat in the Gulf War, this latest wave of presumed prophetic fulfillment abated somewhat. But it always is ready to rush back to major public attention whenever another world crisis emerges. Such interpreters and their systems of specific prophetic fulfillment have proven quite adaptive to changing reality and insistent on the correctness of their reading of the Bible.

The public's thirst for prophetic insight seems unending and the social shifts and dangers that feed it are very real. The cover of the November 23, 1992, issue of *Newsweek*, for example, depicted a fireball from outer space fast approaching the earth. The caption was "Doomsday Science." Apparently the sky is filled with large objects that could threaten earth's life at any time. One popular tabloid recently featured on its cover the story "Hidden Prophecies of the Dead Sea Scrolls."[27] Being revealed in 1996—presumably— was "Doomsday's Exact Date," with the announcement that the final battle between Christ and Satan involves Saddam Hussein of Iraq, who, it was said, probably is the Antichrist. The date of

---

[27]*Sun* (September 24, 1996), 20.

August 13, 2000, will be the end of the world as we now know it, unless this report—as have been many others—is more market-wise than accurate.

Few people today, Christian or not, would fail to recognize the name of Nostradamus (1503-1566), the yet famous French physician and astrologer of the Renaissance. He had to flee the wrath of the Roman Catholic Inquisition and wandered Europe on a journey of self-discovery and awakening "prophetic" powers.[28] Since the sixteenth century his maze of four-line stanzas have been in constant print and their controversial interpretations seem ever more popular as the twentieth century comes to a close. He is inter-preted by some as picturing the 1990s as the final travail of history before the golden dawn of a new age of peace or the black night of total nuclear war in 1999.[29] Well, maybe and maybe not. Prognosticators like Nostradamus surely are intriguing if nothing else. Being intriguing, however, is hardly a central virtue when it comes to Christian faith and life as biblically revealed, especially in Jesus Christ.

The fact that Jesus told his disciples that it was not for them to know the times and seasons (Acts 1:7) should be sufficient word to the wise "not to make fools out of themselves by pin-pointing the time of his [Jesus] coming on a human timetable."[30] It is embar-rassing to the Christian gospel when failed speculations are observed by the world and judged as failures of the faith itself. For instance, a group of Americans appeared on the Mount of Olives near Jerusalem some years ago. They were wearing ascension robes to greet Jesus at his expected second coming. Following their great disappointment, they made the best of their problem by turn-

---

[28]The prophecies of Nostradamus were condemned in 1781 by the Congregation of the Index, the body set up by the Roman Catholic Church for the examination of books and manuscripts.

[29]See John Hogue, *Nostradamum: The New Revelations* (Rockport, Mass.: Element Books, 1994).

[30]Max Gaulke, *May Thy Kingdom Come—Now!* (Anderson, Ind.: Warner Press, 1959), 100.

ing the fateful venture into a business enterprise, building a hotel catering to American tourists. If not consummation, then capitalism. If not the second coming, then the first opportunity that comes along. What suffers in such sordid scenarios is the aborted credibility of Christian witness and the abandoned focus on the self-sacrificing discipleship called for by Jesus.

What, Then, Is "Prophecy"?

What then is prophecy? Is it the presumed mysterious predictive powers of a Nostradamus? Thinking biblically, is it the skill of seeing in the Bible a detailed scheme of God's future intent? How do prediction and current events relate to prophecy as biblically intended? These are central questions with, unfortunately, only controversial answers.

In 1970 the publisher of Hal Lindsey's bestselling *The Late Great Planet Earth* announced on the front cover that the book was "a penetrating look at incredible prophecies involving this generation." That market-sensitive announcement surely was designed and actually did tantalize the reading public. Lindsey's view of biblical prophecy featured examples of Hebrew prophets who were said to have predicted generations in advance certain specific political and social events. A featured example was said to be Isaiah 44:28-45:4 concerning King Cyrus and his generosity to exile-weary Jews. In this book Lindsey chides "so-called Biblical scholars" who try to "late date" such predictions, claiming that the prediction actually was an after-the-fact report that really makes the prophet "a fraud." Assuming that taking seriously the biblical prophets means to take their remaining writings literally as predictive futuring, Lindsey's book proceeds to present "the prophecies which are related to the specific pattern of world events which are precisely predicted as coming together shortly before the coming of the Messiah the second time—coming in power to rule the earth."[31]

---

[31]Hal Lindsey, *The Late Great Planet Earth* (Grand Rapids: Zondervan, 1970), 25, 41.

In its heyday in the eighth to sixth centuries before Christ, prophets in Israel often acted as judges of the covenant, pronouncing divine blessings or curses on the people for their faithfulness or unfaithfulness to God's laws. These prophets were so involved in the implications of the immediate history of God's people that often they are thought of as foretellers of the future. This, however, was not their primary task. Their central role was to look to the future in order to explain the present. They warned that if present trends were not reversed, a negative future would be inevitable. They looked forward to a time when God would act to restore the people to their former glory, despite the desperate circumstances of a sinful present. One day there would be a new Exodus (Isa. 40). A new David would arise to sit on his father's throne (Jer. 23:5). God would even make a new covenant with the people (Jer. 31). Such coming historical events would bring back the "good old days" before Israel forsook God (Hos. 2:14-20). Biblical prophecy, then, seeks to alert those who can hear concerning the work of God to which they are called. Predictions that are designed to satisfy human curiosity are typically little more than arrogant sidetracks that tend to lead away from inspired mission in this world. Serious discipleship must remain in clear focus. There always have been "false" prophets.

In popular usage today, "prophecy" is roughly synonymous with "predicting the future." Some Christians believe ardently that the Bible foretells the course of events in the present and future ages, so that any skilled interpreter can learn secrets of history in advance of their happening. But, as R. B. Y. Scott rightly cautions:

> Such a use of the prophetic scriptures is actually a revival of the ancient heathen practice of divining the future, heedless of the rebuke: "It is not for you to know times and seasons which the Father hath set within his own authority" [Acts 1:7].... [The prophets of ancient Israel] would have been dismayed to hear that some in

this latter day would fail to distinguish the living Word from its incidental setting; that instead of recognizing in their prophecies the timeless message of God to mind and conscience, they would use them as a soothsayer's manual for predicting the future.[32]

Of course, sometimes a Hebrew prophet did indicate what would happen in the future. However, such a prophet invariably did so in immediate relation to the circumstance of the people being addressed in the present. Should God's people not mend their evil ways now, thundered various biblical prophets, such-and-such would happen later as an immediate consequence of their unrepentant moral and spiritual condition. Therefore, it is more appropriate to refer to these prophets as *forthtellers* of the Word of God and its present demands and future consequences than to think of them as *foretellers* of some predetermined future. The predictive component always was subservient to the declarative. The typical prophetic pattern is illustrated by Amos 4:10-12, which may be paraphrased: "You did not return to God despite judgments you suffered for your evil; *therefore*, prepare to meet your God, O Israel!" On the positive side, often prophets reassured a faithful Israel that God would provide a future for them despite the rampant evil attacking them in the present.

In both cases, the prophets were forthtelling the dependability of the God who would act in the future in ways congruent with the divine nature and at least partially in light of the attitudes and actions of people of faith or unfaith in the present. The primary concern of the prophets was not chronology, but the ethical impact of the future on the present. Since the ancient Hebrew prophets were not primarily concerned with matters of mere human calendar and chronology, but with the intended ethical impact of the future on the present attitudes and actions of

---

[32]R. B. Y. Scott, *The Relevance of the Prophets* (New York: The Macmillan Company, 1944), 2.

God's people, George Eldon Ladd summarizes concerning the prophets and their frequent warning of the nearness of the "Day of the Lord":

> The Day of the Lord *did* come; and yet, the Day of the Lord continued to be an eschatological event in the future. This tension between the immediate and the ultimate future, between history and eschatology, stands at the heart of the ethical concern of the prophetic perspective. For the important thing is not what is going to happen and when it will happen, but the will of God, who is Lord of both the far and the near future, for his people in the present.[33]

In fact, biblically speaking, the primary purpose of a future vision is to provide wisdom and resolve for discipleship life in the present. The biblical prophet was the one who was divinely enabled to understand the then-current flow of historical events in terms of "divine concern, divine purpose, and divine participation."[34] Prophecy is God's message to the present in light of the ongoing divine purpose. The Book of Revelation, for example, works from a certainty about God's future to its meaning for the believers in Jesus Christ now living in the present. Crucial for proper understanding is the sequence of tenses when the Lord announces: "I am the Alpha and the Omega...who is and who was and who is to come, the Almighty" (Rev. 1:8). The *now* comes first, informed by what *was* and *will be*. The author works from the context of his vision of the risen Christ already present in the midst of the churches (1:13). Disclosure of God's future actions serves as the basis for issuing a call to obedience in the meantime. Thus, eschatology is not "a projection into the distant

---

[33]George Eldon Ladd, *The Presence of the Future* (Grand Rapids: Eerdmans, 1974), 75.

[34]See B. D. Napier, "Prophet, Prophetism," in *The Interpreter's Dictionary of the Bible*, ed. George Buttrick, et. al., 4 vols. (Nashville: Abingdon Press, 1962), 3:896. Note Amos 3:7.

future; it bursts forth into our present existence, and structures life today in the light of the last days."[35]

John, with prophetic/pastoral concern, wrote the Book of Revelation on behalf of a church in crisis. He interpreted the then-current implications of the presence of the crucified and resurrected Christ. As Frank Carver puts it: "The 'present' Kingdom looks to its 'future,' and the nature of its future impacts the quality of the present."[36] So the primary "prophetic" question should be: "What sort of persons ought you to be in leading lives of holiness and godliness?" (2 Peter 3:11). Like the Book of Revelation, the various New Testament epistles are really prophetic readings of their time of history, witnessing to the future of God in Christ for the sake of the present life of the church in "the present evil age" (Gal. 1:4). Such readings become authoritative guidelines for God's people in any time or place. They share a vision of God's concern, purpose, and participation in all of our times, thus enabling insight, courage, and endurance. This vision is primarily of the sovereignty and faithfulness of God and only secondarily of particular trends and events now current.

God Will Be Faithful

Beginning with Abraham and Sarah and then throughout the whole biblical story, the Hebrew-Christian faith tradition is saturated with divinely-inspired expectation. People of faith, when in personal and national distress, dare to place their trust in the immediate and longterm faithfulness of God. What God has begun God will finish! (Phil. 1:6). God, however, often has been slow (by human reckoning) to bring full realization of the divine will on the historical scene being experienced by humans. God's people have endured suffering and have longed to know when and how God

---

[35]C. G. Berkhouwer, *The Return of Christ*, trans. J. Van Oosterom (Grand Rapids: Eerdmans, 1972), 19.

[36]Frank Carver, in H. Ray Dunning, ed., *The Second Coming* (Kansas City: Beacon Hill Press of Kansas City, 1995), 27.

will act to enforce the divine will and vindicate the faithful. Thus, some believers in all ages have sought to peer forward in order to anticipate better what God soon would surely do.

Again, the Christian doctrine of "last things" often is called "eschatology," a study of the end or the ultimate as context for the "meanwhile" of the continuing present. This study includes much more than just what will happen at the end of time and beyond. It concerns "both (1) beliefs about how God's purposes are realized through the *final* events of individual life and the present age, and (2) convictions about the way that these *ultimate* purposes impinge on and find provisional expressions in our present lives and reality."[37] While hope in God is a central part of true faith, unfortunately the history of Christian hoping too often has been a playground of speculation and even a battleground that has divided believers. Wandering into the arenas of curiosity and even fantasy is all too easy. True biblical hope, however, is more sturdy and longterm than such human guesses about the "signs of the times"—and it has more immediate relevance for the church's mission.

This can be seen in the very organization of the biblical materials. The Jewish canon of sacred Scripture developed in three general stages, the Torah, the Prophets, and the Writings. It is significant that each of these sections of the Hebrew Scriptures ("Old Testament") ends in a similar way. The Torah concludes with the death and burial of Moses (Deut. 34). Moses could not enter the promised land, but he knew that soon the people of God would. The Prophetic section concludes with Malachi and the promise of Elijah's return. The message is persistent and clear. No matter what, there is hope. The Writings section ends with King Jehoiachin released from prison in Babylon. There will be a going home!

The whole biblical canon intends to keep hope alive in all circumstances of human exile. The life of biblical faith is filled with

---

[37]Randy Maddox, *Responsible Grace: John Wesley's Practical Theology* (Nashville: Abingdon Press, Kingswood Books, 1994), 235.

promise. The future is open and God is always faithful. In Genesis, the original fall of humans into sin is followed by the call of Abraham. God will provide a way back for all who have become lost. In the Book of Daniel the message is clear enough. God's faithful people will survive—no matter what! In the Book of Revelation the lightening flashes of persecution finally give way to the wonder of a heavenly vision. Invasions, egotistical emperors, evil "beasts" of all centuries will come and go; but the future that God intends somehow will not be denied forever! Therefore, the consistent message to the faithful is to live accordingly, patiently, faithfully, fruitfully in the meantime.

We humans are not given a mass of detail to satisfy our curiosity about the future. We are, however, given the biblical story that narrates a long pattern of God's acting, preserving, guiding, and finally bringing to fulfillment. Our present believing and living are to be nurtured by our faith in the truth and ultimate implications of the revealing story of God in Israel and in Christ. We should and can be faithful in the sure light of God's enduring faithfulness.

God is known in the biblical story to be present and active in our world. Who is God? "I am the Lord thy God, who brought you out of the land of Egypt" (Ex. 20:2). God is the One who acted historically on Israel's behalf, made of them a people who were no people. God is the alive One, the One who is and who acts to deliver, who manifests power directed by purpose. In contrast to dead idols, "the Lord is the true God; he is the living God and the everlasting King" (Jer. 10:10). God is a living reality, not an inert idea. God is and will be vitally present, "and they shall name him Emmanuel (which means 'God is with us')" (Matt. 1:23b). As known biblically, God is a Subject, not an object, an initiator and thus a Self-revealer to be known by the nature of divine actions. It is this God in whom we hope.

God is free, aware, Self-directing, a chooser, and a purposer. God is living, a willing Spirit, a personal God (Ex. 3:14; Eph. 1:9,

11), the creative and cohesive power in the universe. God is the life-giving Wind that originally swept over the chaotic face of the waters (Gen. 1:2; Isa. 40:12-14). For each of us humans, God is the agent of conception (Ps. 139:7, 13ff; Lk. 1:35) and the sustainer of the breath of life in our bodies (Job 27:3; 33:4). The Spirit of God raised Jesus from the dead and also will "give life to our mortal bodies" (Rom. 8:11). God is faithful! Disciples, inspired by this awareness, are called to be faithful also, hopeful and expectant without ever being escapist and irrelevant to God's ongoing purposes in the present.

The messianic expectations of John the Baptist were not being fulfilled by Jesus in just the way John had anticipated. Instead, the narrative of Jesus' life and deeds caused John to ask what Jesus was doing and who he really was (Matt. 11:2-3). God often is unpredictable[38] and repeatedly fulfills divine promises in ways and times other than our human desires and predictions suggest. Our certainty as believers lies only in looking to Jesus. Therefore, "Christian eschatology at its best affirms that the ultimate fulfillment of God's purposes has already been glimpsed in the loving and merciful ministry of Jesus."[39] On this basis we can rest in faith and live in hope.

In the Wesleyan-Holiness tradition, for example, a preoccupation with knowing the timing and details of God's future has not been typical.[40] The Bible is understood to focus its concern more on God's redeeming grace and our holy living in the present and less on fruitless speculations about the future that easily distract from holy and responsible living. Christ-like life now is enabled in part by confidence in Christ's ultimate triumph over all enemies,

---

[38]This is not to suggest that God acts on occasion contrary to the divine character.

[39]Michael Lodahl, *The Story of God* (Kansas City: Beacon Hill Press of Kansas City, 1994), 211.

[40]See Michael Lodahl's article, "Wesleyan Reservations About Eschatological 'Enthusiasm'," *Wesleyan Theological Journal* 29:1-2 (Spring/Fall, 1994).

even the last enemy, death (1 Cor. 15:26). There is an important link between awareness of the end of the biblical story of God, acting first in Israel and then in Christ, and the current ability of believers to live well and witness effectively in the present scene of this grand redemption story.

Hope in the right future is to be rooted in remembering the past actions of God, the very God whose concern now focuses on the needs of the present. Future speculation by overanxious or just persistently curious believers should yield to the sacrifices of present discipleship. When preoccupation with tomorrow tends to overcome Christ-like ministry today, it surely is time to be weary of speculation!

Glancing Ahead

The prophetic Word of God assures all who will hear and believe that God is loving grace[41] and that God's faithfulness to divine intentions and promises is certain. God, who is both the beginning and end of all things, has come into the present of human experience to reclaim and recreate. The proper focus of Christian eschatology, then, is the present work of God in light of the sure outcome eventually of what is invested in God's work presently. The God of the future is the Incarnation God, the One who in Jesus Christ has now actually come to our world with all of its sordidness and lostness. The people of God are to be the incarnation people, those new creations in Christ now coming to this world in the power of the Spirit of Jesus Christ to embody the present relevance of hope that is found nowhere else.

Insists Brennan Manning, Christian believers are to claim their "belovedness each day and live as servants in the awareness of present risenness." While admitting that "apocalyptic holds a certain morbid fascination for the human mind," Manning observes that "symbols are always vulnerable to over-literal

---

[41]See Barry Callen, *God As Loving Grace* (Nappanee, Ind.: Evangel Press, 1996).

minds" and that specific apocalyptic images usually outlive the circumstances that gave them birth, forcing us to see the sad spectacle of "groups that predict the end of the world over the graves of all former predictions."[42] How sad when future preoccupations overwhelm what is intended to be present ministry.

Here is the central point to be made, the core truth that keynotes all that follows below. The future age already is invading the present evil age (Rom. 12:2; Gal. 1:4; 2 Tim. 1:10; Heb. 6:5). Believers do not wait until the second coming of Christ to experience the "last things." Instead, they have been living in the "last days" since the inauguration of the Kingdom of God now present through the Christ-Pentecost events (Acts 2:17; Heb. 1:2). Traditional Christian theology often has neglected the New Testament emphasis on the eschatological dimension of the present Christian life, leaving believers with an impoverished understanding of Christian living—and making them vulnerable to those who specialize in speculating about the future.

There is today a widespread diminishment of awareness of crucial realities like: the richness of the spiritual resources now available through Jesus Christ and the Holy Spirit; the seriousness of the ongoing warfare of God and the evil powers yet loose in the world and the church's responsibility to be engaged in that warfare; the certainty that no sacrifice for the cause of Christ is ever in vain; and the unshakable confidence in the final triumph of the Kingdom of God, a confidence that liberates the believer to live the life of faith now, whatever the cost. Believers, while looking forward to their final resurrection and heavenly rest, are already to be risen in the sense that they have received resurrection life at their conversions to Jesus Christ (Jn. 3:16, 36; 11:25-26; Eph. 2:6).

Given all of the above, chapter three that follows is intended to help orient the reader to factors that influence the process of biblical interpretation and alter every interpreter's approach to issues

---

[42]Brennan Manning, *Abba's Child: The Cry of the Heart for Intimate Belonging* (Colorado Springs: NavPress, 1994), 146-147.

of eschatology. Then chapter four explores the classic systems of Christian eschatology, leading to chapter five where the person and teachings of Jesus Christ are identified as the proper foundation and structure of authentic Christian eschatology. Beyond that, chapters six through nine direct the attention of Christ's disciples to how hope in God should send believers into this present world as prophetic pilgrims showing a lost world the way to life here and hereafter.

Matters Worth Exploring

1. Why are you, the reader, interested in "prophecy." Is it more a matter of curiosity about coming events or is it a sincere desire to be what God wants you to be for the time *before* the end of the age? Are interest in the future and present discipleship in conflict with each other?

2. Are those believers who are "most spiritual" thereby most able to know the times and events of God's future? Is such knowledge available to any believer?

3. Biblically speaking, what is the focus of true prophecy? Is it predicting specific future events or bringing to the believer a confidence in God's future that frees one to focus on present responsibilities?

4. Explain how one's understanding of eschatology helps determine that person's attitudes toward church, state, and society.

5. In church history there have been many specific predictions about the future and many keen disappointments about the failure of those predictions. What can account for such failures? What lesson should we learn from the fact of their frequent occurrence?

6. Why does the American public's thirst for "prophetic" knowledge seem insatiable? Are Christian believers any different?

7. Are you or your church now facing a real crisis? How might a fresh vision of the faithfulness of God influence the way you react to current events and relate to other people?

Chapter 3

WHAT INFLUENCES OUR INTERPRETATION?

❊

All scripture is inspired by God and is useful for teaching, for reproof,
for correction, and for training in righteousness, so that everyone
who belongs to God may be proficient, equipped for every
good work. (2 Tim. 3:16-17)

❊

Our respect for the Bible as the Word of God means at the outset that we
will be open to allowing the text to declare itself and will resist seeking to
change the literary vehicle to suit our own expectations. . . . The Bible
must be allowed its distance, and this means not trying to overcome
its strangeness by dubious means.[1]

❊

The weariness about some Christians tending to speculate about the future agrees with the concern expressed in 2 Timothy 3:16-17 (above). The purpose of the Bible is not to satisfy human curiosity about what finally will be, but to prepare believers to make a difference in this world in the meantime. Disciples are to search the Scriptures for something other than inspired insight into the coming events of tomorrow. They are to draw from its pages new courage and strength, equipment for ministry, increased resolve to do "every good work." Whatever God intends for the

---

[1]Clark Pinnock, *The Scripture Principle* (San Francisco: Harper & Row, 1984), 106.

long-range, the biblical call is for the church to be faithful in the meantime.

Virtually all Christians say that their perspectives on ministry now and expectations for later are drawn directly from biblical revelation. The problem, then, appears less the lack of commitment to the Bible as fundamental authority and more the nagging question of what is appropriate biblical interpretation. What more warning is needed than the David Koresh tragedy of 1993? As cult leader of the Branch Davidians, Koresh interpreted the Bible in a way that convinced a community of believers that he was Christ and that the end was at hand. He presented himself as the only one who could open the seven seals of the Book of Revelation, thus releasing catastrophic events that would bring the world's end. His followers staked their very lives on the rightness of his interpretation. A violent standoff with agents of the federal government led to a fiery apocalypse, the loss of many lives, and the destruction of the group's compound near Waco, Texas. There is obvious danger in a group of people being isolated and then subjected to twisted methods of biblical interpretation.

Sometimes the following is said in frustration: Why not just read the Bible and take what it says at face value? The answer is that, as an ideal, such an approach appears to be desirable. But there are inevitable difficulties. The Bible is an ancient book originally written by many authors in "foreign" languages and reflecting cultures radically different from our own. Further, we who now read the ancient biblical text bring to our reading, consciously or unconsciously, "modern" presuppositions that influence what we understand the already translated text to be saying plainly as we translate it again through our own experience and available knowledge. The God who inspired the text at is original writing apparently needs to endow the contemporary reader with a wisdom that can enable proper reading, interpreting, and applying.

What influences Christian judgment on end-time matters? Why do Christians equally committed to biblical authority differ so much in their understandings of the meaning of what they read? It somehow was so easy for Hal Lindsey in his 1970 bestselling *The Late Great Planet Earth*. He told his many curious readers that he was "attempting to step aside and let the prophets speak."[2] After all the educators and politicians had been given their say about the future, he judged it time to "give God a chance to present His views." But can we humans set aside our humanness so easily? Can we manage to allow God to speak without our own interpretive limitations somehow subtly entering the picture—even when we sincerely do not want our own perspectives to interfere with the "pure Word of God"? I think not, not even in Hal Lindsey's case. The very dispensationalism represented by Lindsey is itself much more than it claims—the plain and faithful reading of the Bible (see chapter four). It has obvious cultural roots and questionable presuppositions that influence greatly what this interpreter understands as he reads. Recent decades have seen much criticism of this dispensational pattern of biblical interpretation and considerable shifting of positions as its own scholars have had to make some admissions and adjustments.[3]

Often, having reviewed the thinking of a series of biblical scholars about a passage that is variously understood by them, one is tempted to think of the maze of competing perspectives like the sign once seen over an old ironsmith's shop: "All kinds of fancy twistings and turnings done here." Creative explanations for widely different readings of the same Bible text surely call for an exploration of why interpretations often range so widely.

What follows are identifications of sources and kinds of influence on biblical interpretation, particularly in relation to mat-

---

[2]Hal Lindsey, *The Late Great Planet Earth* (Grand Rapids: Zondervan, 1970), 6.

[3]See Craig Blaising, "Changing Patterns in American Dispensational Theology," *Wesleyan Theological Journal* 29(Spring/Fall 1994), 149-164, and a good historical overview by William Charles Miller, "The New Apocalypticism" in H. Ray Dunning, ed., *The Second Coming* (Beacon Hill Press of Kansas City, 1995), 221-245.

ters involving the future (or eschatology in general). As they are discussed, certain of the writer's own presuppositions naturally will be evident. They are chosen consciously over the alternatives because they are believed to be (1) biblically rooted, (2) in accord with the best of contemporary biblical scholarship, (3) happen to be characteristic of the Wesleyan theological tradition (my own), and (4) are judged a wise and proper balancing of the centrality of Jesus Christ for Christian faith in any time and the mission of the church for this present time. These presuppositions are made obvious to the reader because all interpreters have some presuppositions and good interpretation demands openness, self-criticism, and the invited counsel of the larger community of believers.

Place and Tradition

The main problem with the second coming of Jesus is that it has not yet happened. Being delayed now for some 2000 years, expectant Christians have had to reassess in each generation the significance of the history of the world and church up to its own time and then relate that reassessment to its understanding of the Bible's promise about the consummation of all things. The result has been a long line of reinterpretations, each in various ways sincerely attempting to relate biblical prophecy to the particulars of its own time. This ongoing process happened among Jewish leaders in the time of Jesus[4] and then began to appear among the disciples of Jesus as early as the very first generations of Christians.

---

[4]Many of the most respected Hebrew scholars of the first century thought they knew what their coming Messiah would be like and would do. When Jesus actually came, they failed to recognize and thus rejected him. It is easy to look back and ask why skilled interpreters could make such a fundamental mistake. Likely, one day the same will be said of many of us in relation to any of our future projections that later proved false. Note Hendrikus Berkhof, *Well-Founded Hope* (Richmond, Va.: John Knox Press, 1969, 25-26). He argues that only poets are prepared to understand the Bible's eschatological language since it speaks poetically about last things. Truth about ultimate and final things tends to break the bounds of literal language.

The Olivet Discourse of Jesus (Matthew 24-25, Mark 13, Luke 21) contains much of the reported teachings of Jesus related to "end times."[5] A careful comparison of the reporting of this discourse by the three Synoptic Gospel writers is very revealing. Clearly, the wording of the teaching of Jesus and what parts of the discourse are used or unused are influenced by the historical setting, literary objectives, and theological presuppositions of each writer. The passages that speak of the return of Jesus as near are now interpreted differently because they may refer to (1) Jesus' resurrection or (2) his coming in spiritual power on the day of Pentecost or (3) the coming of judgment in the destruction of Jerusalem or (4) his final coming at the end of time.

Lying just beneath almost every verse that reports this discourse of Jesus is the heavy shadow of the Roman destruction of Jerusalem (A. D. 70) and the struggle of the Christian community to understand the delay of the second coming of Jesus in the face of such devastating events. These New Testament writers, influenced deeply by their place in the early tradition of the church's life, were attempting to understand and record what God was saying to the church in the context of its own history and experience. Luke, for instance, describes the conditions prevalent during the destruction of Jerusalem (21:20) and makes a distinction between that awful event and the expected return of Christ. The Christian community, Luke stresses, must remain present in a dramatically changing world—and it has important evangelistic work to do.

Place and tradition also appear to be significant factors for all later Christian interpreters and writers. No one interprets the Bible or writes Christian theology in a social vacuum.[6] One example is the contemporary German theologian Jürgen Moltmann. His work

---

[5]See chapter five for discussion of the teachings of Jesus, including the Olivet Discourse and its eschatological emphases.

[6]A good example is the complex Christian view of Jews that emerged late in the first century and is reflected in the New Testament. See David Efroymson, et. al., eds., *Within Context: Essays on Jews and Judaism in the New Testament* (Collegeville, Minn.: The Liturgical Press, 1993).

in the 1960s launched the "theology of hope" movement that strongly emphasizes eschatology as the key framework within which all Christian theology should be seen.[7] Moltmann lived through World War II, was incarcerated in an English prisoner-of-war camp, learned that hope is key to survival, saw the German state collapse, and finally went home determined that the future would be different. A later reading of the Marxist philosopher Ernst Bloch helped inspire Moltmann's own theological work around the concept of hope. His times and life experiences obviously were crucial to how he came to link the present and future in his understanding of biblical teaching and the current responsibility of the church in providing hope in a deeply troubled world.

The 1960s in the United States was a time for breathing the fresh air of the new frontiers of the John Kennedy era. Soon, however, there came the more polluted air of the Richard Nixon era with its Vietnam war defeat and Watergate political debacle. Cultural shifts do affect religious thinking and Bible reading. Leading Christian voices of the 1960s and 1970s began calling for Christians to escape the walls of the church and make a difference in the streets where the issues of freedom and justice cry out as the Israelites once had in ancient Egypt. Observations easily could be made about influential Christian theologians like James Cone, in the context of African-Americans searching for the right linking of Christian faith and human liberation, and Gustavo Gutiérrez seeking a similar end in a Latin American context.[8] Particular biblical themes dominate their interpretive patterns. Social position shapes the process of biblical interpretation.

A classic study by H. Richard Niebuhr shows the significant power of culture and social class to shape church life and biblical understanding. A person's conception of Christ influences that per-

---

[7] Jürgen Moltmann, *Theology of Hope* (1965, republished London: SCM, 1967).

[8] Gustavo Gutiérrez, *A Theology of Liberation*, 15th anniversary ed. (Maryknoll, N. Y.: Orbis Books, 1988).

son's participation in culture, and the cultural involvement in turn shapes the understanding of faith in Christ.[9] More recently, Justo González has observed that the Bible traditionally has been interpreted "in ways that are oppressive to minorities and to powerless groups, and that serve to justify the actions and values of the oppressors."[10] The secure position of a present establishment is allowed to take away the legitimate future of others. In turn, those on the margins of society tend to champion the biblical hope for a better world—if not here, then hereafter.

Broad theological traditions and assumptions also are clearly influential on how a given interpreter approaches and reads "prophetic" biblical materials. In the Wesleyan theological tradition, interpreters often have been called "reverent agnostics" on eschatological matters. Why? Because their view of divine grace and human freedom encourages them to think of the future as more open and flexible than, for example, a Reformed theologian who is committed to a doctrine of predestination and a propositional view of revealed truth. John Wesley was impatient with "enthusiasts" who focused on future speculations. His fear was that such a preoccupation would detract from the really central and much more surely known matters of human salvation through faith in Christ and God's call to present participation with God's agenda in the power of Christ's Spirit.

Wesley's eschatology was related closely to his teaching about "entire sanctification." It was a "realizable" eschatology since it is God's intent that love for God and neighbor come to maturity in believers who are yet very much in this world.[11] When participating in the Lord's Supper, for example, the early Methodists actively combined the future and present tenses:

---

[9]H. Richard Niebuhr, *Christ and Culture* (1951). See also his *The Social Sources of Denominationalism* (1929).

[10]Justo González, *Out of Every Tribe and Nation* (Nashville: Abingdon Press, 1992), 38.

[11]See Michael Lodahl, "Wesleyan Reservations About Eschatological 'Enthusiasm'," *Wesleyan Theological Journal* (Spring/Fall, 1994), 50-63.

Their realization of the promise in the sacrament fairly shouted a confidence of the heavenly experience whose first-fruits were encountered at the table. This activity did not deny the future reality of the coming eschaton. It served rather to make it a present as well as a future reality.[12]

What we have in this attractive theological tradition are strong orienting concerns, concerns "of humanity over institutional identity, for the margins rather than the centers of control and power, for the future in hope and expectancy rather than some absolutizing of past or present."[13]

The point is not to try to stand free of all conditioning factors in order to be entirely "objective"—an impossible task. The Enlightenment mentality mistakenly has championed, even romanticized this unattainable ideal.[14] The task is to be self-conscious of one's influencing environment, compensate for it as appropriate and possible, and remain tentative and humble about one's own "assured" conclusions. This even applies to theological traditions. The church is a "future-oriented body, intent on realizing the full dimensions of the kingdom of God. When its exegetical task is dominated by a method bound to dogma, it violates its own charter as the people for the future."[15] Norman Kraus is right in arguing that "our definitions of time and history, presuppositions about the nature of 'objective truth,' and our philosophy of language all

---

[12]Steven Hoskins, "Eucharist and Eschatology in the Writings of the Wesleys," *Wesleyan Theological Journal* (Spring/Fall, 1994), 77.

[13]David Whitelaw, "Comparative Patterns of Church Historiography," *Wesleyan Theological Journal* (Fall 1996), 37, n. 27.

[14]See Barry Callen, *God As Loving Grace* (Nappanee, Ind.: Evangel Press, 1996), 44-47.

[15]Robert Lyon, "Evangelicals and Critical Historical Method" in Wayne McCown and James Earl Massey, eds., *Interpreting God's Word for Today*, vol. 2 of *Wesleyan Theological Perspectives* (Anderson, Ind.: Warner Press, 1982), 160.

influence our hermeneutical [biblical interpretation] decisions."[16] It is one thing to read the Bible for what it plainly says to the reader. It is another thing to probe the text with patience, discipline, and within a community of faith in the search for increased insight into what it *really means.*

Time and History

The concepts of time and history held by a biblical interpreter are crucial milestones on the path to biblical understanding. The modern "scientific" concept of time centers in a temporal extension in which everything happens. For the Hebrew prophets, however, time is "filled time." History (His-Story) is that process of God's pivotal actions that finally brings creation to its intended fulfillment. Thinking as moderns and not biblically, too often Christians grasp prophetic biblical texts, compare them with stories seen on the evening news, and find bits of information said to complete the puzzle of what is yet to come. Such literalizing and contextually crafted speculation has brought to the church repeated frustrations, embarrassments (when events fail to meet predictions), and divisions.

The crucial point is that Christian eschatology, properly understood, is itself a philosophy or theology of history, "not a scientific explanation of how and when the universe will cease to be."[17] Saying that eschatology "may be falsely taught so as to pretend that it has detailed keys to contemporary events," Thomas Oden insists that "the teaching of the end of history is a teaching about the meaning of history." It often is taught falsely "so as to detract from the importance of this life or trivialize historical existence or foster the illusion of escape from human responsibility."[18] It is better to view eschatological texts like creation texts, "as

---

[16]C. Norman Kraus, *God Our Savior* (Scottdale, Pa.: Herald Press, 1991), 194.

[17]Ibid., 195.

[18]Thomas Oden, *Life in the Spirit* (San Francisco: Harper, 1992), 373.

images of the future but not as precise pointers."[19] The Bible distinguishes between *chronos*, clock time, and *kairos*, the significant and opportune time (Jn. 7:6-8). A *kairos* day is not just another day, but a day of special importance that moves history toward its goal, a day when God's promise is fulfilled (Acts 7:17) and the biblical story moves on at divine initiative.

Kairotic events, especially the first advent of Jesus, are acts of God that give meaning to all history. They provide the biblical revelation with depth, drama, and direction. Recalling this difference between clock time and pivotal time, we also should distinguish between the chronology and kairology of future events. Jesus said that no one knows the day or hour (chronology) of God's *kairos* (Mark 13:32-33). The role of the true prophet is to discern and proclaim the meaning and present implications of human history in light of the Creator-Consummator whose story penetrates history redemptively. Maps, calendars, crystal balls, and prophecy specialists usually lead astray.

Key questions often are addressed to the Book of Revelation. Where does humanity now find itself in the historical process? What is yet to be expected—and when? What should a responsible believer do in the meantime? The answers received, of course, depend heavily on which basic interpretive view of this book has been chosen (see chapter four). For many Christians a "millennium" is expected soon, a golden age of God on earth either just before or just after the return of Christ. This belief, based on a tiny part of the Revelation text, is justified by reference to a whole system of biblical interpretation that bends the reading of given verses of the Revelation in a particular direction.

---

[19]Clark Pinnock, in Pinnock and Delwin Brown, *Theological Crossfire* (Grand Rapids: Zondervan, 1990), 223. Pinnock expands on this in regard to the creation texts of Genesis ("Climbing Out of a Swamp: The Evangelical Struggle to Understand the Creation Texts," *Interpretation* 43(April, 1989), 143-155. His admonition is to allow the Bible to speak for itself rather than we as interpreters imposing our "imperialistic agendas" onto it.

It is significant to note that one's view of a millennial hope rests in part on the time of one's living. The social optimism of the nineteenth century encouraged one emphasis (postmillennialism) and the social pessimism of the twentieth century has encouraged another (premillennialism). Prior to the Civil War, the young United States had experienced freedom from the domination of England, rapid expansion, and religious renewal. The millennial thought of Jonathan Edwards (1703-1758) was heralded widely. Surely a wonderful period of the reign of God's grace was nearing and would come about through the conversion of the world to Christ. The church would play a central role in introducing this millennium, as would the progressive pioneering of the glorious young nation, the United States. Wesleyan theology, basic to the Methodism so influential in nineteenth-century America, featured an "optimism of grace."[20]

Then came the twentieth century with its increasing urbanization, industrialization, and social pessimism. The immigration of many Roman Catholics to the United States challenged the Protestant domination of American society. New "social sciences" and "evolutionary" thinking challenged treasured assumptions of Christian faith and ushered in a more "secular" setting. The bloody and depressing World War I further eroded social optimism generally. Now the ground was right for the flowering of premillennialism, a view that things are worsening and can only be reversed with the dramatic return of Christ, who then will launch the millennium with divine power. L. L. Pickett (1859-1928), an American holiness leader of his time, issued a militant attack on postmillennialism, calling it an invention of Catholics and the view

---

[20]For example: "So the Holiness Movement in America, as it first came to life in the 1830s and 1840s, was bathed in millennial optimism.... Members of the movement believed that God was graciously and powerfully at work in the world and was quickly bringing history to a triumphant close" (Harold Raser, in H. Ray Dunning, ed., *The Second Coming*, Beacon Hill Press of Kansas City, 1995, 168).

of theological liberals.[21] Times had changed—and so had the preferred Christian pattern of future expectation. The Bible was used as a ready resource in both cases.

So, from the divine viewpoint, what time is it? It is the time between the times, the crucial period between the first and the final comings of Jesus. As the famous Swiss theologian Oscar Cullmann put it in his classic *Christ and Time*, today is part of the time between God's D-Day and V-E-Day. In World War II the first of these days, the massive invasion of Europe by the Allies, was the beginning of the end for the Axis powers. The other was the day when the now inevitable end of the war was actually and fully realized. Likewise, the death and resurrection of Jesus signaled the soon-to-be fully victorious invasion of this evil world by the Kingdom of God. Given Jesus Christ, the outcome is no longer in doubt. Thus, the New Testament focuses more on the *Son* than on *signs* of the times. Concludes Cullmann: "The hope of the final victory is so much the more vivid because of the unshakably firm conviction that the battle that decides the victory has already taken place."[22]

Rather than encouraging anxious speculations about the future, the early church displayed a stubborn and inspiring hope in the midst of present affliction, knowing that suffering produces eternal glory (Rom. 8:17-25; 1 Peter 1:4-9; Rev. 1:5-9). Human history, those first believers were sure, is infused with divine purpose and presence; but it is not merely a "pre-arranged puppet show" (C. H. Dodd) in which the time and order of events is all set in advance. In fact, God "guides the [historical] process within the context of human freedom.... Human choices are real and actually influence the course of history."[23] Biblical prophecy is not to be

---

[21]L. L. Pickett, *The Blessed Hope of His Glorious Appearing* (Louisville, KY: Pickett Publishing Co., 1901).

[22]Oscar Cullmann, *Christ and Time* (London: SCM Press, 1946, rev. 1962), 87.

[23]H. Ray Dunning, "Presuppositions of a Wesleyan Eschatology," in Dunning, ed., *The Second Coming* (Beacon Hill Press of Kansas City, 1995), 196.

seen mechanically as prewritten history that can be sorted out, carefully charted, and preached in advance and in detail.

Revelation, Language, Truth

After a biblical understanding of time and history, interpretation of biblical eschatology is influenced by one's view of the "objectivity" of God's action in history and how that revealing action relates to human perception of the nature of "truth." It also relates to the nature of the language conveying the divine message to human receivers. For instance, how symbolic is eschatological language? Does the Bible provide newspaper-like information that informs us about a literal succession of coming and culminating events, almost like a religious reference encyclopedia of the future? Should the Bible's eschatological language be viewed as "objective" in the sense that it speaks of literal, historical, political, dateable events? How available are the acts of God to public view and scientific investigation? Is the eschaton something historically observable or only existentially significant?

In response to this last question, Rudolf Bultmann (1884-1976) moved away from a literal reading of eschatological texts. Arguing that any literal reading is incredible to modern people, he sought to "demythologize" them into only existential meanings. For the sake of personal relevance, Bultmann adopted a scientific perspective that reduces all spatio-temporal features of the eschaton to "mythological" ones. Thus, he argued, the divine grace in Christ is the new age now, the eschaton already present among us.[24] Eschatology is not an apocalyptic press report of soon-coming events, but the *kairos* of God's revelation to human beings in their

---

[24]See Rudolf Bultmann, *History and Eschatology* (N. Y.: Harper, 1957), 149-155. Bringing the existentialism of Martin Heidegger to bear on New Testament interpretation, Bultmann comments on John 5:25: "For John the resurrection of Jesus, Pentecost and the *parousia* [final and full coming] of Jesus are one and the same event, and those who believe have already eternal life" (*Jesus Christ and Mythology*, N. Y.: Scribner, 1958, 33).

lived presents where decisions have to be made about life in the light either of God or of the world. Bultmann's worldview was Newtonian in nature, one now widely recognized to be outdated in many ways because it stresses too sharply a separation of faith/existence and science/history.

The earliest Christian church did experience and celebrate the *already* of the eschaton, an already that indeed is existentially transforming if received and lived out in faith. The resurrected Jesus was known to be Lord both now and in the future. The new age indeed had come. But persecutions soon appeared and early believers also anticipated the second coming of Christ (1 Cor. 11:26) as an observable event external to present human experience. Religious language is metaphorical. Truth about God's actions in the future is both existential and historical, having immediate and very personal life significance as well as long-term implications for all of reality. Bultmann was right—and wrong.

The key issue is the nature of revelation, the divine self-disclosure about God and God's will and ways. In contrast to a common "fundamentalism" that views revelation as the communication of inerrant propositional truths about God, the Wesleyan tradition insists on a more relational focus that features the reciprocity of divine giving and human receiving in real and conditioned historical circumstances.[25] When biblical writers spoke of the future, they tended to see it as the future of their own times. While truly inspired, they were not detached interpreters giving divinely revealed "eyewitness" accounts of a future wholly disconnected from then present circumstances.

What about eschatological language? Language itself is interpretative. To know and use a given language is to understand time, objects, and events in a certain way. In modern Western culture people have tended to assume a "positivistic" view of lan-

---

[25]See Barry Callen, *God As Loving Grace* (Nappanee, IN: Evangel Press, 1996), 33, 115-116, 138, 145, and 287 where revelation is described as both definitive and dynamic, narrative and relational in nature.

guage. Language is thought to be direct, hopefully a precise and objective reporting of the plain facts of experience. Such an Enlightenment view of language fits well the current technological times, the prevailing mood of American pragmatism, and the anxiousness of many Christians to find in the Bible a clear picture of what comes next in God's plan. But it hardly fits Christian prayer or Christian theology in general (although it supports effectively a fundamentalism that seeks doctrinal precision at the rational and verbal levels). It clearly does not fit the whole Hebrew approach to the nature of truth and religious language.[26]

In fact, biblical stories often are magnificent metaphors that should not be flattened to what is claimed to be straightforwardly descriptive and propositional language. Dealing with the divine drives one to the flexibility and expansiveness of narrative, story, metaphor, and poetry, styles of language found frequently in the Bible, especially in relation to the subjects of eschatology. Biblical revelation concerning the future typically employs metaphors from time and space reality known to ancient Middle Eastern cultures to represent what lies beyond current time and space. God's being and future intent cannot be captured by any or all of our human words, speculations, or creative modern adaptations of "prophetic" biblical writings. The Bible consistently avoids the attempt at any such capturing (subtle forms of idolatry). Rob Staples summarizes well:

> The function of [biblical] eschatological language is not to give us specific information about the timing of future events (such as the end of the world) or of the geography of extraterrestrial places (heaven, hell). The metaphors, symbols, pictures, and images of eschatology serve to create in us an openness to the mystery that lies beyond our power to comprehend or control.[27]

---

[26]See Marvin Wilson, *Our Father Abraham* (Grand Rapids: Eerdmans, 1989), chapter nine.

[27]Rob Staples, "The Theology of the Final Consummation," in Ray Dunning, ed., *The Second Coming* (Beacon Hill Press of Kansas City, 1995), 256-257.

Marvin Wilson agrees: "The Hebrew knew he did not know all the answers. His position was 'under the sun' (Eccl. 8:17), so his words were few (Eccl. 5:2). He refused to over systematize or force harmonization on the enigmas of God's truth or the puzzles of the universe."[28] Such a view takes nothing away from biblical authority; it only allows the Bible to be what it is and say what it wishes to say—quite apart from our anxious, quite "modern," and often very "creative" manipulations of it.

The danger of manipulation certainly exists when it comes to handling given "prophetic" passages in biblical books like Daniel and Revelation. Consider, for example, the complex process of discovering a proper interpretation of the Book of Daniel. Here one faces decisions about the meaning of divine inspiration and the nature of divine revelation and its relation to human language and history. In this regard, one observation deserves close attention. Such decisions often are brought *to the text* from previous understandings and commitments, not truly *derived from it*. Say three current biblical scholars:

> The book of Daniel is an apocalypse. As such, it has one of the greatest messages in the Old Testament: the kingdoms of this world will be replaced by the kingdom of God.... It is pitiful that a work of such grandeur has been trivialized, considered ridiculous or fantastic and not to be taken seriously, or used as the vehicle for all sorts of speculation, systems of the end time, and date setting.[29]

What understandings and commitments do interpreters frequently bring to eschatological biblical texts regarding the nature, origins, and present significance of their futuristic visions and stories? Sometimes "critical" scholars bring the *a priori* conviction that "prophetic" texts cannot be actual predictions of events not to

---

[28]Marvin Wilson, *Our Father Abraham*, 152.

[29]William LaSor, David Hubbard, Frederic Bush, *Old Testament Survey* (Grand Rapids: Eerdmans, 1982), 659.

happen until long after the writer's own time. On the opposite extreme, sometimes conservative scholars bring the *a priori* conviction that "prophetic" texts must be actual futuristic predictions. After all, quasi-prophecies issued pseudonymously would not have been inspired that way by God. Further, it is assumed that such texts must be "pure" and actual history, not any mixture of fact and "fiction" or "myth." However, the actual case is that God can inspire in whatever way God chooses and biblical material is couched in whatever literary style and relation to present history that it is.

All biblical texts should be allowed to speak for themselves, given their own times and assumptions, not those of the present reader. One must be careful to avoid applying modern Western assumptions to ancient Eastern texts. Particular understandings of time, history, revelation, and truth are crucial factors in the outcomes of a given interpreter's work.

Once In Grace, Always In Grace?

In addition to all of the above, often biblical interpreters come from pre-set theological traditions whose systems of belief create the categories of thought into which biblical texts are made to fit. One example will demonstrate adequately how a "tight" system of logic in Christian theology can lead to questionable interpretations of biblical teaching that have significant impact on eschatological matters. There is a Christian doctrine sometimes called the "perseverance of the saints" (popularly known as "once in grace, always in grace"). It is taught by many theologians as a means of assurance for the believer. Their point is that once one is "saved," that salvation is secured eternally by the mercy and dependability of God. This teaching is a good example of how a prior assumption which sounds biblical enough (God is faithful to complete what God has begun) can justify an interpreter's bending of the plain meaning of biblical passages to fit the interpreter's preestablished system of thought.

Two concepts and their interrelationships require careful note in this regard. They are in sharp conflict with each other. Each requires explanation. Once explained, and their conflict clarified, the conclusion will be that the first concept is crucial to authentic Christian believing and the second is made invalid by it. The concepts are (1) the both/and synergism of divine grace and (2) once in grace, always in grace. The first concept focuses on the giving and receiving of divine grace necessarily involved in the mutuality of both partners in a covenant relationship. The other is a commonly-heard Christian claim that intends to honor God by insisting that what God does cannot be undone by mere humans. If God chooses to save, that fortunate recipient of divine grace is given the gift of assurance that such grace never will be removed. If God did it, surely it is unshakably done.

How does the first concept invalidate the second? The synergism of grace rejects the idea that God ever enters into an *unconditional* covenant with any individual or nation—including Israel, any denomination, or any individual. Covenants are between two parties and failure on the part of the human partner invalidates the relationship. This potential of failure surely includes the salvation covenant possible between Jesus Christ and a believer. The plain meaning of at least four discourses of Jesus argues directly for the reality of this potential (Luke 8, parable of the sower; Luke 12, parable of the Lord and his steward; Matt. 18, parable of the law of forgiveness; and John 15, vine and branches imagery).[30]

One vigorous defender of "eternal security" reveals why such a teaching commends itself to him so strongly that he insists, "they who repudiate this truth cast a most horrible aspersion upon the character of the triune Jehovah." His reasoning rests on an assumption heavily conditioned by Calvinistic predestinationism. The

---

[30]For an exposition of each of these passages in relation to the false idea of the "perseverance of the saints," see Robert Shank, *Life in the Son* (Springfield, MO.: Westcott Publishers, 1960), 31-478. He notes some novel and seemingly strained ways in which some interpreters have sought to avoid the rather plain and consistent assumption behind this body of Jesus' teaching.

assumption is implied in his rhetorical questions. "Now is the Father's eternal purpose [that believers be conformed to the image of the Son] placed in jeopardy by the human will? Is its fulfillment contingent upon human conduct? Or, having ordained the end, will He [God] not also make infallibly effectual all means to that end?"[31] The eternal security defender is confident that the right answers are "No," "No," and a strong "Yes!" Other interpreters, equally committed to the biblical emphasis on the both/and synergism of divine grace, are just as confident that the right answers are "Yes," "Yes," and "Not necessarily."

Why does all of this matter? Because those who have responded to the saving grace of God now have a responsibility to be faithful. We believers are responsible to do God's will in this world, nurture the new life given us in Christ, grow up into the full stature of Christ, and reflect to the world the fruit of the Spirit. We have choices—real choices—and our choices matter to God. Of course, we all hope to be eternally secure. The way to that end, however, clearly implied in the words of Jesus (Jn. 15:1-6), rests on the following:

> Throughout his earthly sojourn, the relation of the individual to Christ is never a static relationship existing as the irrevocable consequence of a past decision, act, or experience. Rather, it is a present mutual indwelling of the believer and the Saviour, the sharing of a common life which emanates from Him "who is our life" (Col. 3:4). For the believer, it is a living participation proceeding upon a living faith in a living Saviour. The principle is reduced to its simplest statement in the words of Jesus, "Abide in me, and I in you" (Jn. 15:4).[32]

[31]Arthur Pink, *Eternal Security* (Grand Rapids, Mich.: Guardian Press, 1974), 16.

[32]Shank, op. cit., 42-43.

The three essential truths taught here are: (1) The transforming of disciples by the indwelling of the Saviour depends on the conscious decision of the disciples; (2) The consequence of *continuing* to abide in Christ by the ongoing choice of faith is that Christ *continues to indwell*; and (3) The consequences of failing to abide in Christ are fruitlessness (vv. 4b, 5c) and removal (vv. 2a, 6).

Paul certainly lays great stress on the faithfulness of God who surely is able to preserve Christians in temptation and persecution. He boldly asserts that nothing can separate the Christian from the love of God (Rom. 8:35-39). I. Howard Marshall, however, has done careful exposition of the New Testament teachings and concludes that the evidence "hardly favours the view that the men who finally enter the messianic kingdom or the world to come have been predestined to do so by God who efficaciously causes them to repent and remain faithful to Him."[33] What must be placed side by side are (1) the real possibility of a failure of faith and (2) great confidence in a continuing faith which is sustained by God from the constant fear of falling away. What must be maintained in essential paradox—without pressing the New Testament into a logically rigid system that it does not present or intend—are the preserving faithfulness of God and the real potential of human apostasy.

The point to be made here does not require a detailed exegesis of the relevant biblical passages, as Marshall provides in *Kept by the Power of God* (1969). It only requires awareness that one's view of the working of divine grace and the corresponding role of the believer's faithfulness are very influential on how matters of the future are perceived. Some Calvinistic authors tend to accept the doctrine of final perseverance (eternal security) on previously held philosophical and dogmatic grounds. This doctrine, then, comes to be seen as an inevitable corollary of the assumption of the divine predestination of particular individuals to salvation. On the other hand, the Arminian author typically argues for the possibility of the

---

[33]I. Howard Marshall, *Kept by the Power of God* (Minneapolis: Bethany Fellowship, 1969, originally Epworth Press, London), 193.

loss of salvation as a natural corollary of the previous assumption of the freedom of the human will to accept or reject salvation—before or after it is initially experienced. Once such overarching theological stances are fixed, those holding them have difficulty reading the Bible other than through these dogmatic glasses. Such also is the case with a wide range of eschatological subjects.

Jesus as the Focus

All Christian faith, including its future anticipations, is to be anchored in the Jesus of history.[34] This is a primary Christian assertion. Jesus is the interpretive principle for reading the Hebrew past ("Old Testament") and the future of all creation. The good news is less that Jesus is coming again, though he clearly is, and more that he already has come and now is working out the victory already won. To be eschatological Christians in the proper way is to be both expectant about *then* and responsible about *now* in light of *then*. Revelation is not to be seen primarily as the impartation of supernatural knowledge. It is rather the disclosure of the coming new age that already has dawned in the life, death, and resurrection of Jesus. The entire history of biblical revelation is focused by the New Testament on Jesus of Nazareth. He is the definitive Self-revelation of God, the basis and central content of the apostolic good news, and the hope of the world.

A crucial consideration in proper biblical interpretation regarding the future is the focus of our attention as believers. To really know what is to come, Christians are to look to Jesus more than trying to read the signs of the times. It is in Christ that we see best the nature and extent of God's plan for human history and present discipleship. We discover that the Kingdom of God has cosmic implications that now are being worked out through Christ (Eph. 1:10). The eschaton will be only the fuller revelation of the same Jesus of Nazareth introduced to us in the Gospels. The

---

[34]This basic assumption is elaborated in chapter five.

essence of Christian eschatology is that God in Jesus Christ finally will bring to a proper conclusion the salvation begun in Jesus' life, death, and resurrection. The anticipated second coming of Jesus is to be a "return" since whatever is to come will be fully consistent with the character of the first historical advent of Christ. Believers are to look to Jesus and his call to practical discipleship, not to the skies and the headlines for dramatic signs of what is yet to come.

Furthermore, and contrary to the many "dispensationalist" interpreters of our time, the Hebrew Scriptures (Old Testament) cannot be read appropriately in isolation from the New Testament as if Jesus had never come. Many twentieth-century Christians anticipate the consummation of history in Old Testament terms without realizing that the Old Testament hope already has found fulfillment in Jesus Christ.[35] Jesus transcended the narrow nationalism of many of his Jewish contemporaries. When he returns, surely his actions will not revert to the mindset that he rejected at his first coming. Stephen had it right: "The Most High does not dwell in houses made with human hands" (Acts 7:48). God was finished with a literal Temple-oriented religion in New Testament times and hardly will oversee its rebuilding upon his eventual return. A Jesus-centered reading of God's promises concerning the future does not necessarily suggest their fulfillment in a Zionist nation like modern Israel, just as it did not have such political overtones in the first coming of Jesus.

A biblical presupposition that should guide sound biblical interpretation is that Jesus is the *foundation* of all Christian eschatology. Jesus himself is the eschaton (purpose, end) toward whom the ancient Israelite prophets looked, the fulfillment of God's promises, the first and last One. As Adrio König suggests, Jesus Christ also is the *structure* of eschatology. That is, there are three phases of the history of Jesus, three comings of Jesus, with each of

---

[35]This inappropriate focus on the Old Testament as key to future expectations is especially true of Dispensationalists (see chapter four).

these comings further fulfilling the intended eschaton (purpose, end) of God. (1) Jesus came *for us* in Palestine in the first century as the ultimate expression of God with us (Col. 1:15) and sacrificing on our behalf, the conclusion of the long preparatory plan of God (Heb. 1:1-2). (2) Jesus comes *in us* in the ministry of the Spirit to bring new life, transform the once alienated into covenant partners with God, also further fulfilling in this way God's purpose or eschaton. (3) Jesus yet will come to be most fully *with us* and we with him. Then the servants of Christ will reign with him forever (Rev. 22: 3-5).[36]

In summary, attempting to conceive and even control the unexperienced future, reaching in anxiety or just curiosity for confident chronologies, is less appropriate for Christians than concentrating on the meaning of the crucified and risen Christ for present discipleship. Christ is to be central *now* and central *then*, not some supposed inside knowledge about the particulars of end events (Acts 1:7). The ultimate *parousia* (advent or presence) and *epiphaneia* (manifestation or revelation) of Christ will be a time when "the personal presence of Jesus Christ as he was known in crucifixion and resurrection will be made manifest in our world."[37]

The Spirit as the Teacher

The Bible should be read in a Christ-centered manner, something that can be done properly only with the assistance of the Holy Spirit. God's Spirit, who is the Spirit of Jesus, is key to the illumination needed for discovering the current significance of Scripture for Christian life now and for the anticipation of what will be later. The original Inspirer of the biblical revelation surely is in the best position to assist with a contemporary understanding and application of the Bible. We hear Christ say, "Let anyone who has an ear listen to what the Spirit is saying to the churches" (Rev. 3:22).

---

[36]Adrio König, *The Eclipse of Christ in Eschatology* (Grand Rapids: Eerdmans, 1989), chapters 3, 4, and 5.

[37]C. Norman Kraus, op. cit., 204.

The Bible is authoritative for Christians, but wherein does this authority lie? Approaching the answer requires recognition that many "evangelicals" of recent generations have not evidenced. This recognition sees a close link between the reader of a biblical text and that reader's perception of the meaning and authority of that text.[38] Who and where we are as we read, in fact our whole cultural setting is very influential on what we understand by our reading. Capitalizing on this cultural link without capitulating to its distorting possibilities is a central work of the Holy Spirit.

Christians, especially conservative believers in their reaction to classic liberalism, have tended to be more interested in the *inspiration* than the *illumination* of the biblical text (authority vested in the text as received as opposed to awareness of the text's special significance for life now). Fearing what easily can be the unbridled subjectivism of a reader-driven or contextually-guided interpretation, evangelicals tend to focus on historical exegesis, seeking to affirm and protect the authority of the biblical text as originally inspired. They often "ignore the fact that readers bring interests and presuppositions to the text and settle comfortably into a positivist framework of interpretation, viewing the text as stationary object and the reader as detached examiner."[39]

---

[38]Note: "A Wesleyan hermeneutic, though it gives priority to the Scriptures as the basis of all beliefs, assumes that all truth is existentially perceived and appropriated. One does not simply come to the Scriptures with a blank mind and then rationalisticly interpret the Bible. For the Bible is always interpreted through experience, tradition and reason. This is not a subjectivizing of the biblical revelation, but a frank acknowledgment that all truth is mediated in a larger context, rather than merely through a logical and rationalistic framework. This personal-relational dimension is a decisive exegetical and theological presupposition for a Wesleyan hermeneutic. Hence the crucible of life is the laboratory for testing our interpretation of Scripture" (Laurence Wood, "The Wesleyan View" in Donald Alexander, ed., *Christian Spirituality: Five Views of Sanctification*, InterVarsity Press, 1988, 95-96). Also see Donald Thorsen, *The Wesleyan Quadrilateral: Scripture, Tradition, Reason & Experience as a Model of Evangelical Theology* (Grand Rapids: Zondervan, 1990).

[39]Clark Pinnock, "The Role of the Spirit in Interpretation," *Journal of the Evangelical Theological Society* 36:4 (December 1993), 492.

Many leaders of European Pietism in the seventeenth and eighteenth centuries taught that only the spiritually prepared biblical reader will understand the text properly. In other words, there is an intimate connection between holiness of text, holiness of interpreter, and quality and significance of interpretation.[40] More recently, and with good reason, Mary Ford has rejected the characteristic Enlightenment ideal of reading Scripture in an "objective" way. Rather, the knowledge that is intended for conveyance by the Bible, spiritual knowledge of God and of the path to restored relationship with God and God's contemporary work in the world, comes only through a faith-full reading that is inspired by the Spirit and conducted in the context of the believing community.[41] Therefore, Stanley Grenz rightly calls for "the reorientation of the doctrine of Scripture under the doctrine of the Holy Spirit."[42]

The model of the ancient Apostles' Creed is wise, making the Triune God the organizing principle for systematic theology and addressing the content and interpretation of revelation within and not prior to consideration of the being and work of God. In this way the Bible comes to be seen as a dynamic instrument of the Spirit's work, not a static deposit of propositional truths or future predictions to be considered in advance of and even separate from a focus on the past and present work of the Spirit. Instead of exclusive attention being given to the past action of the Spirit in inspiring the biblical authors (insuring the adequacy of their writing in relation to divine intent), there also is need to recognize the Spirit's present work in speaking through the Scriptures to illumine appro-

---

[40]For instance: "For the early Pietists, illumination transformed dead faith into living faith;. The living faith is from the light of the Holy Spirit" (Dale Brown, *Understanding Pietism*, rev. ed., Evangel Publishing House, 1996, 70-71).

[41]Mary Ford, "Seeing, But Not Perceiving: Crisis and Context in Biblical Studies," *St. Vladimir's Theological Quarterly* 35:2-3 (1991), 122.

[42]Stanley Grenz, *Revisioning Evangelical Theology* (InterVarsity Press, 1993), 114. These paragraphs are indebted in part to this work of Grenz, especially his chapter 5.

priate interpretation and fresh application. Believers are to listen to the biblical text (historic meaning) and live in front of the text (present significance). Both tasks require the work of the Spirit of God.

The canon of biblical materials is itself the result of the Spirit's inspiration of original composition and illumination of Israel and the church as they sought ongoing meaning in changing circumstances. Church perception of relevant meaning today rests both on initial divine inspiration, a tradition of divine illumination in the church, and the ongoing illumination work of the Spirit. There is a close relation between Scripture and the believing community, to the extent of saying that, energized at all stages by the Spirit, the Bible is both a *product* of the community of faith and a constant *resource* for that community's fresh belief, application, and expectation. Consequently, "a closer connection between inspiration and illumination would lead evangelicals to a more profound, Spirit-focused rather than text-focused understanding of the nature of biblical trustworthiness."[43] According to 2 Timothy 3:16-17, God "inspires," breathes into the Scripture, thereby keeping it alive, faith producing, and church directing as times and cultures change.[44] The culturally specific *significance* of the biblical texts sometimes changes, but not its *meaning*. Distinguishing the difference is an essential work of the Spirit.

This ongoing illumination of the Spirit of God need not be an open door to unchecked subjectivism among Christians. Brevard Childs provides one helpful way of avoiding this persistent danger. He approaches biblical understanding by examining the process of

---

[43]Ibid., 124. Also see F. F. Bruce, *The Canon of Scripture* (InterVarsity, 1988), 281-282.

[44]The simple and rigid logic of the verbal (inerrancy) theory of the Bible's inspiration is inadequate to convey the mutually interactive relationship between Bible and Spirit. If the Spirit only inspired and then fixed forever the very words of Scripture (the exact "facts" of revelation), then we are taken "back to the Jewish scribal position, which assumed that the prophetic Spirit had been withdrawn from Israel" (Norman Kraus, *God Our Savior*, 158). Such is not the case with the Pentecost people, the church of Christ's Spirit.

the original formation of Scripture as we now have it, particularly the patterns of interpretation and reinterpretation evident over the generations within that very process. Scripture displays examples of its own reinterpretation in ways judged by the faithful community of the past as appropriate to the ongoing and authoritative work of the original inspiring and then later illuminating Spirit. The Spirit enables the interpretation of the Bible as authoritative Scripture through "the canonical context of the church."[45] This view is hard on a "dispensationalist" mentality (see chapter four) that sees fixed promises of God made to Israel long ago, promises that yet will be fulfilled literally and precisely as predicted—despite the claim of the New Testament that such promises already are fulfilled in Jesus Christ and his faithful church.

The Scriptures play the foundational role of being the "constitution of an ongoing community"[46] because they are the product of the faith's formative stage and because they provide the narrative that yields the pivotal events and foundational realities that make the church God's church. In the Bible is the revelation of God's work in the world, the very revelation that the Spirit is prepared to use to bring new life and hope and to form true Christian community in every time and setting. Through the retelling of this

---

[45]Brevard Childs, *Biblical Theology in Crisis* (Philadelphia: Westminster Press, 1970), 104. Drawing on Edmund Clowney, *Preaching and Biblical Theology* (1961), and assuming the Protestant principle that the Bible is its own best interpreter, Richard Lints expands helpfully on three "horizons of interpretation," the textual, ephocal, and canonical (*The Fabric of Theology*, Eerdmans, 1993, 293-310). These horizons are (1) the immediate context of a biblical passage, (2) the context of the period of revelation in which it falls, and (3) the context of the entirety of biblical revelation. Under the guidance of the Spirit, these horizons help an interpreter discipline the questions asked of a text and determine the current relevance of the points made in a text. Regarding any passage, one asks: Is it in the flow of the biblical story of salvation? What does it add to the story? How is it illumined by looking at it in light of the whole of the story, especially Jesus Christ? The Spirit's role is crucial in answering such central questions.

[46]Francis Schussler Fiorenza, "The Crisis of Scriptural Authority," *Interpretation* 44 (October, 1990), 363.

biblical revelation of primal events,[47] "the Spirit re-creates the past within the present life of the community. And the texts thus provide paradigms and categories by means of which the community under the direction of the Spirit can come to understand and respond to the challenges of life in the present."[48] According to Jürgen Moltmann:

> Scripture points beyond itself to the history of the coming kingdom of God. This history is the history of the Spirit, which brings together God's people for the coming kingdom, communicates the powers of healing, and preserves and establishes creation for the day of glory. Holy scripture is no self-contained system of a heavenly doctrine, but promise open to its own fulfillment.[49]

Charles Wesley put it well in his hymns that were intended to be sung or prayed before the reading of Scripture. For instance:

> Come, Holy Ghost, for moved by Thee
> The prophets wrote and spoke;
> Unlock the truth, Thyself the key,
> Unseal the sacred book.[50]

---

[47]Of central significance are the exodus, exile, and messianic expectation of the Hebrews, and the life, teachings, death, and resurrection of Jesus.

[48]Stanley Grenz, *Revisioning Evangelical Theology*, 127.

[49]Jürgen Moltmann, *History and the Triune God*, 67.

[50]As quoted by T. Chrichton Mitchell, *Charles Wesley: Man with the Dancing Heart* (Kansas City: Beacon Hill Press of Kansas City, 1994), 137-138.

Matters Worth Exploring

1. Do you agree that biblical materials, while the revealed Word of God, also are the written products of faithful Christians who were influenced both by their time and place of writing and by the inspiration of God's Spirit?

2. Even though most details about "final things" are not defined clearly by the Bible, Christians typically justify their own speculations by the use of biblical materials. Do such justifications often tell more about the interpreters and their times than about what the biblical writers clearly intended?

3. How do private presuppositions color how biblical interpreters understand what they read? Note this example. On September 13, 1996, I spotted this headline on the front page of *The Indianapolis Star* newspaper: "Christ Resigns As Police Chief!" My first thought (as a theologian) was: "Has Jesus also decided to quit being King of Kings and Lord of Lords, or has he just tired of being police chief?" I was operating out of a wrong mindset and thus had read wrongly the headline. Actually, the headline was about a police chief by the name of Donald Christ.

4. Think about the world in which you now live. How might it be influencing your understanding of the meaning of particular biblical passages? What is one example?

5. How does the popular "once in grace always in grace" teaching illustrate the danger of tight systems of logic and prior theological commitments controlling the process of biblical interpretation?

6. If Christ is the center of Christian faith, the foundation and structure of Christian eschatology, should a Christian's attention be more on what God has done in Christ and is seeking to do now through Christ's Spirit and less on speculation on what is going to happen at the end of time?

Chapter 4

SHIFTING SYSTEMS OF EXPECTATION

❧

Then I saw an angel coming down from heaven, holding in his hand the key to the bottomless pit and a great chain. He seized the dragon, that ancient serpent, who is the Devil and Satan, and bound him for a thousand years, and threw him into the pit, and locked and sealed it over him, so that he would deceive the nations no more, until the thousand years were ended. (Rev. 20:1-3)

❧

Warns one interpreter concerning a particular millennial theory:"It affects some of the most important points in Christian doctrine. It is subversive of the whole aim and mission of the church. Its advocates become so obsessed with it that they believe they find reference to it on almost every page of the Bible.[1]

❧

Admitting to a weariness with a long line of aborted future speculations by well-meaning Christians in all centuries, and recognizing the numerous factors that influence biblical interpretation, an approach to Christian "systems" of expectation is made here with considerable caution. The intent is not to provide the available options so that a reader can choose the best, thus encouraging a uniformity of expectation worked out in an extensive eschatological system. Nor is there intent to add to the already too

---

[1]Russell Byrum, *Christian Theology* (Anderson, Ind.: Warner Press, 1925, rev. ed. 1982), 520.

large body of speculation by setting up one more aborted plan of premature predictions or devising my own systematic scheme of future expectation. Five core beliefs appear basic and adequate: God already has come in Jesus Christ; the Spirit of Christ came to the church at Pentecost and remains as power and wisdom for the church's mission; the Lord one day will return to judge and consummate all things; the primary task now is for the Christ-anchored and Spirit-filled church to be faithful in the meantime.

With such core beliefs in mind, there should be caution about all patterns of future speculation which appear to have only slight biblical credibility at best and which tend to use up precious Christian time and energy on subjects other than the present challenges of Christian living and church mission. The call of Christ is to serious discipleship, not to eschatological system building. It is not my intent to belittle such systems or act arrogantly like I have superior insight into the exact meaning of every verse of the Bible that bears on the future. Even so, surely Jesus' own modesty about the time of his own return stands as a model for the proper eschatological modesty of the faithful. John Calvin, for instance, thought it "rash to inquire into matters unknown more deeply than God allows us to know."[2] In relation to confident assertions about supposed prophetic insight, it is troublesome indeed that proponents frequently fail to recognize the limited and genuinely debatable nature of their own interpretations and speculations.

Two of my own presuppositions are stated immediately. (1) It is my intent to lift up Jesus Christ as central and definitive for all eschatological subjects, hoping thereby to keep first things first. I urge that any speculation keep faithful to the foundation of all Christian eschatology, Jesus Christ. (2) It also is my intent to be sensitive to the church's call to be on mission in the present time. Therefore, I tend to resonate with Carl Braaten's self-declared task of "constantly promoting the relevance of eschatology for church

---

[2]As quoted by Heinrich Heppe, *Reformed Dogmatics* (London: George Allen and Unwin, 1950), 695.

renewal and Christian ethics." Such relevance, he says, "is to believe that the essence of things lies in their future; nothing that exists is exactly as it ought to be; everything is subject to the call for radical conversion; and all are heirs of the promise of fulfillment."[3]

A central feature of most Christian systems of expectation is the concept of a coming "millennium." One brief biblical passage stands at the heart of differing expectations of the second coming of Jesus and the events expected to somehow surround that glorious event. It is the passage mentioning a thousand years. According to Revelation 20:1-3:

> Then I saw an angel coming down from heaven, holding in his hand the key to the bottomless pit and a great chain. He seized the dragon, that ancient serpent, who is the Devil and Satan, and bound him for a thousand years, and threw him into the pit, and locked and sealed it over him, so that he would deceive the nations no more, until the thousand years were ended. After that he must be let out for a little while.

Such a rare biblical reference to a millennium (one-thousand year period) has spawned much speculation among Christians, but with little practical result. Systems of expectation come and go and necessarily are adjusted constantly to fit evolving reality.

Extraordinary value has been seen by believers over the centuries in books like Esther, Daniel, and Revelation. Their messages of hope in the face of violent persecution have bolstered courage in various centuries and political circumstances. Esther enabled the survival of the Jewish people in ancient Persia. Her story was treasured by European Jews treated harshly in the Middle Ages, and it was hated by Hitler and helped fire his attempt at a "final solution" for the Jews in twentieth-century Europe. Jesus prevailed even over Roman crucifixion. As told in the Book of Revelation, the

---

[3]Carl Braaten, *Eschatology and Ethics* (Minneapolis: Augsburg Publishing House, 1974), 6.

thrilling story of his triumph then and also at the coming end of time inspired the persecuted Polycarp (c.70-160) as he was burned at the stake. These biblical books, arising from given sets of circumstances, had immediate relevance in the initial settings of their writing, as well as usefulness for the synagogue and church in much later times that resembled the original circumstances.

The Book of Revelation, for instance, a frequent source of shifting eschatological systems of Christian expectation, was not written in the twentieth century or even with the twentieth or twenty-first century primarily in mind. John was called to write a message of comfort to troubled Christian people of his time. The book's relevance for the renewal and encouragement of today's church is of keen concern to contemporary Christians, of course— and clearly the book offers such potential. But the first question to be answered is what John's writing meant to Christians of the late first century. Only then can one begin to grasp what it ought to mean to believers many centuries later. The central intent of the ancient writer was *relevance for that present time.*

Bankrupt Utopias

One strain of popular wisdom claims that waiting and hoping turns many people into fools. By longing for tomorrow, they miss their todays. But biblical hope does not detach the human spirit from the present through unfounded delusions based on futuristic preoccupations. On the contrary, God's promised future is pulled into the present and "places the experienced present in the dawn of God's future."[4] Believers are "born anew to a living hope through the resurrection of Jesus Christ from the dead" (1 Pet. 1:3). Such hope is inspiring and fortifies believers for hard times. Severe persecution and outbursts of fresh hope have been frequent across the centuries since the time of the earliest church. Sometimes the hope has lost its way and become intensely predictive and delusionary

---

[4]Jürgen Moltmann, in D. Musser and J. Price, eds., *A New Handbook of Christian Theology* (Nashville: Abingdon Press, 1992), 239.

in nature, leaving behind a trail of frustration. A balanced eschatological perspective is difficult to maintain.

One of the earliest instances of Christian hope failing to balance properly an assurance of God's certain future and a focus on God's present mission in the world was instigated by Montanus. He was a Christian convert from Asia Minor who called for intense spirituality of believers in the face of growing formalism and worldliness in the official church. Just beyond the middle of the second century after Christ, claiming a special revelation from God and reading the New Testament in a very literalistic manner, he prophesied that the heavenly Jerusalem would soon come to Phrygia. Many Christians responded to his exciting sense of certainty, sold all their belongings, and moved to Phrygia. The dramatic prediction did not happen, encouraging critics to discount the Christian faith altogether. Montanus was virtually excommunicated when the Synod of Iconium in 230 A. D. refused to recognize the validity of Montanist baptism. Other such movements within the Christian community would arise across the centuries to follow. Some eventually were considered "orthodox" in general, but with their eschatological speculations more questionable and dated.

In the sixteenth century, for instance, Martin Luther thought of the Roman Catholic Church as a source of Antichrist. He rejected all hope of a future millennium and looked in his lifetime for a cataclysmic end of time to be initiated by the return of Christ. Here was Luther's view:

> It is my firm belief that the angels are getting ready, putting on their armor and girding their swords about them, for the last day is already breaking, and the angels are preparing for the battle, when they will overthrow the Turks and hurl them along with the pope, to the bottom of hell. The world will perish shortly.[5]

---

[5]Conversations with Martin Luther. See Hugh T. Kerr, *A Compend of Luther's Theology* (Philadelphia: Westminster Press, 1963), 244.

It did not happen either how or when expected.

Joseph Smith (1805-1844) claimed that he experienced visions calling him to restore what he thought of as the true Christian religion. He announced that an angel had guided him to a set of golden plates buried near the Smith farm in upstate New York. Translating the strange script "by the gift and power of God," Smith published the "Book of Mormon" in 1830. This charismatic figure and presumed religious record of ancient North American inhabitants launched the Church of Jesus Christ of Latter-day Saints and Smith's own tumultuous private life that was ended when he was assassinated by a mob in 1844. He is only one of numerous such figures representing apparent streaks of fresh prophetic light that, once having made a dramatic public appearance, fade quickly into the general darkness.

The twentieth century has given cause for numerous utopian movements to emerge inside and outside of Christianity. The nuclear age has brought unprecedented dread to the world's masses. Beginning with the eighteenth-century Enlightenment and proceeding into the twentieth century, numerous critics have scorned the traditional Christian hopes for Christ's second coming and heaven, calling them ignorance, fear, and irrelevant escapism. In at least one sense these critics have been right. To allow a future hope to wrench one free of a serious obligation to participation in the present is indeed abortive of the mission of the church itself. Even so, faith in the God of creation and redemptive purpose implies a directional plan headed toward some substantial fulfillment beyond the limited accomplishments of this evil age. The balance between the end hoped for and the present now faced is crucial.

Marxist utopianism emerged as the dominant reality for a large percentage of the human population of earth for much of the twentieth century. It motivated whole societies with a revolutionary and secularized version of the biblical hope. As the twentieth century ends, however, disillusionment has virtually destroyed any widespread belief in this alternative to Christian faith. Communism now has crumbled into a massive social failure and frustrated hope that most of the world now recognizes. Nonetheless, Ernst Bloch has developed a neo-Marxist view driven by a hope for a future that transcends all alienation. Not God, but a revolutionary proletariat presumably will bring judgment on capitalist oppressors and thus bring about a socialistic new heaven and earth.[6] "Presumably" is the key word.

In recent generations Christians often have been urged to adopt a "liberal" theory of human and social progress. Education is to replace eschatology. Science is thought to be a surer path to knowledge than special revelation. Human reason is to rise while Christian theology yields to some secular utopianism. Under this pressure, Christian eschatology soon deteriorated into a "harmless little chapter at the conclusion of Christian Dogmatics."[7] What some day will be became seen as so controversial among Christians that it could be placed in an "optional" category and basically ignored. But ignoring God's future is necessarily to impoverish the doing of God's will for the present. There is an inherent and foundational connection between the Christian's hope in the coming God and the present meaning of being Christian and being the church God intends in this world that still remains.

Things have changed. It now is recognized widely that Christian eschatology no longer can afford to be seen as limited, insignificant, harmless and nice, an impossible mass of conflicting theories, an optional afterthought to the heart of Christian theology. Competitive liberal visions of the ideal future have been shattered in the face of two world wars, nuclear weapons, the Holocaust, and impending ecological disaster due largely to human greed, hate, and waste. Theories of a better and better world through technology and education are virtually bankrupt. Marxism has collapsed, having failed to deliver its grand promises. Theorists

---

[6]Ernst Bloch, *The Philosophy of Hope*, 3 vols. (Cambridge, MIT, 1985).

[7]Karl Barth, *The Epistle to the Romans*, trans. Edwyn Hoskyns (London: Oxford University Press, 1933), 500.

now talk longingly of a post-liberal and post-modern world, something to follow the collapsing one we have known. The disastrous results of both failed communistic societies and failing affluent, consumerist societies somehow must be reversed. The realities of our world need to be addressed by a hope that is neither naively utopian nor irresponsibly escaping into a currently irrelevant anticipation of an otherworldly realm.

Unfortunately, escapism is all too evident in the church as it searches for relevance and a prophetic voice in these difficult times. Hal Lindsey speaks of a future that is to end in a nuclear holocaust of God's judgment.[8] Claiming to interpret biblical teaching from a privileged prophetic position, he and many others capitalize on news headlines and the public's confusion, fear, and virtual biblical illiteracy. They publish calendars and descriptions of events announced as ordained by God to end this evil age. The true church is to hope because it will be able to avoid the coming horrors of the "tribulation" by special action of God that will sweep the church away to a better place while terror is unleashed below. Meanwhile, as this plethora of prophecy fills bookstores and airwaves, the world and its peoples languish in hunger and hatred, in self-indulgence and militarism—and the end is not yet. A true Christian theology of hope must assist Christians to avoid the twin dangers of social disillusionment, and thus an abandonment of the church's social mission, and an otherworldly inwardness that easily aborts the now in favor of private "experiences" and God's later time.

The biblical story of God in Israel and in Christ certainly does move along a clear path to a sure consummation. Its focus, however, is not on satisfying the curious believer and horrifying the stubborn unbeliever. It does not intend to distract the church

---

[8]Hal Lindsey, *The Late Great Planet Earth* (Grand Rapids: Zondervan, 1970). This brand of apocalypticism is critiqued sharply and rightly by Daniel Migliore (*Faith Seeking Understanding*, Eerdmans, 1991, 236).

with a game about which Bible verse appears fulfilled by which newspaper headline. The biblical revelation is hardly an eschatological game in which all the answers are lying in a pile before us, only needing to be sorted out and turned over whenever we are ready to see all the hidden sides of what is about to be.

On the contrary, the biblical story argues that the church should address constructively the many horrors of the present. The faith naturally yearns for a final fulfillment of the peace, justice, and reconciliation already brought in Christ. But its eschatology should be a vision of the future that intends to send sacrificing and reconciling believers into the problems of the present as agents of a better future. Living Jesus' way, the church is to be engaged in healing, reconciling, and peacemaking. Theology should guide Christian believers into service, not tempt them with energy-draining speculation about God's future. The gospel is now! The future will take care of itself in God's good time and way.

An important caution is in order. Focusing on the present meaningfulness of faith and avoiding confusing and dividing speculations about the future should not lead to a denial of the reality of the future. Equally as problematic as escaping the present responsibility of Christian discipleship by an inordinate focus on the future is escaping the sobering fact of the future by an inordinate focus on the present—as though now is all there is or ever will be.[9] The eschatological present ushered in by the first coming of Jesus is critical; but Jesus' first coming does not substitute for the eschatological future that will be ushered in by his second coming.

Paul Tillich is one Christian theologian who gives up too much by saying that the eschaton is no longer "an imaginative matter about an indefinitely far (or near) catastrophe in time and

---

[9]This is the problem with the eschatology of Rudolf Bultmann. To him the "mythical" eschatology of the New Testament is untenable since the soon return of Christ never took place as the New Testament church expected. But we no longer need this mythical framework anyway, he concludes, since the coming of Christ should be interpreted in anthropological or existential terms, not cosmological ones.

space." What is the eschaton for the Christian? He claims that it is only "an expression of our standing in every moment in face of the eternal."[10] Tillich fails to affirm that the Christian hope also remains a hope not to be separated from coming events in time and space, even if detail is not presently available and should not be pursued as a justified preoccupation of curious or anxious believers. The biblical narrative of God-among-us is a story with beginning and end, both on the stage of real, trans-personal history.

Millennial Models

Many Christians focus inordinately on trans-personal history, seeking whole systems of understanding of what yet will be. Escape from present discipleship responsibility comes in many forms. One is extensive speculation about the future. Often such speculation centers around a given millennial theory.[11] A "millennium" (one-thousand year period of righteousness and peace, presumably on earth)[12] is mentioned briefly only in Revelation 20.[13] On this modest biblical base, the subject has become a great preoccupation of countless Christian leaders across the whole of the church's existence.

For instance, Joachim of Fiore (c.1135-1202) was a Cistercian monk who lived in Italy. He developed a speculative approach to reading the periods and progress of human history within the plan of God by dividing history into three eras, using as

---

[10]Paul Tillich, *Systematic Theology*, vol. 3 (University of Chicago Press, 1963), 395.

[11]For further study of the basic millennial views, see Robert Clouse, ed., *The Meaning of Millennium: Four Views* (InterVarsity Press, 1977).

[12]The word "millennium" derives from the Latin *mille* (thousand) and *annus* (year). Among Greek-speaking Christians the word "chiliasm" is common, derived from the Greek *chilia* (thousand).

[13]George Eldon Ladd, a premillennialist, acknowledges that "the only place in the Bible that speaks of an actual millennium is this passage" (in Robert Clouse, ed., *The Meaning of the Millennium*, 1977, 32).

his model the Trinity of God. The age of the Father, he taught, corresponds to the Old Testament dispensation. The age of the Son corresponds to the New Testament dispensation (the church), while the age of the Spirit will be the final establishment of peace and unity on earth, initiated by the rise of new movements of the Spirit that would renew the church. Joachim went so far as to date these periods. Each consisted of forty-two generations of thirty years each, with the age of the Son due to end in 1260 A. D., to be followed immediately by the radical new age of the Spirit. Joachim's scheme anticipated many of the millenarian movements of our own day.

The Book of Revelation is used often in support of all millennial models. Frequently it is claimed that it anticipates an end time when Christians will endure suffering and a "great tribulation" (7:14; 12:17) when a beast or Antichrist will kill the saints (11:7; 13:7, 15). Christ's return will signal the judgment of the beast and the triumph of the saints (15:1-4). Mentioned briefly is a thousand-year reign of the saints with Christ (20:4-6). However, the meaning, interrelationship, and sequencing of these "events" is perplexing and controversial. One might well argue that these were intended to constitute a series of images intended for the encouragement of oppressed believers and not for the development of a precise predictive plan of coming events. Even so, numerous Christian interpreters have sought to discover such a plan and to relate it to the trends of their own times.

The times do help shape perspective on such elusive matters. The apparent prominence of four major millennial views in differing periods of church history illustrates this key point.[14] In brief,

---

[14]Proponents of each theory often find their views significantly valued in various periods of church history when other interpreters, looking at the same evidence, do not. One should be cautious about reading back to much earlier times the highly developed millennial theories prominent in the twentieth century. George Marsden, for instance, observes that clear distinctions in terminology between "premillennialism" and "postmillennialism" do not seem to occur before the nineteenth century, and "amillennialism" was not so termed until the twentieth century (*Fundamentalism and American Culture*, N. Y.: Oxford, 1980, 240).

the millennium has been understood figuratively by some as the present reign of Christ through the gospel and ministry of the Holy Spirit, by others as the reward of the martyrs in heaven, and by many others more literally as a yet future period of Christ's rule on earth before or after he returns again. The main schools of millennial thought tend to separate from each other on whether certain biblical texts point literally or symbolically to a future earthly reign of Christ, whether any such reign will occur before or after his glorious return, and whether the Old Testament promises to Israel are fulfilled in Christ and the church or in a revived nation of Israel near the end of time. Each school of thought is characterized by a particular view of history and thus the attitude that ought to characterize the church as it seeks to pursue its mission in this present world. Following are brief overviews of the four most prominent millennial models of Christian expectation.

1. Postmillennialism. Millennialists teach that the Kingdom of God will assume a very visible expression in a literal, millennial (1,000 years) reign of Christ on earth. Some of them, *postmillennialists*, hold that Christ will come again only after (post-) such a welcome millennium has evolved on our earthly scene. Christ is to reign now through the successful efforts of an obedient church that "Christianizes" wayward societies through gospel witness, faithfulness, and the power of the Spirit.

During the seventeenth century, for instance, the Puritans of England and New England tended to read the Old Testament prophecies as pictures of the church destined to enjoy great evangelistic success. They came to believe that the Holy Spirit would bring a worldwide revival before Jesus returned. The threshold of this revival was thought to be at hand in their time. Jonathan Edwards (1703-1758) was a significant influence in causing many American Christians to believe that the preaching of the gospel and use of the ordinary means of grace would usher in a glorious millennial era before the return of Christ. The expectation of a worldwide establishment of the Kingdom of Christ is reflected in Isaac Watts' great hymn, "Jesus Shall Reign Where 'er the Sun."

Adam Clarke (d. 1832), one of Methodism's great early theologians, maintained a postmillennial tendency as he commented on Revelation 20:2. "There is no doubt that the earth is in a state of progressive moral improvement; and that the light of true religion is shining more copiously everywhere; and will shine more and more to the perfect day."[15] The English Presbyterian minister Matthew Henry had popularized postmillennialism in his celebrated commentary, *An Exposition of the Old and New Testaments* (London, 1708-10). While John Wesley (1703-1791) did not develop and defend any system of eschatological thought, his writings also tend to be in keeping with a postmillennial frame of reference.

The church's obedience in embodying and witnessing to the gospel, it is argued, will lead to a millennium of righteousness and peace prior to the climax of history, Christ's return.[16] The voice of the Spirit is heard calling the church to vigorous engagement with the world and is known to be providing assurance that the fruit of such labor will become visible in present structures and relationships. Postmillennialism typified much of the Wesleyan-Holiness biblical interpretation of the nineteenth century. Highlighted in this revivalist tradition was a transformationist view calling the church to responsibility as an active agent of the Spirit of God in the renewal of individual and social life by the received grace of God. This tradition featured "perfectionism" and an "optimism of grace."

In the postmillennial view, God is championed as sovereign over history and calling the faithful to advance the divine reign

---

[15]Adam Clarke, *Commentary and Critical Notes* (Cincinnati: Applegate, 1856, 4 vols.), 4:1074.

[16]For example, see Walter Rauschenbusch, *A Theology for the Social Gospel* (1917). Some interpreters criticize the optimism of this position, fearing that it leads too easily to a "humanistic" reliance on other than divine enablement to bring God's Kingdom to present reality.

through the power of the Spirit and before the return of the Son. Viewed positively, this perspective nurtures faith's optimism and inspires aggressive mission to the world.[17] Left unbridled, postmillennial optimism runs the risk of separating itself from its distinctively Christian source and degenerating into a blind utopianism[18] or even a shameful use of violence—it was used, for instance, to support the justifications of the Crusades. The Christian hope is not to be an end of realism in the face of continuing human sin. In fact, given the dramatic evidence of human sin that surfaced so dramatically with World Wars I and II, the postmillennial view virtually disappeared. It began to sink in April, 1912, with the shocking loss of the Titanic, the "unsinkable" luxury liner, a microcosm of the proud new world that crashed into an iceberg on the North Atlantic. Money, fame, and high technology plunged into a vast icy darkness that had no mercy and was hard on hope.

2. Premillennialism. While there is an invigorating, mission-minded optimism about postmillennialism, other Christians, *premillennialists*, read the ending of the biblical story somewhat differently. They certainly are evangelistic, but also are more pessimistic about present possibilities for the progress of the divine

---

[17]In fact, one interpreter of postmillennialism concludes: "The dynamism and optimism engendered by this view fostered what are usually regarded by Christians as the most important developments of the last two centuries: the Evangelical Awakening; the modern missionary movement; and the building of a worldwide church" (Ian Rennie, in Armerding and Gasque, eds., *Dreams, Visions and Oracles*, Grand Rapids: Baker Book House, 1977, 43). A more contemporary exponent of postmillennialism is J. Marcellus Kik (*An Eschatology of Victory*, Philadelphia: Presbyterian and Reformed, 1971).

[18]In part as a result of the Enlightenment mentality and the sweeping social changes of the industrial and technological revolution of the nineteenth century, a "liberal" stream of Protestantism arose. While hardly guilty at all times of being blindly utopian, its eschatological emphasis clearly shifted away from focus on events of the end time to a central concern for this world and the development of a social theology for the church's significant service to this world. Prominent leaders were Friedrich Schleiermacher (1768-1834), Albrecht Ritschl (1822-1889), and Adolf von Harnack (1851-1930).

reign in earthly affairs. They think instead that Christ is scheduled to return before (pre-) an earthly millennium. His return, in fact, is what will keynote a dramatic defeat of the evil forces through a divine intervention that then allows an earthly expression of the wonderful reign of God for 1,000 years. This divine reign will come not through the cumulative faithfulness of the church, but only through God's direct and dramatic intervention. The church in the meantime is to be faithful and patiently endure, knowing, however, that its efforts never will usher in the reign of God in this earthly life. God alone will bring the Kingdom at Christ's return. Those who will enjoy the millennial blessings are Abraham's spiritual children of all ages, the church.

This general view appears to have been common among the Ante-Nicene "Fathers," although it soon came to be challenged by Origen, Augustine, and the Greek "Fathers." Classically, premillennialism has traced all of human history on the pattern of six one-thousand-year periods, corresponding to the six days of creation, plus another thousand as the day of rest that the Lord first inaugurated and will again be at Christ's return. Toward the end of the sixth "day," the persecution and suffering of believers will increase, to be climaxed by the reign of the Antichrist until Christ appears suddenly to slay Antichrist, bind Satan, and establish the millennial period. The millennium will be a time of peace and righteousness during which many Jews will finally accept Jesus as their Messiah. There will be separate resurrections for different groups, one at the beginning and one at the end of the millennium, followed by the final judgment and the re-creation of the heavens and earth as God's eternal Kingdom.

Premillennialism holds particular appeal for Christians living in days of disaster when the cry of the faithful is for a speedy return of Christ to vindicate his suffering people. For instance, this prophetic view emerged in the Peasant Wars (1524-25) that accompanied the Continental Reformation. Then the premillennialism of Johann Alsted (1588-1638) found a positive response among some contemporary Puritans facing a government staunchly opposed to their views.[19] The watershed of the French Revolution and the Napoleonic wars in the generation between 1789 and 1815 also gave rise to the expectation of the soon return of Christ, with a literal millennium on earth to follow.

3. Dispensationalism. A significant variation of premillennialism, arising with the thought of John Nelson Darby (1800-1882) and especially influential in recent decades, is dispensationalism. Darby, an early leader of the Plymouth Brethren in Great Britain, was distressed by the lethargy of the Irish Anglicanism of his day and he found the somber note of premillennialism appropriate to his experience. The variation that he developed emphasizes strongly a literal interpretation of key portions of the Bible's eschatological language, believing that all the Old Testament promises to the Jews will be fulfilled during the coming thousand years, including their restoration to the land of Israel and the rebuilding of the Temple in Jerusalem.[20] Dispensationalism centers in a literal interpretation of select Old Testament prophecies and then fitting the New Testament into them. God is said to have dealt with humanity through several covenants and seven distinct dispensations, with number five being the dispensation of law (Ex. 19:8), six that of grace (Jn. 1:17), and seven that of the Kingdom (Eph. 1:10).

Dispensationalism spread rapidly in the United States after the publication of the second edition of the *Scofield Reference Bible* in 1917 and the charts that then appeared in *Dispensational Truth* by Clarence Larkin in 1918. It has become a complex scheme of Christian expectation with growing variation among its

---

[19]Alsted's influential book was *The Beloved City* (1627). It influenced the Anglican scholar Joseph Mede, whose work then joined Alsted's in reviving the premillennial thought that accompanied the Puritan Revolution of the 1640s.

[20]The founding of the modern State of Israel in 1948 was, of course, seen by such interpreters as dramatic evidence of the correctness of this view and the soon-coming of the other expected prophetic fulfillments.

numerous adherents. Craig Blaising presents an analysis of classical, revised, and progressive dispensationalism, noting a current questioning or even rejection of the central "two peoples" theory.[21] This theory separates Israel and the church, seeing them as two distinct peoples of God with different covenants in effect simultaneously. Dispensationalists typically have taught that the church was created almost as a temporary divine afterthought once God's chosen people, Israel, had rejected the Messiah. The church is a "parenthesis" in God's prophetic plan and soon will be "raptured" away to heaven when God finally gets back to finishing the fulfillment of the original plans for Israel. The millennial blessings are for the restored nation of Israel.[22]

Historical premillennialism stresses the New Testament as key to the Old. The church, God's heavenly people, fulfills God's Old Testament promises to Israel, God's earthly people, and the millennial age is essentially Christian and has no necessary relation to the restoration of national Israel in Palestine.[23] Dispensational premillennialism, however, emphasizes the authority of the Old Testament in millennial matters, including the mil-

---

[21]Craig Blaising, "Changing Patterns in American Dispensational Theology," *Wesleyan Theological Journal* 29:1-2 (Spring/Fall, 1994). Kenneth Grider refers to dispensational premillennialism as "the one millennial view to which Scripture stands most clearly opposed" (*A Wesleyan-Holiness Theology*, Beacon Hill Press of Kansas City, 1994, 533).

[22]To the contrary, the New Testament and the church are hardly to be seen rightly as an interlude, a detour from the main track of the Covenant rooted in the original promise to Abraham and delivered to Moses. A true reading of the Old Testament is found with those who have repented and been recreated by the Lord Jesus (2 Cor. 3:14-16). A Jew now is a matter of the heart (Rom. 2:29). In Christ there now is neither Jew nor Greek, for all are one in Jesus Christ (1 Cor. 12:13; Gal. 3:28; Col. 3:11).

[23]Even if Paul did expect a national conversion of Israel at the end (an unclear assumption), he does not say a word about any return of the Jews to Israel, about the rebuilding of Jerusalem and the Temple, about any visible and political rule of the returned Christ on this earth. In Paul's picture of the future there appears to be no room for all of this speculation. See Herman Bavinck, *The Last Things*, trans. John Vriend, ed. John Bolt (Grand Rapids: Baker Books, 1996, chapter five).

lennial reign referred to in Revelation 20:1-10. The Old Testament promises to Israel concerning a future national glory in Palestine are yet to be fulfilled (or began being fulfilled in 1948 with the founding of the modern State of Israel). Thus, the coming millennial age has a distinctly Old Testament and Jewish character. In recent decades, dispensationalism has become a common Christian view among a wide range of conservative Christians, especially those emphasizing on their popular radio and television programs that prophetic fulfillment is happening before our very eyes as the twentieth century ends.

4. Amillennialism. There are still other Christians, *amillennialists*,[24] who do not anticipate any thousand-year golden age of the political reign of Christ on earth, after or before the return of Christ. The negative *a* in a-millennial probably is an unfortunate prefix since most adherents of this view do not reject completely all millennial concepts, usually only the ones that are seen as excessively literal in their biblical interpretation, politically oriented in their expectations, and draw attention away from the central significance of the faithfulness of the church in the interim between the first and second comings of Christ. Augustine was an early amillennialist, believing that the millennial period was not totally in the future, but that, since Jesus Christ already had bound Satan, the millennium was just another way of describing the blessings of the age of grace, the gospel, and the church. For over one thousand years, or past the Reformation of the sixteenth century, amillennialism was the basic prophetic view of Christians.

The focus of amillennialism is not on presumed knowledge about future tribulations, raptures, and multiple resurrections, but

---

[24]The term *amillennialism* is something of a misnomer since this position does not argue against a millennium altogether, only against the expectation of a literal, earthly-historical millennium not already present in part in the presence and power of the Holy Spirit.

primarily on the present reign of Christ launched by the resurrection of Jesus and the subsequent outpouring of the Spirit at Pentecost. In regard to the potential effectiveness of gospel witness in the present, amillennialists reject as extreme and biblically unwarranted both the optimism of the *post* view and the pessimism of the *pre* view. Rather, it is understood that the biblical revelation presents the proper Christian attitude toward the present world as neither utopian nor despairing. Christians should be sober and realistic about the success of the gospel in this present age—but without such caution being crippling to aggressive mission. The Kingdom of God never will arrive in its fullness within the current confines of a corrupted creation. Even so, God's call is for the church to be a redeemed and redeeming people who focus on what God already has done in Christ, celebrate the new life now available in the Spirit, and through faithful discipleship become a sign of hope for all who will yield to the grace of a new creation, God's Kingdom that in part already has come.

Of all the millennial views, the amillennial is the one most interested in the church as itself an eschatological phenomenon (see chapter six). The church is to be the fulfillment of many if not most of the prophecies of the messianic Kingdom. Revelation 20:1-10, the only biblical passage speaking directly of a thousand-year reign of Christ on earth, is understood to be taking the reader back to the beginning of the church in New Testament times. The defeat of Satan began with Christ's first advent, especially with his atoning work (Jn. 12:31-33). The thousand years, typical of biblical symbolism, is understood as an undetermined period extending from the first coming of Christ in Bethlehem to the second coming at the end of the age.

Here is a perspective modest in its speculations and neither overly optimistic nor pessimistic about the possible progress of the visible reign of God in our present age. God is known to have broken into our world already, inaugurating the divine reign and making possible a canceling of the power of sin through the work of the Spirit. The fullness of the Kingdom is expected to arrive only when Christ returns, concludes the historical process, judges, and brings eternity into being. The hope of that coming reality, rooted in and shaped by Christ's first coming, provides the vision and energy required to be God's people now.

This amillennial view picks up central themes of the gospel message and appears to fit well the structure of the biblical revelation. The Kingdom of God will not come in its fullness in this world by human cooperation with God's plan, but neither is the Kingdom simply the divine gift for which believers only wait in passive anticipation. Neither unchastened optimism nor despairing pessimism fit the God whose grace is all-sufficient and who now is working in a world where evil should never be taken lightly and divinely-given freedom is still a reality. If the church is faithful in the meantime, yielding to the guidance and power of the Holy Spirit, it will be "successful" penultimately, even though ultimate success will come only by God's grace beyond human effort and historical time.

There, of course, is weakness in any pattern of future expectation. Some amillennialists tend to overly "spiritualize" future expectations and insist on an unbiblical disjunction between the "physical" and the "spiritual." Physical health and political justice are clear concerns of the Hebrew tradition and should be part of Christian faithfulness in the time between Jesus in Bethlehem and Jesus coming in final victory at the end of the age. Some amillennialists fall easily into a church imperialism by identifying too closely the Kingdom of Christ and the "visible" church (as did Augustine and John Calvin). Some also tend to take away from Christian expectancy of Christ's second coming by seeing this coming already realized, at least in part, by the gift of the Holy Spirit to the church soon after Jesus ascended. Thus, "the view advanced by Calvin and Barth that we are already in the last days (since we are living in the period between Christ's resurrection and second advent) is acceptable so long as a role is still given to the last day (as distinct from the last days)...."[25]

The Role of Historical Context

Millennial theories, especially the varieties of premillennialism, have evolved into complex systems of vivid expectation, each working from its own set of presuppositions about adequate biblical interpretation.[26] Each has had its time of prominence in the Christian community, with none gaining an ecumenical consensus. It is rather obvious that the circumstances being experienced by the church and general culture in a given time are influential on how the church of that time views the nature and nearness of its future hope.

Premillennialism was typical of the early church,[27] consistent with that church's status as a persecuted minority awaiting divine intervention and vindication. By contrast, Augustine was the first prominent teacher of amillennialism. He lived after Emperor Constantine had reversed the fortunes of Christians in the Roman Empire. Christian faith had nominally permeated the culture known to Augustine, tempting believers to see the millennium as already arriving, the millennial promise being fulfilled in the life of the church itself.[28] At the Council of Ephesus

---

[25]Donald Bloesch, *Essentials of Evangelical Theology* (San Francisco: Harper & Row, 1979), 2:197.

[26]For good reviews and critiques of these millennial positions, see Millard Erickson, *Contemporary Options in Eschatology* (Baker, 1977) and Stanley Grenz, *The Millennial Maze* (InterVarsity Press, 1992).

[27]While this is a common observation, it should not leave the impression that the early church "fathers" had access to the same range of developed millennial theories available today and deliberately chose the premillennial over the other options.

[28]In the Church of God movement (Anderson), F. G. Smith (*The Revelation Explained*, 1908) and Lillie McCutcheon (*The Symbols Speak*, 1964) have taught from this general perspective. They use the literature of Daniel and Revelation as a biblical context for understanding the rise and role of the Church of God movement in God's plan (a use now questioned by other key biblical interpreters of the movement like Otto Linn, Kenneth Jones, Boyce Blackwelder, John Stanley, and Marie Strong). None of these interpreters, however, have been inclined to be rash date-setters.

in 431 A. D., belief in a literal millennium was condemned as superstition, demonstrating the persuasiveness of Augustinian eschatology at the time. In his *City of God*, Augustine pictures the church as the sixth day of the seven day-ages of the world. The church era is the millennium of Revelation 20.

Many leaders of the American holiness movement in the nineteenth century were postmillennialists. Their optimism of grace led to belief that personal motives could be turned to perfect love and the sinful cities could be transformed. In fact, belief in the inevitability of progress has been a cardinal doctrine of Western culture generally since the eighteenth century. As knowledge increases, it has been assumed, humankind could and would take increasing control of nature and surmount social ills. But economic depression and two world wars in the twentieth century culminated a sobering process that helped turn most conservatives back to premillennialism.[29] Many believers now sense that "civilization" is tottering on the edge of extinction and will be saved only by a dramatic divine event, the return of Christ. Biblical scholarship more recently has encouraged a move away from literal millennial expectations (pre- or post-) to more of an amillennialism that embraces the apparent fullness of the New Testament view of the *already/not yet* of the Kingdom's

---

[29]See Donald Dayton, *Theological Roots of Pentecostalism* (Hendrickson Publishers, 1987, chapter six). He details the earlier process of this shift in the nineteenth century. The optimism of progress basic to postmillennialism, encouraging mission and social action, suffered after the Civil War from the negative results of waves of immigration, the rise of biblical criticism, and the dehumanizing effects of urbanization and industrialization. In recent decades liberation theologies have renewed the focus on the power of God and the potential of the transformation of this present world by concerted Christian action. They tend to reflect an optimistic world view like the older postmillennialism. The Believers' Church tradition does not share such optimism about society's potential redemption and often balks at working primarily through established structures of the state to effect Christian ends (see, for instance, the writings of J. Denny Weaver).

realization.[30] Even so, the ethos of the times has a way of over-whelming the popularly perceived significance of scholarly stances.

Again, it is important to recognize that one's view of such matters often derives from more than "what the Bible plainly teaches." Social forces influence views of reality, the sources of hope, and sometimes what we come to believe the Bible actually does teach. To some degree we all are creatures of our times. Note, for instance, Richard Hughes' insightful recounting of the story of the Churches of Christ in America. He explores "the premillennial controversy" and the eventual "demise of the apocalyptic perspective." Why the big change? Especially during the World War I era, "the heart and soul of that change involved a fundamental reappraisal of human potential."[31]

Affirmed here is the assumption that Jesus Christ should be viewed as the center of Christian eschatology (see chapter five). Accordingly, it probably is best to recognize...

> no difference of time or essence between the kingdom of God which came in Jesus and the so-called thousand-year reign. The latter is a figure employed by John [Book of Revelation] to convey the truth that Jesus has overcome Satan and ever increases his kingdom in triumph despite the repeated assaults of a Satan who goes about as a roaring lion, against whom the church is so safe that the gates of hell will not prevail against it (Matt. 16:18).[32]

---

[30]For a critique of premillennialism, see Russell Byrum, rev. ed., *Christian Theology* (Anderson, Ind.: Warner Press, 1925, 1982), 533-540. For a contemporary Wesleyan scholar who affirms a "realized millennialism" similar to the amillennialism typical of the teaching tradition of the Church of God (Anderson), see J. Kenneth Grider, *A Wesleyan-Holiness Theology* (Beacon Hill Press of Kansas City, 1994), 535-540.

[31]Richard Hughes, *Reviving the Ancient Faith* (Grand Rapids: Eerdmans, 1996), 149.

[32]Adrio König, *The Eclipse of Christ in Eschatology* (Grand Rapids: Eerdmans, 1989), 137.

The Book of Revelation is understood best when it is recognized that it was written for a church under persecution. The burning question of believers then was: Is Jesus really Lord given the delay of his promised return and the evil yet loose in the world? In Revelation 20:4-6 the answer given is "Yes!" Jesus indeed is Lord during this prolonged time before his final coming in complete triumph. The painful interim is a millennium, symbolically an indefinite period of waiting, believing, enduring, and serving, being faithful in the meantime. Satan is bound throughout the period, alive and active, but limited and unable to destroy the church. He was defeated with Christ's incarnation, the first coming of Jesus, and one day, when Christ returns, this defeat will be finalized for all to see. A series of apocalyptic images in the Book of Revelation conveys reassurance to the people of God that Christ is going to be victorious over all opposition, including the system of emperor worship at the time of the book's writing and whatever rises to take its place in any and every other time that still may come.[33]

Evidence of the subtle complexities of and possible interrelationships among the several millennial models is seen as Donald Bloesch proposes a "postmillennialism within the framework of a modified amillennialism."[34] He does not call the church to a "romantic optimism," but to "a summons to confidence and courage in the knowledge that Christ has utterly defeated the powers of evil, and this defeat will become more and more manifest as the church fulfills the great commission." This stance sounds overly technical in how it is labeled, but its meaning is crucial. The

---

[33]Ray Summers reaches the following conclusion in his commentary on the Book of Revelation: "This message is peculiarly relevant today—the call to choose the eternal rather than the temporal; to resist temptation, to refuse to compromise with pagan secularism, to place the claim of conscience above all demands against it; to cherish the confidence of ultimate victory for the kingdom of God, not only in the reign of Domitian [Roman emperor] but also in every other chaotic period of world history, including the twentieth century" (*Worthy is the Lamb*, Nashville: Broadman Press, 1951, 93).

[34]Donald Bloesch, *Essentials of an Evangelical Theology* (San Francisco: Harper & Row, 1979), 2:199.

key phrase is "as the church fulfills." Christ already is victorious; now, in the meantime before his second and final return, the church is to be faithful to its God-given mission in this world.

The Bottom Line

What is the ultimate lesson to be learned from the complex, controversial, and often divisive history of millennial theories? What is the bottom line? What do Christians know for sure? What really matters? Ray Dunning's conclusion is clear and surely correct. "The reality of Christ's second advent, the consummation of the Kingdom, and the eternal abode of the saints are precious truths of the faith, firmly grounded in the Word of God; but the real significance of these doctrines is aborted when they are made the object of such theorizing that seeks to pry into mysteries that transcend our present state of knowledge, or construct systems that depict history in advance." The constant danger is that curious and anxious believers will be grasped by "a preoccupation that will divert from the preaching of the gospel that God has *already* decisively won a victory over sin and Satan in this present age so that He can deliver from all sin here and now."[35] This is a caution fully consistent with the biblical revelation.

Christians should stop *speculating* and start *serving*! Biblical scholars should have learned long ago that "the important thing is not that Christ's return is near, but that it is *intended*—by a God whose faithfulness is well-known."[36] The Apostle Paul freely confessed that the faithful will struggle with the weakness of the flesh and be tempted to wish that such life could be exchanged very soon for the coming joy of heaven (Rom. 7:24; 2 Cor. 4:7-12, 5:1-5). His longing, when twisted just a little, becomes a blind-alley escapist stance leading to the irrelevance of believers in the present world.

---

[35]H. Ray Dunning, *Grace, Faith, & Holiness* (Beacon Hill Press of Kansas City, 1988), 588-589.
[36]Stephen Travis, *The Jesus Hope* (InterVarsity, 1976), 50.

Such subtle but significant twisting was seen by A. G. Mojtabai and reported in her *Blessed Assurance: At Home With the Bomb in Amarillo, Texas*. Fanny Crosby's loved hymn "Blessed Assurance, Jesus Is Mine!" has been drawn on by this author with a deliberate sense of irony. Amarillo is an American city that has adapted to the presence nearby of a nuclear weapons assembly plant. Many of the city's Christian citizens have found ways to be relatively comfortable as a major target if there should be nuclear war, a war prepared for locally every day, a war that cannot be won and must never be fought. What is the source of this comfort? According to Mojtabai: "It is hard to name the precise tense in which so many Christians live; whatever it might be called, it is not the present tense. The present is merely an interim."[37] According to many "evangelicals" in Amarillo, faithful Christians are to evangelize, fill their lamps with oil, stay clean in a polluted world, be ready and expectant and believe that nothing will really be solved until Jesus comes again. God then will destroy this earth by fire, but the faithful, it is commonly believed, will be lifted off the earth before the conflagration begins (a "tribulation"). The Book of Revelation too often serves for such believers as a dream of miraculous rescue and as a license for opting out of political struggle with the prevailing evil of their own times.

In 1 Thessalonians 4:13-18 the Apostle Paul makes clear that the Lord's coming again is the basis of hope for believers who should comfort each other with this hope. The intent is comfort, not contention; it is determination to be faithful whatever transpires, not divisive based on differing views of coming events surrounding the Lord's return. The Wesleyan theological tradition has tended toward moderation and tolerance in the debates over such things as millennial theories and the many colorful and controversial issues related to them. Thus, the combative nature of many of the eschatological debates in other circles has not led to the divi-

---

[37]A. G. Mojtabai, *Blessed Assurance* (Boston: Houghton Mifflin Company, 1986), 153.

sions often seen in Reformed and fundamentalistic denominations. Heard often in Wesleyan circles is the motto: "In essentials, unity; in non-essentials, liberty; in all things, charity."[38] In Wesleyan theology, "addressing speculative questions beyond issues that have soteriological [salvation] implications is inappropriate."[39] What is primary is a position that avoids preoccupation with future speculation and seeks rather to focus on the present realization of the Kingdom already come in Christ.[40]

What then is an approach to "end things" that looks ahead in real hope, but also looks in a way that inspires the believer to Christian responsibility in the meantime? Rather than becoming committed to any shifting "system," note this balanced perspective:

---

[38]This pattern of moderation is explored at length by Stephen Johnson, "Wesleyanism as Conciliatory in the Eschatological Debate," paper presented to the Wesleyan Theological Society, Bethany, Oklahoma, November, 1993.

[39]H. Ray Dunning, *Grace, Faith & Holiness* (Kansas City: Beacon Hill Press of Kansas City, 1988), 569. Kenneth Collins expands the point. Wesley's "strong soteriological [salvation] interest was evident throughout.... He much prefers to view eschatology as having great practical import in the sense that it is, for the most part, the continuation of the salvation already begun in this life" (*A Faithful Witness: John Wesley's Homiletical Theology*, Wilmore, Ky.: Wesley Heritage Press, 1993, 189). Martin Luther, before Wesley, also understood eschatology through soteriology. The starting point for eschatological thinking for him was the experience of conversion by grace through faith.

[40]The Church of God (Anderson) movement has remained close to the balance, modesty, and practical concern of John Wesley. He had an "inaugurated" concern, the coming Kingdom having current personal and social significance beyond mere waiting for a final intervention of God. Losing this biblical balance, unfortunately, has been the experience of many of Wesley's theological descendants. Some of his liberal descendants have settled for realized eschatologies (losing the future dimension), while many of his more conservative descendants have been drawn to the futurist, dispensational eschatologies that distort the present dimension. Adding a Believers' Church witness helps insure the balance, with its focus on the nowness of the Kingdom and the resulting demands of radical discipleship, without denial of the future dimension.

We should ever watch against temptation and pray for divine strength. We should cultivate a passion for righteousness, individual and social. We should work while it is day, knowing that the night cometh when no man can work. We should be so eager for the coming of our Lord, that if he should come tomorrow we would not be taken by surprise. We should so hold ourselves in restraint, that if his return should be delayed a thousand or ten thousand years, we would not be disappointed. And our hearts should be ever filled with joy at the prospect of his coming and the certain triumph of his kingdom.[41]

There are a few, but only a very few references in the New Testament to the "last days" and the "signs of the times."[42] The five references to "last days" all appear on close inspection to be referring to the general time of the biblical authors rather than to some distant future such as our own times. The key verse is Matthew 16:3: "You know how to discern the face of the heavens, but you do not know how to discern the signs of the times." Jesus had no intention of satisfying curiosities about the future, especially ones that were designed to distract from current responsibilities. He was scolding the Pharisees and Sadducees for being good forecasters of the weather and yet awful recognizers of the really important, an awareness of all that pointed to the presence of the Kingdom of God in his own ministry.

How egotistical it is, then, for current interpreters to assume that Matthew 16:3 alerts twentieth-century Christians to the real meaning of what is going on now in Iraq, Iran, Russia, and the European Common Market. In fact, the Bible's point in even men-

---

[41]Edgar Young Mullins, *The Christian Religion in its Doctrinal Expression* (Philadelphia: Roger Williams, 1917), 471-472.

[42]Acts 2:17; 2 Tim. 3:1; James 5:3; 2 Pet. 3:3; and Heb. 2:1. For an interpretation of these, see Roger Hahn in H. Ray Dunning, ed., *The Second Coming* (Beacon Hill Press of Kansas City, 1995), 33-36.

tioning "signs of the times" was to guide its initial hearers and readers to understand that, in the coming of Jesus, God had fulfilled the long stream of divine promise. Reading rightly the signs of the times should have led faithful seekers to a stable in Bethlehem. The end of the "last days" still lies in the future, and there is little we can know about it until it comes; but what we must know is that the purpose and plan of God that will be fulfilled by the *second* coming of Christ already has been put in motion by the *first* coming of Christ (see chapter five).

Christian eschatology is not only, maybe not even primarily about *last* things, what will happen at the end of time. Authentic eschatology should be linked directly to the whole redemptive plan of God. It should be based squarely on the foundation of the person and work of Jesus Christ in the first century. Old Testament prophecies should be interpreted directly in light of their fulfillment in Jesus Christ, not isolated from him and related to a future nation of Israel as though Christ has not yet come.

Believers today must avoid the blind alley of distracting speculation. Disciples intending to be seriously about the Lord's business can function well without knowing for sure the meaning of 70 weeks, 10 horns, tribulation, or the exact identity of the Beast or Antichrist. But they cannot be effective disciples without knowing that Jesus is the Lord *now* and that *now* is the time to grow up to the full stature of the fullness of Christ, both as individual believers and as the church together on mission as Christ's representatives in the world. The New Testament frequently witnesses to the central importance of the future of God in Christ for the *present life* of the church.

The Kingdom of God as now present is only partially fulfilled and stretches toward its certain consummation in the future; nevertheless, its focus is on how that future confidence is to impact the Kingdom quality of the present. All contrived interpretations and self-serving speculations that push the focus elsewhere are devilish diversions to be avoided.

The church of the second century after the life, death, resurrection, and departure of Jesus struggled with two competing extremes of prophetic interpretation and finally judged each to be inappropriate. Since each is prominent today (under various names), noting how the church responded long ago may be helpful in how the church of today should react. The church then came to see as wisdom a course between the extreme views that often were called "Gnostic" and "Adventist." The Gnostics spiritualized the Christian faith, even to the point of rejecting the literal Incarnation of Jesus, and instead posited a bodiless Christ and no concretely actual end time. All eschatological categories were taken to be present realities of experience. The goal of God was said to be realized as Christians are released from their material imprisonment and reunited with their spiritual origin and destiny. The Adventists, on the other hand, tended to claim special revelations of the immediacy of Christ's return and interpreted New Testament eschatological passages in an excessively literal manner.

What eventually came to be the almost universal teaching of the early church regarding end times was summarized in the straightforward language of the Apostles' Creed: "From there He [Christ] will come to judge the living and the dead.... I believe in the resurrection of the body, and the life everlasting."[43] Gnosticism is clearly rejected here (resurrection *of the body*), with avoidance of any official perspective on the timing and literalisms common to Adventist enthusiasms. Again, the bottom line involves the wisdom of emphasizing the present significance and related responsibilities of the Christian gospel instead of allowing any distraction by fruitless speculations about future details. This more recent perspective of Wolfhart Pannenberg is helpful:

---

[43]One of many commentaries on the Apostles' Creed is Wolfhart Pannenberg, *The Apostles' Creed in the Light of Today's Questions* (Philadelphia: Westminster Press, 1972). Pannenberg notes the creed's stress on the resurrection of the body in contrast to the Greek belief in immortality of the soul.

The people who are now baptized into the death of Christ and who in dying are bound to his cross, have through their communion with Christ the hope of partaking in the future in the new life of the resurrection of the dead, which has already appeared in him and which already gives those who are baptized power for a new life in faith and hope (Rom. 6:4ff). The forgiveness of sins and life in faith, hope and love, through the power of the Holy Spirit, are the present dawn of future life in communion with God....[44]

Systems of expectation shift often and commonly are influenced by time and place as well as by biblical teaching. Even so, the realities noted by Pannenberg constitute the faith itself and are stable in the midst of all the shifting.

Prophetic systems aside, the prime reality that nurtures authentic Christian hope is that in Jesus the dawn of the coming future already has broken over the tortured horizon of human history. To a consideration of this dawning we now turn.

Matters Worth Exploring

1. Why do Christians seem so determined to build complex systems of future expectation? Why is it that such systems keep shifting in at least their details?

2. How much solid biblical evidence is there for believing in a future millennium, a literal thousand-year reign of Christ on this earth? Is it the case that the "evidence" comes only from one brief passage in the Book of Revelation and then is said to be implied elsewhere?

---

[44]Pannenberg, op. cit., 170.

3. How does one decide which if any of the classic models of God's future are to be accepted as truly biblical? Is this choice among them important in the whole scheme of Christian living today? Is it a possible threat to such faithful living?

4. How can we as the church be motivated by the vision of God's ultimate future in a way that will cause us as believers to be about the Lord's business *in the present time*, no matter how long the delay until Christ does come again in glory?

5. The twentieth century has witnessed the failure of cherished utopian dreams. Marxist utopianism, for instance, has suffered a dramatic collapse in recent years as communism failed miserably—with the whole world watching the Berlin Wall being torn down in 1989. Do such failures help prepare the frustrated world for the hope of the Christian gospel?

6. After reviewing the several systems of Christian expectation, what should be the Christian's *bottom line*?

7. What is affirmed by the Apostles' Creed about God's future actions to consummate the world? Is what is affirmed in this creed biblical and enough, or is there more that can and should be known and proclaimed by Christians today?

Chapter 5

TEACHINGS AND SIGNIFICANCE OF JESUS

❧

"The time has come," Jesus announced in Galilee.
"The kingdom of God is near." (Mark 1:15)

❧

Creation is the arena of the Kingdom, history is the drama of the Kingdom, Christ
is the essence of the Kingdom, the church is the community of the Kingdom.
Individual believers are agents of the Kingdom, and the return of Christ
will usher in the consummation of the Kingdom.[1]

❧

Jesus stands at the very center of the Christian faith. Who Jesus was and what he taught about hope's fulfillment became central to Christian faith and life. His life on earth was lived in the midst of intense Jewish anticipation because they were occupied by yet another foreign power, Rome, and believed that somehow God would act decisively on their behalf. They looked for the dramatic coming of their Christ, the One anointed by God to save them from their harsh situation. Although many of the first-century Jews did not realize it, Jesus came fulfilling their expectation. The fact that he did not fulfill many of the popular expectations in the expected ways of social-political vindication of the Jews led directly to his violent death. Christians, however, soon found even

---

[1]Gilbert Stafford, *Theology for Disciples* (Anderson, Ind.: Warner Press, 1996), 95.

his death to be a source of new hope because of their belief in his subsequent resurrection. In fact, the bodily resurrection of Jesus "was the theme of every Christian sermon; it was the master-motive of every act of Christian evangelism; and not one line of the New Testament was written...apart from the conviction that He of whom these things were being written had conquered death and was alive for ever."[2]

The trend in the nineteenth century among many Christian scholars was to view Jesus as only the moral educator of humanity, a model and mentor for us all. But as the twentieth century approached, Johannes Weiss and Albert Schweitzer rediscovered the "apocalyptic" character of the preaching of Jesus. The Kingdom of God was the "master-thought" of Jesus,[3] an "eschatological" notion of central importance. To ignore this eschatological context is to fail to understand his significance. This context, however, must be understood with care or the resulting perception of his significance will be skewed badly.[4] The challenge includes understanding the nature, timing, and present as well as future implications of the arrival of the Kingdom of God.

Teaching Discourses in Matthew

The Gospel of Matthew is a good place to learn about the teachings of Jesus, including those having to do with the future of the Kingdom of God and its relation to the present of Jesus himself. This Gospel can be seen as narrative christology, a telling of the story of the true identity of Jesus in the context of his being an

---

[2]James Stewart, *A Faith To Proclaim* (N. Y.: Charles Scribner's Sons, 1953), 104-105.

[3]James Stewart, *The Life and Teaching of Jesus Christ* (London: SCM, 1933), 53.

[4]Albert Schweitzer went on to argue that the Kingdom did not come as and when Jesus expected. Jesus' "perfectionistic" ethical teachings had been intended by him only for the presumed brief interim before the end and thus are not directly relevant for believers today. This current chapter does not agree with such an argument (for critique of Schweitzer's thesis, see John Howard Yoder, *The Politics of Jesus*, 2nd ed. 1994, Eerdmans).

extension of the story of God's preparation for Christ in the history of the Jewish people. Matthew begins with a Jewish genealogy that leads to Jesus. Jesus is presented as "Israel's new David, as the fulfillment and zenith of God's history with His people Israel."[5] The one all-important difference between Saul the Jewish Pharisee and Paul the Christian apostle was Paul's new evaluation of the person of Jesus. Rooted in the Jewish past, this Jesus also came to be seen as the very presence of God's future.

The Gospel of Matthew presents a series of major teaching discourses of Jesus. The fifth and final one is the "Olivet Discourse" found in chapters 24 and 25. As Jesus' ministry on earth was nearing its end, he is presented by Matthew as offering to his disciples a private farewell address. This address consists of three primary topics: (1) Jesus' second coming and the events that will precede it (24:1-35); (2) the crucial need for true believers to live in watchfulness and readiness as they await the end (24:36-25:30); and (3) the final judgment of all people and things, the judgment over which Jesus will preside after he has come again to conclude all history as we now know it (25:31-46).

Here is an excellent place to get our bearings, raise the perennial questions, and get good perspective on how the early church gained insight and strength directly from the remembered teachings of Jesus. The future was very much in view. The earliest Christian community was sustained by a vibrant hope in the soon-return of Jesus. But, understandably, some second- and third-century Christians already were asking about the unexpected delay of the promised coming again of the Risen Christ (2 Peter 3:3). The Gospel of Matthew, probably written around A. D. 80-90, addresses this pressing issue for a needy and waiting church.

What were and still are the key questions addressed as Matthew recorded Jesus' teachings in a particular way for the church, both then and now? They are: How will the end come?

---

[5]Michael Lodahl, *The Story of God* (Kansas City: Beacon Hill Press of Kansas City, 1994), 129.

How should faithful believers live in the meantime? What happens after the end has come in terms of judgment, reward, and punishment?

1. The "How" of the Kingdom. Matthew's account of the teaching of Jesus about "end things" (chapters 24 and 25) is "apocalyptic" in form and flavor. Apocalyptic texts flourished in Israel in the centuries just before and after the birth of Jesus. Examples in the Bible are portions of the books of Daniel and Revelation. Characteristic of this way of thinking is a viewing of current history as hopelessly in the grip of evil. A solution to this evil is not available except through a cataclysmic intervention by God to crush the evil and usher in the new age of God. God invites humans to participate in the drama of the dawning divine Kingdom. Since, however, it is *God's* Kingdom that is dawning, its coming is not being controlled by religious zealots, political revolutionaries, or military strategists.

Hans Küng writes at length about Jesus' relationship to the four main religious/social groupings in the Jewish society of his time (groups that by differing names are found in all times).[6] The question is how God's people should participate in God's coming. The Sadducees were allied with those in religious and political power. They were the clever accommodationists. Jesus was not one of them, not a priest, scribe, elder, or power broker. The Zealots sought in God's name to overturn the oppressive status-quo by violence if necessary. Jesus had much opportunity in this regard, but was not one of them, choosing poverty and deliberately passing by the violence option. The Essenes sought escape from an impure world by a spiritual retreat from all apparent compromise. Jesus was not one of them. He ate with the impure and sought out the compromised, saying that is why he had come. Finally, the Pharisees were religiously elite conservatives, doggedly devoted,

---

[6]Hans Küng, *On Being a Christian* (Garden City, N. Y.: Doubleday & Co., 1976).

the proud protectors of received tradition. Jesus was not one of them, although he loved his Hebrew heritage and intended to fulfill rather than separate from it.

The first Christian disciples had to reorient their understanding of the way God expresses power in the midst of human history so that they could have the mind of Christ in their own living. "If they had been endowed with the gift of the Spirit before that gift had manifested its full range of meaning in Jesus," warns Ray Dunning, the early Christians "would have doubtless become raging nationalists, swinging weapons like Samson of old."[7] While life in the Spirit is essential, so is it crucial that such life be understood as one with the historical story of Jesus. Jesus coupled the role of the "Son of Man" with the "Suffering Servant" (Isa. 52, 53) to become a Messiah of a unique kind. He would combine the glory and power of the one with the sacrifice and suffering of the other.

The Spirit of God sends the believing community on mission in the Spirit's way. This way is the way of Jesus. The community of believers in Jesus goes forward in the Spirit, that is, in the present power of the messianic age already dawned in Jesus Christ. The Spirit "moves us through enemy territory toward God's final victory, along the way offering us a quickening foretaste of the glory to come." But, concludes Leonard Allen, the Spirit's leading is into, not out of this present world. The Spirit always directs us "to the Crucified One and thus into the way of the cross." So we who really believe are put on mission *for* Christ, *by* the Spirit of Christ, and *like* Christ. Like Christ? Yes, "the Spirit implants in our hearts the strength to follow the way of weakness, the power to receive and care for the powerless, the peace to endure and absorb hostility."[8] Such is the vocation of those who follow the way of the cross, the way of the resurrected Jesus, those who would be faith-

---

[7]H. Ray Dunning, *Grace, Faith & Holiness: A Wesleyan Systematic Theology* (Kansas City: Beacon Hill Press of Kansas City, 1988), 415.

[8]C. Leonard Allen, *The Cruciform Church* (Abilene Christian University Press, 2nd ed., 1990), 163.

ful in the meantime, daring to serve sacrificially until the time of service is no more.

2. In the Meantime. Matthew presumes the already obvious. There was a delay in the Lord's expected return that was disturbing to many disciples. The response of the Gospel writer to this awkward and confusing circumstance was to reinforce the hope and recall for readers how Jesus taught his disciples to wait. When those first disciples of Jesus approached him with their question about details of the future, the Lord replied with a gentle firmness: "It is not for you to know the times or dates the Father has set by his own authority. But you will receive power when the Holy Spirit comes on you; and you will be my witnesses. . .to the ends of the earth" (Acts 1:7-8; see also Matt. 24:36). His focus appears to have been on mission in the world, not speculation about the future beyond this world.

Matthew prefaced his report of Jesus' end-times narrative with Jesus' warning to "watch out that no one deceives you," implying that the events to come may not transpire according to what looks to believers like a well-plotted divine story-line with a good and rapid conclusion. There would be room for doubt, apparent ambiguity, confusion among interpreters of the future, and even deceit by some supposed prophets. Whatever some would claim, "no one knows about the day or the hour" (25:36). The point is not for disciples to know the plan in detail, but to be alert, ready, patient, and prepared to endure faithfully and fruitfully in the meantime. The intent of Jesus was that his disciples should keep watch and begin living in a certain way because they believe that he is coming soon to fulfill, judge, and reward.

Pregnancy is a helpful metaphor for proper Christian discipleship. The life of faith is a time of measured waiting for the coming wonder of God's working. The young Mary had waited wonderingly as an amazing new life, even the beginning of a new age matured within her. Her pregnancy is at the core of the Christian message. Are we not all so chosen? "We are hailed," writes Wendy Wright, "to receive into ourselves the seed that God wishes to plant there. We say yes and the life of God begins its course of gestation in us. We become the ground out of which the incarnate God flowers in the world."[9] Such pregnancy is a time of waiting. What is yet unseen wants to come to light. What is gestating wants to be born—and it will, in its own time and way! Waiting is part of the process.

Christ's promised return in final triumph was a sure, compelling, even an imminent expectation of the early church. According to Jesus, however, it would be unexpected in its timing. When Matthew was writing, in the eyes of the young church the soon return of Jesus already had been delayed long enough, an awkward circumstance requiring some explanation and encouragement. The issue Matthew addressed was how best to deal with delay, keeping real faith alive and the focus on mission to the world for Christ. While there is some reference to future judgment and the return of Christ, the clear emphasis of the parables told by Jesus is on the presence now of the future Kingdom—"the Kingdom of God has come upon you" (Matt. 12:28; Luke 17:20). In some vital sense the future already is here and has been since the Jesus events in first-century Palestine. There is no real delay at all, only time for faithfulness in the meantime.

In the Book of Revelation there is further addressing of the church's in-the-meantime questions. With the young church already suffering persecution, the pressing questions were whether Jesus really was Lord and whether Satan really was a defeated foe. The answer given by John the Revelator is a clear "yes!" to both questions. According to Revelation 20: 4-6, there will be an indefinite (symbolic "thousand years") time before the final presence and full vindication of the glorified Christ and his faithful people . Even so, Jesus is Lord even now. The many nows in which the faithful find themselves waiting and suffering are times when,

---

[9]Wendy Wright, "Wreathed in Flesh and Warm," *Weavings* II:1 (Jan./Feb. 1987), 18.

despite appearances, Satan is *bound*—at least to the extent that evil has no opportunity to completely obliterate the church.

What are the faithful to do in the meantime—now that Jesus has been resurrected and Satan bound, but when the ultimate vindication of Jesus and his faithful disciples is still delayed? Matthew offers a collage of brief pronouncements and comparisons in 24:36-44. This collage establishes clearly the view of Jesus about the *need to be ready*. Then come three parables told by Jesus that elaborate more fully his understanding of the meaning of disciples being ready. A servant's readiness is pictured in terms of proper care for a master's household (24:45-51), especially when the master unexpectedly stays away for a long time (v. 48). The issue of having proper provisions for the potential of a long wait is clarified with a story about wise and foolish maidens (25:1-13), some of whom were so expectant that they forget to keep oil in their lamps. Then there is the story of the "talents" (Matt. 25:14-30), where readiness is pictured in terms of the resourcefulness expected of servants in handling assets entrusted to them. So Christian disciples, anxious for Christ's return, are to display a *proper* anxiousness by caring for the Master's business now, gathering ample provisions for what is to come, and being resourceful stewards in the meantime.

The parable of the sheep and goats (Matt. 25:31-46) makes vividly clear that waiting for God's eventual future requires a central concern for living lives of compassion and justice in the meantime. Faithful disciples are to treat others as though they were Christ! Thus, according to Jesus, the essence of keeping watch for the Lord's coming again is how we who believe relate to our brothers and sisters in this world of injustice and misery. What is the Bible's purpose in its teaching about the end? It is "not to satisfy our curiosity about the future but to teach us how to live as we await the end."[10]

---

[10]Jon Paulien, *What the Bible Says About the End Time* (Hagerstown, MD.: Review and Herald Publishing Association, 1994), 89.

3. The End and Beyond. Once Matthew had made very clear the priority need for disciples to be ready and resourceful about God's business in the now of their lives, he concluded by offering a dramatic picture of the event that will bring to a close all history as humans have known it since their forced departure from the Garden of Eden. This event will be a second coming of the Son of Man, the *parousia* or ultimate presence of the Christ with us. Christ's coming again will establish clearly in the public arena what people of faith already know, namely that *Jesus is Lord.* According to Philippians 2:9-11:

> Therefore God also highly exalted him [Christ] and gave him the name that is above every name, so that at the name of Jesus every knee should bend, in heaven and on earth and under the earth, and every tongue confess that Jesus Christ is Lord, to the glory of God the Father.

The publicness of this final coming (24:30-31) will not be restricted to the spiritually fortunate. It will not first be a secret *parousia* for the benefit of the elect. When it happens, all people of the earth, living or dead at the time, will know what is happening. But only the faithful of all the ages will be caught up into the glorified presence of their Lord (1 Thess. 4:13-17).

Immediately following the great *parousia* (24:29) will come the cataclysmic end of the world order as it now is known. After that comes the judgment. All the nations will be gathered for judgment after the event of Christ's eventual return (25:31-46). Since the good news of God in Christ is to be preached to all people (24:14; 28:19), all humankind will be held accountable at the end. The exalted Jesus is the One who comes, reigns, and carries out the divine judgment. This final judgment involves the coming home of the "blessed" (25:34-40) and the painful departing of the "accursed" (25:41-46). Eternal life is life with Jesus and his beloved community in the new age God creates, a life in which all of God's wonderful promises are fulfilled forever. God's objective all along has been to redeem and restore—that is the core meaning of Christ's cross and the mission of Christ's church. But human choices matter and there finally will be accountability. The dark side of Christian hope is that some will spurn God's reign, refuse God's grace, not practice mercy "to the least of these," and thus on that final day will be separated from God's blessing forever.

One must move beyond the reporting in the Gospel of Matthew to learn about Jesus and the issue of resurrection after death for humanity in general. For centuries before Jesus, the Hebrews had conceived of life after death as a shadowlike existence in Sheol. By the time of Jesus there was a range of Jewish views. The Sadducees, accepting only the Torah as Holy Scripture, denied resurrection (Mark 12:18; Acts 23:8). The Essenes appear to have believed in the immortality of the soul, while the Pharisees were anticipating a kind of bodily resurrection. Jesus himself appears closest to the Pharisees on this subject, discussing resurrection only once in the Gospel accounts (Mark 12:18-27). Resurrection life, he taught, is inconceivable in human terms (Mk. 12:25; cf. 1 Cor. 15:35-50). It also is inevitable since God is "God of the living" (Ps. 73:23-26). Jesus presupposed life after death and anticipated his own resurrection. Soon the earliest Christian preaching would highlight the God who had "raised Jesus from the dead" (Acts 13:33-34; Gal. 1:1) and "who gives life to the dead" (Rom. 4:17).

Reviewing the New Testament presentation of Jesus the Messiah reveals that eschatological significance is emphasized. There are at least five end-time aspects. First, in Jesus the messianic age has dawned (Acts 2:16; 3:18, 24) in his ministry, death, and resurrection (Acts 2:23). Second, by his resurrection, Jesus has been exalted to the right hand of God as messianic head of the new people of God (Acts 2:33-36; 3:13). Third, the Holy Spirit's presence is the sign of the eschaton already with us, as well as the proof that Jesus currently reigns in heaven in power and glory (Acts 2:33). Fourth, the messianic age will shortly reach its consummation in the return of Christ (Acts 3:21). Fifth, an invitation is always extended by the Spirit for people to receive Christ and the life of the age to come (Acts 2:38-39).[11]

The result is that the life of the early Christians was essentially an eschatological existence. That is, they knew themselves to be living "between the times." Already, by God's grace, they had become people of God's future, privileged to be living the life of the future in the present age. The earliest Christian historians and theologians announced what they considered the central fact: the age to come had dawned in the first coming of Christ (Acts 2:16-17; Heb. 1:2; 1 Tim. 4:1; 2 Tim. 3:1; 1 Jn. 2:18). Eduard Schweizer provides a good summary:

> When Jesus calls on his disciples to keep watch, he is calling on them to take the reality of God so seriously that they can come to terms with its sudden appearance at any moment within their lives, precisely because they know that this reality will one day come unboundedly in the kingdom of God.[12]

The Book of Revelation is a powerful presentation of confidence in that eventual day. In its distinctive apocalyptic language that requires special understanding and careful interpretation, we are given a testimony *from* and initially *for* first-century Christians concerning the lordship of Jesus, the ongoing conflict with evil powers, and the eventual future. There is dramatic reassurance that the reign of the exalted Jesus, "the Lamb who was slain," is full of promise for the faithful, some of whom now were experiencing being slain themselves. But one finds here no encouragement for those who want to decode the future and seek license to escape the negatives and responsibilities of the present. The Revelation to

---

[11]See the classic work by C. H. Dodd, *The Apostolic Preaching and Its Developments* (New York: Harper, 1944), 38-45.

[12]Eduard Schweizer, *The Good News According to Matthew* (Atlanta: John Knox Press, 1975), 468.

John is not fundamentally a book of future predictions. Rather, it offers a prophetic vision that focuses on the present as an arena of conflict between the dominion of Jesus Christ and the arrogant Roman order, which was the then-current expression of the evil powers. It is a call to Christians "to endure in their faith in Jesus' heavenly reign and to repent for placing their security in any other power."[13] It is a vigorous call for believers to be sure of their hope and then be faithful in the meantime.

Jesus Inaugurates a New Age

A study of the goal of the biblical revelation concerning human history's process, meaning, current status, and coming climax is called *eschatology* (study of the goal and end). In Christian perspective, eschatology is a focused assessment of the movement of cosmic and human history in the special light of the advent of Jesus Christ. Eschatological reasoning "inquires into how creatures who, having their beginning in God, and having fallen and received redemption in God, have their final destiny and end in God."[14] Biblically speaking, the key concept is the Kingdom of God.

Jesus proclaimed the imminent coming of the Kingdom of God, even in his own person and ministry. His message had two important emphases. The messianic salvation anticipated by the Hebrew prophets was being fulfilled in his own person and ministry; there yet remains a later consummation when this salvation will be perfectly accomplished in an age yet to come. The "Kingdom of God" (Greek *basileia*, Hebrew *malkuth*) at least means the active reign or rule of God as opposed to the concrete idea of a specific realm being ruled. God's rule, of course, exists universally by virtue of who God is; but functionally, given human freedom and sin, it exists in this evil age only when people submit

[13]David Tiede, *Jesus and the Future* (Cambridge University Press, 1990), 88-89.

[14]Thomas Oden, *Life in the Spirit: Systematic Theology*, vol. 3 (San Francisco: Harper, 1992), 369.

themselves to it. The Kingdom actually has come in Jesus, in whom full submission to God was present. The announcement to Mary was that God would give to Jesus the throne of David and Jesus would reign forever, his Kingdom having no end (Lk. 1:32-33). That is, "before the eschatological appearance of God's Kingdom at the end of the age, God's Kingdom has become dynamically active among men in Jesus' person and mission."[15] To understand the Kingdom's present meaning and future nature requires understanding the person and work of Jesus. He should be the defining center of all Christian eschatology.

The Gospel of Mark presents Jesus as the definitive inter-preter and fulfillment of Israel's prophetic tradition. God continues to contend with humans who remain in active opposition to God's will and reign. While God's full sovereignty and final judgment are never in question, neither God nor humanity is locked in any fatal-ism or fixed cosmic calendar. History, including the future, is "a dynamic arena of the relationship between God's reign and human will."[16] Indeed, the future is as secure as God's faithfulness, but exactly how the future develops depends in part on the repentance and faith of humanity in relation to the current reign of the Lord Jesus Christ (Acts 28:23-31).[17]

How near is this end? The New Testament materials suggest an ambiguous answer. The two letters addressed to the Thessalonians, for example, seem to have somewhat different emphases in this regard. First Thessalonians 5 follows the common apocalyptic motif that the end will come "like a thief in the night," so that there always should be a sense of urgency and a need to be ready for what could come any moment. But in 2 Thessalonians

---

[15]George Eldon Ladd, *The Presence of the Future: The Eschatology of Biblical Realism* (Grand Rapids: Eerdmans, 1974), 139.

[16]Tiede, op. cit., 72.

[17]See Barry Callen, *God As Loving Grace* (Nappanee, Ind.: Evangel Press, 1996), 73-80 and 114-121, for discussions of the vulnerable way God has chosen to work in the world and the possible effectiveness of prayer in actually changing what God does in given instances.

we find a detailed scheme of final events, implying that the end is not at all near. While this scheme does not lessen the need for believers always to be ready, it does suggest a longer timetable before the end actually will come.

Beyond the question of the timing of the Kingdom of God is the equally crucial question about the nature of its eventual coming. Biblical scholarship has made considerable advance over the intensely rationalistic atmosphere of the Enlightenment mentality that encouraged criticism of any focus on "last things" as more superstition than revelation. In recent centuries, eschatology for many believers became only a theological curiosity, or merely a realm of moral values toward which society is advancing (Albrecht Ritschl), or nothing more than a network of symbols ("myths") to be interpreted existentially (Rudolf Bultmann). But Johannes Weiss and Albert Schweitzer rediscovered the apocalyptic character of the preaching of Jesus and argued that the Kingdom of God is primarily an eschatological vision.

One cannot escape a serious dealing with apocalyptic eschatology by engaging in modern "historical" reconstructions of the life and thought of Jesus without inadvertently attributing to Jesus one's own assumptions and social visions.[18] For instance, Jesus was more than the moral educator of men and women and their fumbling human societies (as he often was depicted in the nineteenth century). The New Testament presents him as the inaugurator of a new age. Concerning this "new age," however, the question of timing has been a persistently troublesome one. Four general positions have emerged:

1. Kingdom Realized. The Kingdom of God already has been realized in the coming of Jesus, with no future Parousia (second coming) now expected (C. H. Dodd).[19]

---

[18] See Albert Schweitzer (1875-1965), *The Quest of the Historical Jesus* (1906).

[19] R. H. Fuller has subjected Dodd's theory to rigorous examination and found it inadequate (*The Mission and Achievement of Jesus*, London: SCM, 1954, 20-25).

2. Kingdom Postponed. The Kingdom of God was placed on hold when the Jews rejected Jesus. It now awaits the last days for its appearance on earth. Classical dispensationalists argue that these last days began with the founding of the modern State of Israel in 1948 (Charles Ryrie).

3. Kingdom Inaugurated. The Kingdom of God was inaugurated with the first coming of Jesus and now is active in human history, especially in the church, although its full realization still lies in the future (O. Cullmann, R. H. Fuller, G. E. Ladd).[20]

4. Kingdom Yet Future. The Kingdom of God remains entirely in the future and one day will intervene disruptively in the midst of human history (J. Weiss).

The view taken here is the general inaugurated position, with the present responsibility of Kingdom-enabled discipleship a special concern. God is the Alpha and the Omega, both the Creator and Consummator of all history. Rather than being the last in a series of theological topics, eschatology "highlights the final hope that frames and radically contextualizes all other temporal affirmations."[21] Such an assessment of history provides a vision of hope that saves sinful and oppressed people from being overwhelmed by historical disillusionment. Jesus believed firmly that God's gracious reign would ultimately triumph. When proclaiming the nearness of the Kingdom of God, he probably was not declaring the soon end of the world so much as that, in his own ministry, God's

---

[20]John Wesley's view often is commended for the creative tension it seeks to hold between the present and future dimensions of the Christian hope. For Wesley's eschatology, Randy Maddox prefers the designation "processive." This adjective highlights the present significance and dynamic nature of God's ongoing work of transforming grace (*Responsible Grace*, Abingdon Press, Kingswood Books, 1994, 235-236).

[21]Ibid.

promises to Israel were coming to fulfillment. The words and works of Jesus were evidence of the Kingdom already being at hand (Isa. 35:1-10; Matt. 11:1-15)—without exhausting the Kingdom's future meaning. Several difficult New Testament texts are made clearer when it is understood that the Kingdom of God is "the dynamic working of God's rule in the world in advance of the eschatological consummation."[22]

God's Kingdom in its fullest reality and final consummation awaits the second advent of Christ. That is not yet. In the meantime, as the result of Christ's first advent, the Kingdom now is an inaugurated reality that people are called to enter (Mk. 9:47; Matt. 21:31-32). Recognizing the kingly presence of God in the present time, the Kingdom of God is an invitation for all who will to live in the power of this divine presence, consciously deciding for this reign (Matt. 13:44-46) and doing God's will (Matt. 6:10, 7:21-23). God's Kingdom will be fully understood and realized only at the eschaton, the very end of time itself. Nevertheless, already this Kingdom's reality and power are at work, breaking into the human present from God's future.

The Gospel of John emphasizes that new existence in Christ by the Spirit is to be a *present reality*. Life in the Kingdom of God is now, not merely a hope reserved for the future. The believer already has made the transition out of death into life (Jn. 5:24). Said Jesus, "Now the judgment of this world takes place, now the prince of this world will be thrown out; and I, if I am lifted up from the earth, will draw to myself all people" (Jn. 12:31). The believer knows resurrection in and through Christ in the present time (Jn. 5:21, 24 and 11:25). Rudolf Bultmann concludes that this focus on presentness precludes a future fulfillment also, but his exclusion fails to do justice to the biblical evidence. John takes seriously both the consequences for present time of the work of Jesus and affirms that the present action of

---

[22]George Eldon Ladd, *The Presence of the Future* (Grand Rapids: Eerdmans, 1974), 158.

the risen Lord extends to future horizons (Jn. 5:17, 11:25). The Johannine eschatology is understood best through this Evangelist's central insight that eschatology for Christians is *Christology*. That is, "to the Son is committed the carrying out of the eternal purpose of the Father; this he has achieved, he is achieving, and he shall achieve *eis telos*"[23] (at the end).

The church of the Christ, the body of the newly created believers in Christ, is called to live the new life now, and live it in hope as it continues to remember and embody the crucified and resurrected Christ by the ministry of the Spirit of God. The Kingdom of God, yet to come in its fullness, should be viewed as now present "as the new redemptive order established by the Christ and Pentecost events that inaugurated the eschatological last days promised in the Old Testament and consummated when Christ returns."[24] Summarizes Jürgen Moltmann:

> The present power of this remembrance and this hope is called "the power of the Spirit," for it is not of their own strength, reason, and will that people believe in Jesus as the Christ and hope for the future as God's future…. Faith in Christ and hope for the kingdom are due to the presence of God in the Spirit.[25]

Paul refers to the Spirit of God as the "first fruits" or "down-payment" of the final resurrection (Rom. 8:23; 2 Cor. 1:22; 5:5; Eph. 1:13-14). Into our troubled human present has broken God's future! What then of the resurrection of Jesus Christ? It was more than an isolated event in which one individual overcame death by the re-creating action of God. It was "the death of the old aeon and the birth of the new aeon. Hence to be in Christ or in the Spirit

---

[23]George Beasley-Murray, *Word Biblical Commentary*: John, vol. 36 (Waco, Texas: Word Books, 1987), lxxxvii

[24]Boyd Hunt, *Redeemed!: Eschatological Redemption and the Kingdom of God* (Nashville: Broadman & Holman Publishers, 1993), 68.

[25]Jürgen Moltmann, *The Church in the Power of the Spirit* (N.Y.: Harper & Row, 1977), 197.

(which we have seen to be synonymous) is to be in the age to come and to participate in its power."[26]

The present experience of the Spirit of God features the resurrection power of Jesus, the risen Christ. Jesus' disciples, once aware of his resurrection, knew that it was really just the beginning of God's coming future for all who believe. Given the richness of their Jewish heritage and now the dramatic saving events of God in Christ, God was propelling the faithful into the future. They were learning that "to be a Christian was [is] to be a risk-taker. Every day they could expect that God's Spirit would do creative things in making Jesus' presence real."[27] To live in Christ is to live by God's loving grace, through the Spirit of God, as an extension of the emerging post-resurrection life of Jesus. To do so together as the body of Christ is to be the church, the community of the Spirit on mission in the present.

The teaching of the resurrection in John's Gospel includes both a future eschatological event and a present spiritual reality. Both this future and this present reside in Jesus Christ. John makes clear that whoever believes in Jesus, though dying physically, shall live again; and whoever accepts the blessing of present spiritual life in Christ shall retain that relationship even beyond physical death (Jn. 11:25-26). The offer is for the believer to enjoy a future eschatological reality in the present. The age to come and this present age are now overlapped so that a person can draw on the blessing and power of God's coming future for purposes of redeemed living and Christ-like serving even now. Arguing for such a present reality, however, does not logically lead to the negative conclusion of C. H. Dodd. He argues that the resurrection of Lazarus illustrates that eternal life through Christ is a present possession "and no longer a hope for the last day."[28] In fact, by God's grace it is both!

---

[26]H. Ray Dunning, *Grace, Faith & Holiness: A Wesleyan Systematic Theology* (Kansas City: Beacon Hill Press of Kansas City, 1988), 476.

[27]Alan Kreider, *Journey Towards Holiness: A Way of Living for God's Nation* (Scottdale, Pa.: Herald Press, 1987), 204.

[28]C. H. Dodd, *The Apostolic Preaching*, 170.

Accepting the intended "nowness" of the anticipated "will be" sets a distinctively divine context for the Christian understanding of all things and all time. What is the Kingdom of God? In part,

> 'Tis a kingdom of peace, it is reigning within,
> It shall ever increase in my soul;
> We possess it right here when He saves from all sin,
> And 'twill last while the ages shall roll.[29]

The prayer that Jesus taught his disciples (Lk. 11:2-4), the "Lord's Prayer," has as its whole thrust a petitioning for God's future reign to be *present reality* in very practical ways—Thy Kingdom come now, on earth, bringing forgiveness, daily bread, and the ability for believers to survive temptation, all because believers recognize God as Loving Father and hallow the divine name. Jesus accepted the conviction of Israel that God's reign would be fully evident one day, with all divine promises finally fulfilled. This future and its security, however, are not centered in a complex pattern of predictions about specific future events, but focus on faith in the God of Israel, now come in Christ, the God who keeps divine promises and offers the future and its security as a gift that allows forgiven and fruitful living, Christ-like living *now*.

In concluding his masterful study of Mark 13, George Beasley-Murray chooses an excellent quotation to summarize Mark's recounting of the early church's expectation of the nearness of Christ's return and its relation to their present discipleship responsibilities in the meantime. The early disciples had

> the eschatological attitude of those who stake their all
> on the sovereignty of God in the sovereignty of Jesus

---

[29]Refrain of the hymn "The Kingdom of Peace" by Barney E. Warren, as in *Worship the Lord: Hymnal of the Church of God* (Anderson, Ind.: Warner Press, 1989), 481.

Christ and, like Jesus himself, in his Spirit, enable the power of God's sovereignty to be perceived, and cause God's sovereignty to reach human beings in its healing power—and at the same time to await its fulfillment from God through Jesus Christ.... It is realized and concretized on the way of following in cross bearing (Mark 8:34-38), on the path that is free from anxiety because it is radical trust in God and his Son Jesus Christ in the power of the Holy Spirit (13:9-11), a way which leads to death and to the hoped-for resurrection promised in Jesus Christ.[30]

Did Jesus Predict A.D. 70 or 1948?

If the first fruits of God's coming Kingdom should be present reality, believers nonetheless have remained curious about the time when this divine Kingdom will be evident fully and forever. In the Olivet Discourse, Jesus told his inquiring disciples, "For then shall be great tribulation, such as was not since the beginning of the world to this time, no, nor ever shall be" (Matt. 24:21). These anxious disciples wanted to know when the Jerusalem Temple would be destroyed. Jesus gave them a clear sign about when to flee from the coming danger. Referring to Daniel's prophecy (9:27), the disciples were to flee into the mountains when they saw the "abomination of desolation" stand in the holy place (Matt. 24:15-16). Luke's record of this statement adds some detail about the event that should trigger the fleeing. It would be when Jerusalem is surrounded with armies (Lk. 21:20-21). Jesus wept over Jerusalem, knowing what soon would befall her "because you did not know the time of your visitation" (Lk. 19:41-44).

The terrible event was not far away. In 70 A.D. a Roman army led by Titus desecrated the Temple in Jerusalem, placing

---

[30]R. Pesch, *Naherwartungen* (1968), quoted by George Beasley-Murray, *Jesus and the Last Days* (Peabody, Mass.: Hendrickson Publishers, 1993), 475.

ensigns there and making mock sacrifices on them. Some decades later the Romans, tired of Jewish revolts, destroyed the city and the Temple, even plowing up the ground and renaming the land "Palestine" after the ancient Philistines, the historic enemy of Israel. For the many Jews caught in the devastation, the suffering was almost unspeakable, including mass starvation, slaughter, even cannibalism that saw Jewish parents consuming their own children. The account by Flavius Josephus in his *Jewish Wars* is long, detailed, and gruesome.

Beyond these terrible events in Palestine around A.D. 70, it appears clear that Jesus further anticipated an end to all history as we know it, a general resurrection (Mk. 12:25-27), a great judgment (Matt. 5:21-30), and a final separation of the saved and the lost (Matt. 13:24-30, 25:31-46). But did he predict 1948, the year the modern State of Israel was founded? Given the "prophetic" environment today, it appears necessary to address this common claim, presumably based on the teaching of Jesus. The claim is worded this way by Hal Lindsey: "Jesus promised us that the generation that witnessed the restoration of the Jewish people to their homeland would not pass until 'all these things'—including His return to Earth—would be done. The Jewish people declared the rebirth of their nation in 1948."[31]

Lindsey represents a popular viewpoint among one large group of Christians in the latter half of the twentieth century. Called "dispensationalism," it was first given systematic articulation by the Irish Anglican clergyperson John Nelson Darby, then made popular in America with the publication in 1909 of the *Scofield Reference Bible*. This view makes a sharp separation between God's Old Testament and New Testament people, one being God's national people (Israel) and the other God's spiritual people (the church). Though the first people rejected their Messiah, there is said to be coming a "tribulation" to prepare

---

[31]Hal Lindsey, *Planet Earth—2000 A. D.* (Palos Verdes, California: Western Front, Ltd., 1994), 3.

today's Israel to receive its Messiah at his return, with a millennium then serving as the time during which God finally will fulfill the Old Testament promises to Israel. These promises are read quite literally and usually are associated with the nation of Israel founded after World War II. In recent decades there have arisen "progressive" dispensationalists who have softened some of this scheme's classic views. They have recognized, for instance, that there is some real continuity between Old Testament Israel and the church and they have repudiated the tendency toward highly specific end-times speculation. But even they argue that ethnic Israel still has a special place in the present and future of God's program in human history.[32]

Against this whole prophetic scheme, even when modified, there should be a deep concern about the tendency to put the life, death, and resurrection of Jesus into a secondary category by a preoccupation with what is yet to come. The New Testament proclaims that Jesus' death was central to God's plan of human redemption. Jesus, as Alpha and Omega, has a special relationship with the whole of the world's history. He is both Lord of creation and the "end," the goal and decisive meaning of all history. The church's founding was a consequence of this saving grace and became God's intended new vehicle for proclaiming it to all the world. The church is not merely an interim arrangement until God gets back to finishing an original plan for a geo-political Israel. In fact, the whole thrust of the teaching of Jesus appears to counter any such thinking. The Kingdom of God "is not food and drink but righteousness and peace and joy in the Holy Ghost" (Rom. 14:17). First-century Jewish assumptions about the true Messiah coming to overthrow Rome and restore Israel's national independence was a fundamental misunderstanding of prophecy and the key reason

---

[32]See Craig Blaising, "Changing Patterns in American Dispensational Theology," *Wesleyan Theological Journal* (Spring/Fall, 1994), 149-164. For a good review that seeks to sort out all "evangelical options," see Stanley Grenz, *The Millennial Maze* (InterVarsity Press, 1992).

why Jesus was rejected and crucified. If Jesus had not come to "vindicate" them, those Jews expecting such a military Messiah naturally would reject him as not the one for whom they waited.

Did Jesus predict the founding of the modern nation-state of Israel? Hardly. He focused rather on the coming of God's Kingdom, coming already in his own ministry, coming in hearts newly committed to the will and ways of God.[33] In fact, Jesus almost surely had in view the destruction of Jerusalem to come soon after his own earthly ministry. "The desolating sacrilege" is his phrase as reported by Mark and Matthew (Mk. 13:14; Matt. 24:15). Luke is most clear about this tragic event very early into the life of the Christian church (21:20). He describes conditions prevalent at the destruction of Jerusalem in A.D. 70, noting however that this shocking event was not to be understood as the end of time. As a matter of fact, historical events (A.D. 70 or A.D. 1948) are not in themselves a sure sign of Christ's soon coming again.[34]

It is difficult for interpreters to decide how best to sort out the extent to which New Testament texts that speak of the "signs of the times" had primary reference to the actual historical event in 70 A.D. or to the end of all historical events yet to come. Clearly the actual event of Jerusalem's destruction by Rome became a prevailing archetype for interpreting the general denouement of all things (Dan. 12:1; Matt. 24:21-22; 2 Pet. 3:9). Wars, famines, earthquakes, persecutions, apostasy among former believers, and the frightening emergence of counter-Christs have been frequent in all

---

[33]Note this from George Eldon Ladd: "It follows that if Jesus proclaimed the messianic salvation, if he offered to Israel the fulfillment of her true destiny, then this destiny was actually accomplished in those who received his message. The recipients of the messianic salvation became the true Israel, representatives of the nation as a whole. While it is true that the word 'Israel' is never applied to Jesus' disciples, the idea is present.... Jesus' disciples are the recipients of the messianic salvation, the people of the Kingdom, the true Israel" (*The Presence of the Future*, 250).

[34]See Brevard Childs, *The New Testament as Canon: An Introduction* (Philadelphia: Fortress Press, 1985), 111.

centuries of the church's history. They "belong to the structure of this dying world—ascension to Parousia" and their signs "exhort us to be aware of our finitude and sin and to be constantly awake to the hope of God's own coming."[35] The popular dispensationalist claim that literal Israel is the "clock of prophecy" is misguided. The New Testament wants the attention of believers to be on Jesus Christ, not on some expected reorganization of the nation of Israel.

Focusing on particular current events like the founding of modern Israel tends to distract believers from the truly significant events of the divine salvation plan, the crucifixion, resurrection, and continuance of Jesus Christ (the present work of the Holy Spirit). The phrase "the last days" is not used in the New Testament for some future period, but of those days in which Jesus and the apostles acted. The last days dawned centuries ago. Indeed, Christ "had been chosen by God before the creation of the world and was revealed in these last days for your sake" (1 Pet. 1:20). We who believe always are to be living in the last days, on the alert, and on mission by the power of Christ's Spirit. The New Testament writings presume that with Jesus the world had entered into a new, an eschatological era. Viewed from the Old Testament perspective of promise, now is the time of fulfillment (1 Pet. 1:10-12). This "last days" time of the Spirit is bounded by the Christ-event of the first century and the coming consummation, the return of Christ in victory and final judgment in whatever year or century it finally may come.

The eventual return of Christ to conclude all historical time is no more eschatological than was his first-century ministry, sacrifice, and triumph over even death. There is no biblical reason to regard that which happens to the Israel of our day as fulfillment of prophecy. The eschaton accomplished *for* Israel by Jesus Christ must now be *attained* in Israel by its coming to faith in the Messiah (Eph. 2:11-18). The hope that Paul holds out for Israel in Romans 11:25-27 is a hope for salvation in the same way that Gentiles are

---

[35]Thomas Oden, *Life in the Spirit* (San Francisco: Harper, 1992), 414.

saved. It is not a hope for a national and political restoration. The "signs" of Jesus' second coming appear to have been given to the first disciples of Jesus (1) to warn that trouble would be their lot as long as history lasts, (2) to caution against any preoccupation with precise dates of expectation, and (3) to assure them of God's faithfulness regardless of trouble and uncertain timing of the end.

Christ the Resurrected King

The resurrection of Jesus made dramatically clear that the future belonged to this man, God's Messiah, and not to the Temple and Torah institutions of Judaism or to the political and military power of any Caesar. Preaching about the crucifixion and resurrection of Jesus was "a stumbling block to Jews and a folly to Gentiles," but "to those who are called, both Jews and Greeks, Christ the power of God and the wisdom of God" (1 Cor. 1:23-24). The early Christians joyously declared that "Jesus is Lord!" Though the world crucified him, Jesus was and remains the key to the future promised by God.

If the teaching of Jesus is not to be understood as a pattern of predictions about an historical period far removed from his own time, our own for instance, one understanding of the mission Jesus accomplished is full of "eschatological" insight. Revived in modern times by Swedish theologian Gustav Aulén (1879-1977) is the Christus Victor model of atonement.[36] Aulén's view of Christ's work emphasizes the military metaphor (e. g., Col. 2:15). Christ has liberated humanity from binding powers and himself has emerged victorious in the resurrection. The atonement issue highlighted is not only release from the guilt of sin through justification before

---

[36]Gustav Aulén, *Christus Victor*, Eng. trans. 1931 (reprinted by Macmillan, 1969, with a foreword by Jaroslav Pelikan). See also Aulén's *The Faith of the Christian Church*, 2nd Eng. ed. (Philadelphia: Fortress, 1960), 196-213. Several contemporary Mennonite theologians champion this atonement model as biblically faithful and directly compatible with traditional concerns of the Believers' Church tradition (John Howard Yoder, J. Denny Weaver, John Driver, Thomas Finger, and Norman Kraus).

God through the sacrifice of Jesus. Human sin is recognized as having resulted in humans being released by God into the control of satanic forces, working in personal and institutionalized forms.

According to most traditions of the Western church, the sin-releasing atonement accomplished by Christ is grounded exclusively in the death of Jesus and not in his resurrection. The resurrection, while surely crucial, is understood only as divine authentication of the work of Christ. But Christ both died and rose for us (Rom. 5:10). Beyond forgiveness for past guilt, the goal of God in Jesus was and still is to create anew in place of the "old that has passed away" (2 Cor. 5:17). The resurrection of Christ from the dead is the beginning of the new creation.[37] This is why the Orthodox Church of the East has proclaimed forgiveness at the Easter festival and celebrated Easter as the feast of atonement.

The triumph over sinful forces featured in the Christus Victor atonement view is intended to be seen eschatologically. That is, the good-versus-evil war already is won in principle, but with real battles still going on and yet to be fought—although there is a liberating present awareness of future victory. The evil powers are still active and influential. Paul says that we are enslaved to the "elemental spirits of the universe" (Gal. 4:3, 9; Col. 2:8, 20). These spirits apparently include the law, which can become deceiving and enslaving, and sin that takes us captive (Rom. 7:11, 23). The church still is engaged in a hostile conflict with such enemies. This conflict may persist stubbornly, probably until the end of time. Even so, eventual victory is already known. Christ's grave is empty!

The New Testament teaches that Jesus constantly had to overcome Satan (Matt. 4:1-11, 12:22-32, 27:37-44). Liberation from evil powers is a pervasive New Testament theme (Gal. 1:3; Acts 10:38), with all powers finally to be subordinated to Christ (1 Pet. 3:22; 1 Tim. 3:16). A classic statement of the Christus

---

[37]Release from the controlling power of sin ("sanctification") was a central concern of John Wesley.

Victor atonement model is Hebrews 2:14-15: "Since, therefore, the children share flesh and blood, he himself likewise shared the same things, so that through death he might destroy the one who has the power of death, that is, the devil, and free those who all their lives were held in slavery by the fear of death." Early Christians rejoiced that, in the cross and resurrection of Jesus, God somehow "disarmed the rulers and authorities...triumphing over them in it" (Col. 2:15). The victory motif captures well the biblical story of God's long conflict with enslaving evil powers, beginning with the dramatic exodus from Egypt, a primary paradigm of faith and salvation throughout the Hebrew Scriptures. Christ's victory over the rulers and authorities is at the heart of one of the earliest Christian confessions of faith (Phil. 2:9-11).

The battle goes on and is not limited to "otherworldly" evil powers that function only in the spiritual realm. The crucifixion death and resurrection victory of Jesus occurred in the physical, historical world in which we now live. God's victorious Kingdom continues to have both reality and visibility wherever and whenever God's people live according to the example of Jesus and in the power of Jesus' Spirit, giving present visibility and reality to the Kingdom of God. The biblical revelation views the work of Christ as establishing "a new social order which stands over against—in confrontation with—the structures of the world."[38] Such standing against is possible only because of the liberating victory of Christ on our behalf.

---

[38] J. Denny Weaver, "Atonement for the Non-Constantinian Church," in *Modern Theology* 6:4 (July, 1990), 309. This new social order is the church, the minority ecclesiology as emphasized in the Believers' Church tradition. Note that this atonement model has been subjectivized in ways that Weaver finds abortive of the full biblical intent for a visible, social demonstration of the victory of God. Rudolf Bultmann and Paul Tillich used the theme of victory by focusing on existential forces that deprive modern humans of "authentic existence." In this way, the atonement of Christ tends to be reduced to a subjective victory within human consciousness only. American revivalism often has encouraged a similar reductionism. The biblical narrative is far more outward and historical than this.

This view of Christ's work probably was popular in the post-apostolic period because it spoke forcefully to Christians of both Jewish and Gentile origin, many of whom knew much about oppressive military and spiritual powers. Justo González calls this the "classic" atonement model. He judges that the human problem is not fundamentally that we owe a debt to God (satisfaction) or lack necessary knowledge or inspiration to love God (moral influence), theories related closely to socio-political issues prominent in church life long after biblical times.[39] Such theories often have functioned to support the control of ruling classes in many cultures. Rather, the primary human problem is enslavement to evil, "and it is no coincidence that the 'classical' view of atonement began to recede into the background when the church became powerful."[40] Says Clark Pinnock: "We must keep the cross and resurrection together and jointly prominent. Evangelical theology has been biblically deficient in its treatment of the resurrection of Christ. It treats the cross soteriologically [as central to effecting human salvation], but seldom the resurrection. It is a remarkable omission in evangelical theology."[41]

The sacrifice of the cross and the victory of the resurrection of Jesus addresses the guilt as justification, provides the power as sanctification, and assures the consequences as eventual glorification. The Kingdom of God has been inaugurated in Christ on our historical scene and its firstfruits are to be the liberation, reconciliation, restoration, and commissioning of Kingdom citizens for new life in the world. Our human understanding of the proper focus of Christ's atonement should not be limited to a resolution of the guilt of past sin. It also is being set free for life now, life dedicated to God's mission in this world.

---

[39]See Justo González, *Christian Thought Revisited: Three Types of Theology* (Nashville: Abingdon Press, 1989).

[40]Justo González, *Mañana: Christian Theology from a Hispanic Perspective* (Nashville: Abingdon Press, 1990), 154.

[41]In Pinnock and Delwin Brown, *Theological Crossfire* (Grand Rapids: Zondervan, 1990), 148.

Why was Jesus crucified? For our sins, we immediately and rightly respond. Note, however, that the evil powers to which Jesus was handed over and which Jesus conquered on our behalf included political forces. The penalty for a range of severe violations of religious laws among the Jews was stoning. The stoning symbol of salvation for Christians is a cross. The cross was Rome's method of executing political crimes. Jesus was accused of "forbidding us to pay taxes to the emperor, and saying that he himself is the Messiah, a king" (Lk. 23:2). He was killed for presumed rebellion against the ultimate authority of a human empire.

Surely an overcoming of such arrogant worldly authority is included in the Christian good news. Jesus reversed the whole arena of worldly power and offers liberation to the oppressed in the midst of their worldly oppression. By the cross, Jesus "disarmed the rulers and authorities and made a public example of them, triumphing over them" (Col. 2:15). Concludes Theodore Jennings: "If our faith has no relation to this public and political sphere, then our faith has no relation to the historical cross of Jesus."[42] Kwame Bediako of West Africa insists that the death and resurrection of Jesus have enthroned Jesus on the "stool of power" with God. Kings of the earth may still reign, but now they are "desacralized" by Christ's rule. Christian loyalties are changed. In a culture where ancestors long deceased are still claimed to have significant reality, Bediako says that "once Christ has come the ancestors are cut off as the means of blessing for we lay our power lines differently."[43] One belongs to a new kingdom, and King Jesus is Lord of all!

The defining center of Christian eschatology, then, is Jesus Christ. In his earthly ministry the Kingdom of God came (Matt. 12:28). In his death and resurrection the judgment of the end has already begun (Jn. 12:31; Rom. 8:3). Through his continuing min-

---

[42]Theodore Jennings, *Loyalty To God* (Nashville: Abingdon Press, 1992), 109.

[43]As quoted by William Dyrness, *Learning About Theology from the Third World* (Grand Rapids: Zondervan, 1990), 169.

istry the disciples of Jesus experience heaven now (Eph. 2:6). In the most comprehensive of all passages about him, Colossians 1:15-17 declares that creation, history, and the final future are all Christocentric. The expectation of what God will do grows out of the knowledge of what God already has done in Jesus Christ. That is, Jesus Christ is the source, cohesion, and goal of all created things. The resurrection of Jesus is the reassuring model and its power the only capable cause of our own eventual resurrections as mortal persons. It, therefore, should be the starting point for Christian eschatology.

All of the exhortations of Jesus about "the end" were intended to have practical, ethical meaning, calling persons to current responsibility in the fellowship of Christ's new body on earth. Jesus came announcing and bringing the Kingdom of God. One day Jesus Christ will also consummate the Kingdom on the coming occasion of his glorious return. Before that consummation comes, however, the role of the church in the present should remain a central consideration. The liberation and hope of Jesus' resurrection should lead to the current faithfulness of believers bound together by Christ as his new body, the church. Therefore, we now turn to a consideration of Christian hope as it ought to relate to present history.

Matters Worth Exploring

1. Jesus introduced God's Kingdom in a distinctive way, one not expected or accepted by many of his own people before or after the first century. What was that distinctive way?

2. The Gospel of Matthew records what Jesus taught about how his disciples are to wait in the time before his coming again. What is the right way to wait as faithful Christians?

3. How is the resurrection of Jesus foundational to the present mission of the church in an evil world and the source of hope for life beyond this world?

4. It is said that being a Christian is to be freed to be a "risk taker," an extension of the post-resurrection life of Jesus. Are you now experiencing such freedom and Jesus-life in the Spirit? Why are so many people who are called "Christians" not particularly reflective of the distinctive life modeled by Jesus?

5. Is the founding of the modern State of Israel in 1948 the "clock of prophecy"? Why is considering it as such questionable given New Testament teaching about this age and the next?

6. Are our own times the "last days" any more than any time in which disciples of Jesus have or yet will seek to serve faithfully in the face of the active powers of evil still loose in this world?

7. Christian eschatology is "Christocentric." What does this mean?

Chapter 6

HOPE WITHIN HISTORY

❧

So is my [God's] word that goes out from my mouth:
It will not return to me empty, but will accomplish
what I desire and achieve the purpose for
which I sent it. (Isaiah 55:11)

❧

But if the Christian hope is reduced to the salvation of the soul in a heaven
beyond death, it loses its power to renew life and change the world, and
its flame is quenched; it dies away into no more than a gnostic yearning
for redemption from this world's vale of tears.[1]

❧

In chapter three we spoke of presuppositions that influence each person's reading of the Bible. When approaching matters of eschatology, this chapter suggests that one basic presupposition that clearly should be allowed to influence Christian thinking is the heritage of the Jewish tradition. It was the very soil from which Jesus the Messiah came and in which the Christian faith initially

---

[1]Jürgen Moltmann, *The Coming of God: Christian Eschatology* (Minneapolis: Fortress Press, 1996), xv. George Eldon Ladd puts it this way (*The Presence of the Future*, 331): "The Kingdom of God cannot be reduced to the reign of God within the individual soul or modernized in terms of personal existential confrontation or dissipated to an extraworldly dream of blessed immortality. The Kingdom of God means that God is King and acts in history to bring history to a divinely directed goal."

flowered. To reject this heritage out of hand as "old" and now entirely superceded is premature and often has led to serious theological error among Christians.[2] Jesus said that he had come to fulfill, not eliminate his own Hebrew heritage (Matt. 5:17). That heritage linked closely the hope of tomorrow and social responsibility in the history of today.

One Jewish key to establishing a mission-laden Christian hope is a steady focus on the divinely-intended meaningfulness of present history. History was understood by the ancient Jews as the arena and story of God at work in the world. Eschatology, then, is the "systematic-theological reflection on history as the narrative of God's activity in bringing humankind to God's intended goal."[3] The call to Christians is to join redemptively in the ongoing divine narrative, not shun history's significance in lieu of the coming time beyond time.

Recalling Adrio König's manner of developing the history of Jesus in accomplishing the redemptive purpose of God, the first phase is what God once did *for us* in Christ and the second is what God now seeks to do *in us* through the Spirit of Christ. So,

> ... the eschaton realized for us has yet to be realized in us. We must be brought to the point of accepting the end of our hostility toward God; we must begin to experience our freedom from sin and freedom for God and neighbor; we must begin to live actively as God's true servants and offer our lives for his service.[4]

If justifying sinners through the death of Jesus is the central meaning of what God did *for* us, then sanctifying us through the transforming power of God's living Spirit is what God seeks to do *in* us and

---

[2]See Marvin Wilson, *Our Father Abraham: Jewish Roots of the Christian Faith* (Grand Rapids: Eerdmans, 1989), especially chapter ten.

[3]Stanley Grenz, *Theology for the Community of God* (Nashville: Broadman & Holman, 1994), 780.

[4]Adrio König, *The Eclipse of Christ in Eschatology* (Grand Rapids: Eerdmans, 1989), 97.

then *through* us in the world. Jesus now acts in the real history of our time to make God's reign visible and concretely real. The Kingdom of God does not belong to this world (Jn. 18:36); nonetheless, it is more than a "spiritual" idea, more than a peace in the souls of redeemed people now satisfied to ignore a Christ-like engagement with the politics, demon possessions, and harsh injustices of the places and times of our earthly lives. Howard Snyder laments that after 1890 "social gospelers secularized this kingdom vision and conservatives spiritualized it."[5] Reinhold Niebuhr concludes that Christians living in the ambiguities of this world tend "to destroy the *dialectic of prophetic religion*, either by sacrificing time and history to eternity or by giving ultimate significance to the relativities of history. Christian orthodoxy chose the first alternative, and Christian liberalism the second."[6]

The biblical challenge is to embrace the power, healing, and vision of God's eternity without abandoning a Christian hope that has good news for real human history in the times and places where it still must be shared and lived. "Eternal life" is to be already present as God's gracious enabling now of the reign of God that will be realized fully only then. Eternal life for the Christian is existence in the presence of God and living now and forever in accord with the purposes and will of God. Such life now, lived in the hope of the risen Christ in the midst of the ongoing crucifixion of our historical times, means "already acting here and today in accordance with that world of justice and righteousness and peace contrary to appearances, and contrary to all historical chances of success."[7]

A Distinctively Christian Humanism

It is important to take careful note of the impact that any cultural setting has on how life is lived. This includes the way reli-

---

[5]Howard Snyder, *The Community of the King* (InterVarsity, 1977), 28.

[6]Reinhold Niebuhr, *An Interpretation of Christian Ethics* (London: SCM Press, 1948), 151.

[7]Jürgen Moltmann, *The Coming of God: Christian Eschatology* (Minneapolis: Fortress Press, 1996), 234.

gious faith is conceived and practiced. No person believes in a cultural vacuum. Sometimes the cultural impact on particular religious perspectives and practices is so subtle and pervasive that it is not even recognized. Sometimes the impact is so dramatic and evident that it either is celebrated openly or resisted vigorously, often stimulating either the official establishment of a given faith or the persecution of that faith by the dominant culture. Christian hope intends to send believers into their cultures with a distinctive and relevant good news designed to make a real difference.

Christianity has experienced all varieties of cultural relationships in various times and settings. For proper perspective on crucial subjects like faith's relationship to human history, the material world, and the human body, Christians should review their own theological heritage critically and re-emphasize the normative teachings of its Hebrew roots. Especially is this the case because of the problems which have been created over the centuries by the negative and lingering impact that aspects of one particular culture has had on the Christian faith.

The Judeo-Christian religious tradition has experienced a dramatic, volatile, and theologically influential relationship with classic Greek culture, particularly with its philosophic thought structures. Not long after the world-changing exploits of Alexander the Great (c. 330 B.C.E.), an aggressive and even violent process began which was designed to impose aspects of Greek culture on the population of Palestine. This process finally sought to outlaw and supplant various traditional Jewish beliefs and practices. After reluctant accommodation by many Jews to the goals of this brutal process, the Maccabean Revolt followed (c. 165 B.C.E.). It managed to tear the Jewish community of Palestine free of this forced "Hellenization" which so obviously meant to undermine the very foundations of Jewish faith and life. A Jewish counter-culture had reasserted itself in order to provide protection for the integrity of its traditional way of believing and living.

The successful Maccabean Revolt, however, was not the end of this struggle. Hellenization entered a more subtle and more pervasively influential phase as it soon came to interact with the early Christian community. Christianity, flowering out of Jewish soil, had declared itself universal in nature and mission. Its self-understanding compelled disciples of Jesus to go to all the world. There was to be an openness to "Gentiles" as well as Jews. A complex process began which saw much interaction between the cultures of the Mediterranean world and the distinctive faith of Christians.

One result of this interaction was at least a partial Hellenization of Christian theological thought. Christians encountered an old, rich, and sophisticated philosophic tradition which they wanted to impact for Christ. One method of encouraging effective impact was the attempt to explain the Christian message in Greek philosophic categories of thought, hoping thereby to enhance communication of the good news. But impact went both ways. The nature of the Christian message was shaped in subtle ways by the dominant Greek culture that it was seeking to impact for Christ. As early Christian "apologists" sought to express their faith to the larger world, they tended to develop their thinking by the use of concepts and arguments readily understood and appreciated by the best philosophic schools of those times. These Christians, on mission to the world, also found themselves influenced by those they sought to teach. Justin Martyr (c. 100-164 A.D.), for instance, "built a bridge between Christian revelation and Greek learning that allowed much of Greek wisdom to be accepted and incorporated into Christian theology."[8]

One point of such alteration involved the Christian's understanding of the material world, the human body, and their place in the plan of God. The Jewish roots of Christian faith differed fundamentally from central aspects of the Greek philosophic worldview. Generally speaking, the Greek worldview assumed an

---

[8]Thomas N. Finger, *Christian Theology*, vol. 1 (Scottdale, Pa.: Herald Press, 1985), 15.

incompatibility between the realms of the divine and the material world. Since it was assumed that the divine Principle could never come into the material corruption of this world, human union with God could be achieved only as persons separated themselves from "worldly" things and experienced the purely immaterial, spiritual realities. The soul, thought of as the divine dimension of persons caught temporarily in fleshly and historical corruption, was to seek freedom from its prison-house of bodily flesh. Biblical faith, on the other hand, looked at these things very differently. It not only saw the possibility, but proclaimed the voluntary entrance of God into the material world. The sovereign God, wholly "above" his own creation, nonetheless demonstrated genuine care about real human history by entering its arena with redemptive intent. The heart of the Hebrew Scriptures pictures the world-entering God enabling exodus from Egypt, the possession of land, and return from exile.[9]

Moving to the New Testament, God is said to have come to the world in the lowliest way possible, a helpless baby in desperate surroundings. God was believed to have created this world, to have called it good, to have demonstrated intense love for it and continuing involvement with it. Such a faith perspective was literally "incarnational" because God had become voluntarily "enfleshed" in Jesus (an inconceivable thought to the Greek mind). Jesus turned to Isaiah 61 to interpret in expressly social terms his own fulfillment of the messianic expectation. God, he said,

> has sent me to bring good news to the oppressed, to bind up the brokenhearted, to proclaim liberty to the captives, and release to the prisoners; to proclaim the year of the Lord's favor, and the day of vengeance of our God; to comfort all who mourn.... (Isa. 61:1-2)

Believers seeking to be like the God now come in Jesus Christ knew themselves called to be appreciative of and involved

---

[9]See Walter Brueggemann, *The Land: Place of Gift, Promise and Challenge in Biblical Faith* (Fortress Press, 1977).

redemptively with material reality, right down to the levels of the human body and human history. Their teaching about the physical resurrection of Jesus was scorned by the dominant Greek culture (Acts 17:32) because it seemed unthinkable that a spiritual man like Jesus, once freed from the flesh by death, would again accept voluntarily its terrible burden.

If Christians are committed to the authority of their Hebrew-oriented biblical rootage, as opposed to later theological and philosophical developments of their faith, then the essentials of such rootage are of crucial concern. These essentials include a respect for the material world in general, for God's active involvement in the historical process, and for the well-being of the human body in particular. Marvin Wilson discusses at length this "visceral Hebraic perspective on human nature," noting that, biblically speaking, human beings are "whole" beings with "one's physical, psychological, and spiritual functions...one indivisible entity."[10] This is in sharp contrast to the Greek concept of persons having a "soul" separate from the body. To the Hebrew mind, a person, rather than *having* a soul, was understood *to be* a living soul. Any true life of the spirit had to be *body* life. Any real hope had to have some obvious relation to the material reality of this world.

The nature and will of God were known to the ancient Jew through what was believed to be the divinely inspired interpretations of the real events of human history. There was a disposition toward being passionate and fully human people who, because of their faith, were directed *to* this world and not *from* it. History was real. God was deeply involved in it by gracious choice. Politics was important. Ethics was not optional. Economic justice was obligatory. The artistic, dramatic, and musical were appreciated and used often as aids in worship. Since the physical world was seen as real, good, and created and highly valued by God, it was

---

[10] Marvin R. Wilson, *Our Father Abraham* (Grand Rapids: Eerdmans and Center for Judaic-Christian Studies, 1989), 139.

believed that one should never deny it, destroy it, misuse it, or limit its proper involvement in the fullness of life.

As the Song of Songs of the Hebrew Scriptures makes vividly clear, even passion-filled poetry verging on idealized sexual eroticism within the marriage relationship was judged worthy of being remembered and celebrated. God had sanctified human flesh as part of the highpoint of his creative activity. Our human bodies and troubled times are worthy of respect, attention, contemplation, and effort on behalf of their intended fulfillment within God's will and way. While not to be worshipped as divine itself or violated through sexual promiscuity or material deprivation, the human body was to be recognized, enjoyed, cared for, and celebrated as a precious and beautiful gift of God. It was not to be separated from the "soul" and thus relegated to the realm of the nonspiritual. Humans as complex and unified beings are the ultimate work of the very hands of God. In fact, high compliment was paid to the human body when the Hebrew did not hesitate to use references to human body parts ("hands" of God, for example) as ways of describing attributes of God himself.

Spirituality for the Hebrews did not mean a turning inward in denial of the reality or value of the world. Marvin Wilson puts it well:

> True piety was not simply the private nourishing of the virtues of one's soul. Rather, it meant to be fully human, every fiber of one's being alive, empowered in passionate and inspired service to God and humanity.... The Hebrews experienced the world of the spirit as robust, life-affirming, and this-worldly in character.[11]

The richness of life was relished. Questions of justice and liberation were frequent and urgent. There was to be holiness in the here and now. It was God's world to be experienced without guilt. As Paul later put it, "to the pure, all things are pure, but to

---

[11]Wilson, op. cit., 176.

those who are corrupted and do not believe, nothing is pure" (Titus 1:15).

What perspective does the Bible give to the contemporary Christian who lives in a hedonistic world where pornography is more evident than piety? Some think the biblical faith encourages a withdrawal from the world because they associate evil and shame with the human body and sexual activity, things so often being perverted for self-gratification or just evening entertainment. The understandable call, then, is to abandon such "worldly" pursuits as art and politics, in effect to avoid all appearance and unnecessary risk of evil by ceasing to function in many areas of ordinary fleshly and civic life. This approach welcomes much of the earlier Greek thinking and thereby flies in the face of the central witness of the biblical heritage.

Of course, we as Christians have been called to be *not of* the world; but we also very much have been called to be *alive in the world* as new, fully functioning, life-changing creations. The biblical faith calls for more than defensive reaction to popular perversions of God's revealed intentions. It calls for proclamation through word and deed of what was intended and is possible in all aspects of human life.[12] Creation is good; it is to be enjoyed as a gift of a loving God. Life is beautiful and should be received by faith in its fullness—without shame and with deep gratitude. Judgment after this life will not be separated from divine awareness of what was done in this life at the basic levels of visiting, feeding, clothing, healing, and liberating those in such need (Matt. 25:31ff).

Anything which is truly "human" sounds admirable enough. In today's setting, however, human*ism* verges on being a popular anti-religion. It was understandable and appropriate, then, for the

---

[12]See Robert Tuttle, Jr., *Mysticism in the Wesleyan Tradition* (Francis Asbury Press, 1989), for an excellent study of how John Wesley combined the quest for fulfillment of the inner life with great sensitivity to the realities of the world of his time.

Board of Trustees of Anderson University to have made the following judgment:

> There is today a widespread and influential approach to truth and value, an approach which can be called "secular humanism." It has been formalized in documents like "Humanist Manifestos I and II" (1933 and 1973) and is popularized in many forms. It tends to exalt inordinately both human reason and potential, while failing to acknowledge the existence and relevance of God in all such matters. This secular humanism is alien to the assumptions of the Christian faith and to the very foundations of a Christian liberal arts college.[13]

To be fully faithful to the biblical heritage, however, it is important to go beyond a negative critique of the clearly unacceptable. A contemporary Christian lifestyle, as well as Christian involvement in implementing programs of higher education and social reform, should demonstrate the positive which emerges from faith in the now incarnate God who loves his creation and always seeks its redemption and fulfillment. Recognizing this need, the University's Board of Trustees went on to make clear that the institution's educational philosophy "does not subscribe to secular humanism. It seeks instead to approach the human condition in light of God's revelation of Himself and His will in Jesus Christ."[14]

A distinctively Christian humanism often has been affirmed as possible and essential as Christians seek to live in hope and fulfill their biblical heritage by being on God's mission in God's world. This special "humanistic" approach to all aspects of life has been defined helpfully in this way:

---

[13]Report to the General Assembly of the Church of God, June 16, 1981, 7.
[14]Ibid.

Christian humanism is the interest in human persons and the positive affirmation of human life and culture which stems from the Christian faith. It shares with other humanistic philosophies the motive of discovering and supporting whatever enhances human existence, but is distinctive in finding the source and goal of human powers in God, the Creator, Redeemer, and Spirit. Where secular forms of humanism focus on "merely" human interests, deliberately excluding transcendent factors from consideration, Christian humanism seeks an understanding of the whole range of human experience in the light of God's revelation to humanity in the person and work of Jesus Christ.[15]

Christians look forward in hope. Their hope is centered in Jesus Christ. It is a hope that brings God's future into the present where God's people find God still at work. Disciples of Christ are to seek an embodiment of the will and ways of God, to be holy as God is holy. They know that they should work while it is day, since accountability lies somewhere just ahead. They find themselves sent into all the world, aware of the finiteness of this time-space existence and of their own mandate to be faithful in the meantime.

Blessed are the History-Makers

God, of course, originally created history itself and without question remains sovereign over its few glories and many agonies. But who controls our human understanding of the meaning of history? Unfortunately, there is much truth in the claim that "all history is written by the winners." The dominant political and military leaders usually manage the flow of information to the public and put their official "spin" on what should be seen by the public as

---

[15]Joseph Shaw, et. al., eds., *Readings in Christian Humanism* (Augsburg Publishing House, 1982), 23.

significant. "History" is regularly created in this manipulative and self-serving way. In sharp contrast, in ancient Israel much of the view of that peoples' history which has survived in the Bible was shaped by the prophetic few, the daring voices from the margins of establishment perspectives.

Jeremiah is an excellent example. He lived through that dramatic time when Jerusalem was destroyed (587 B.C.E.) and official "public history" in Judah came to an abrupt end. When temple and king are gone, who is left to say what is real and what is not? "In every generation," insists Walter Brueggemann, "the people who make the time-line, the people who sponsor and benefit from the headline, want to manage the process, deny the hurt, eradicate the ambiguity."[16] Those at the margins of society have little voice and experience much pain.

Jeremiah, however, was anything but an establishment history-maker. He asked the hard questions: "Why does the way of the wicked prosper? Why do all who are treacherous thrive?" (Jer. 12:1). But he also made history "from below" by having confidence that there is an unbreakable fiber of justice and righteousness which finally cannot be violated, mocked, or eliminated. God's will is not the same thing as the way things are; it remains redemptive, undefeated, remarkably tenacious to the eyes of faith. Jeremiah shaped new history by crying out against those who sought to domesticate God, and those others who in despair thought that the domestication efforts have worked. God is both distant and close at hand (Jer. 23:23), right in the thick of things while beyond being dominated and destroyed by those things that make up our real lives. There is hope, and God's people are to be its daring heralds.

Those rare history-makers with eyes fixed on God's future "have some sense of the flow of the historical process in the long

---

[16]Walter Brueggemann, *Hope Within History* (Atlanta: John Knox Press, 1987), 57. This present chapter owes part of its inspiration to this insightful book.

haul and are very sure where history is headed."[17] Even though little Judah resisting huge Babylon was futile, Jeremiah nonetheless was not a voice of despair. He could articulate God's future out of the very disaster at hand (cf. Isa. 45:18-19). The prophet of God was sure that there would be a new day "wrought not by political strategy but by God's free capacity to work beyond visible constructs. It is that freedom of God which gives a future and a hope."[18] In the New Testament Jesus is represented as the real maker of history rather than those who merely managed the religious tradition (cf. Matt. 23:27). Those who carried out his crucifixion were sure that such an ultimate act would end abruptly the unsettling ministry of the unusual man from Nazareth. They were wrong. Even death fails to have the last word in the working of God.

The Christian good news heralds with joy that God in Christ is both the believer's past and future. It affirms that God is the beginning and the end and that the divine presence is real and potentially transforming in current historical circumstances as well as ultimately. Even now, liberty is proclaimed to the captives (Lk. 4:18) because Satan was dethroned when Jesus was raised from the dead. Jesus Christ, yet to come again, already is Lord over all earthly powers (Rev. 17:14, 19:16). He may have ascended to the right hand of the Father after the resurrection, but Jesus remains present as the Spirit of Christ. Jesus Christ, the beginning and the end, is powerfully active in every present until the end of all time. We now are in the "end times," the times when the Spirit is being outpoured (Joel 2:28; Acts 2:17). The Spirit's ministry is eschatology now in action as its pledge and first-fruits (Eph. 1:14; Rom. 8:23).

The challenge for Christians is to truly live in the light of Christ's second advent, remaining faithful here and now, working *within history*, but also *from beyond history*, to overcome the

---

[17]Ibid., 66.
[18]Ibid., 68.

demons of the world by the power of the God who already has come among us in Christ and yet remains with us in the presence and power of the Spirit. Corporate America may proclaim that "progress is our most important product," but Christian faith believes in a hope made real by divine grace, not progress which is the "product" of human achievement. Hope is trust in what we cannot see fully and never can produce ourselves. Since hope in God does focus on justice in our time and place, working toward that end is essential. What is justice? Justice is "a dance that people are free to do when they hear the music of God's future being played in the present."[19] The church is to be God's eschatological people, a new humanity, the fulfillment of God's original intent for Israel, a light to the nations. A proper eschatological perspective is what enlivens the church's vision in the present and on behalf of the present out of the resources of the future.

A key aspect of African-American Christianity, like the faith of the Hebrew Scriptures, is belief in the inseparability of the material and spiritual dimensions of life. Hope and history are linked. In the theological career of James Cone, for instance, there has been "a movement from the rejection of otherworldliness, to a critique of distorted otherworldliness, to an appreciation of the role of eschatological vision in the liberation struggle of the oppressed."[20] This linking of hope in God's future and responsibility in the painful now of human history is a continuation of the longstanding vision of the biblical narrative.[21] While Latin American liberation theologians like J. P. Miranda are understandably critical of the traditional view of death and eternal life for shifting Christian focus away from the injustices of this world to a solution only beyond this life, African-American theologian James

---

[19]Thomas Long, in Barry Callen, ed., *Sharing Heaven's Music: The Heart of Christian Preaching Today* (Nashville: Abingdon Press, 1995), 201.

[20]James Evans, Jr., *We Have Been Believers* (Minneapolis: Fortress Press, 1992), 149.

[21]See Walter Brueggemann, *Hope Within History* (Atlanta: John Knox Press, 1987).

Cone still insists that belief in an afterlife is appropriate, but certainly agrees that such eschatology can and must engage the present historical order.[22] Future hope gains proper significance when it enables believers to even risk death in order to overcome present oppression and injustice. It is inspiring to read the script of an interview with James Earl Massey which Henry H. Mitchell conducted and, in Massey's honor, titled "Veteran Inhabitant of the World We Hope For."[23]

Christian feminist perspectives on eschatology typically stress that any ultimate hope must include commitment to a just and egalitarian (gender and otherwise) transformation of the created order. Rejecting other-worldly, merely futuristic eschatologies, they tend to adopt an inaugurated view, preserving the biblical balance between the *already* and the *not yet* of the Kingdom of God. In this spirit of championing the transformative potential of the Kingdom's already dimension, Donald Bloesch, while strongly reemphasizing the importance of indebtedness to the Protestant (magisterial) Reformation, nonetheless notes: "We must include the Anabaptists, with their pronounced stress on the Christian life." The Reformation message of justification by the free grace of God "becomes rationalization for sin and cheap grace unless it is united with the New Testament call to radical discipleship, the salient emphasis of the Anabaptists."[24]

Such an emphasis on radical discipleship is seen in the Hebrew Scriptures, where there is refusal to eliminate as central the present implications of any hope of salvation beyond death. Justo González argues forcefully for abandoning any lingering "gnosticism" that devalues the significance of the reality of present, material existence: "In the 'books of Moses,' God's 'salvation'

---

[22]See James Cone, *A Black Theology of Liberation*, 2nd ed. (Maryknoll, N. Y.: Orbis Books, 1987).

[23]Barry L. Callen, ed., *Sharing Heaven's Music: The Heart of Christian Preaching* (Nashville: Abingdon Press, 1995), 203-219.

[24]Donald Bloesch, *The Future of Evangelical Christianity* (Doubleday, 1983), 115.

is the deliverance from Egypt. In Judges, 'salvation' is a success-ful uprising against oppressors. In Isaiah and several of the prophets, it is freedom and return from exile. In the Psalms, it is the destruction of one's enemies. If all of this has nothing to do with 'real salvation,' then it is difficult to see why these books are considered sacred and inspired Scripture."[25]

The crucial concern of the biblical story is that the dynamics of the Kingdom of God *in* history do not get swallowed up in the longing for and symbols of eternal life anticipated *beyond* history. The Kingdom of God is rightly preached as an anchor of hope for the believing individual after death and even after the end of all human history. It is this and it is more. It also is the power of that future of God to manifest itself now in political and social terms, in the struggle for peace with justice, for true community and free-dom here in this earthly life. Believers cannot "earn" their own sal-vation by any form of "good works." Even so, judgment finally will be in terms of what we believers have done with our lives—feeding the hungry, clothing the naked, etc. (Matt. 25:31-46). Claiming to believe without living accordingly is a lie (1 Jn. 4:20). The future toward which the Christian journeys by faith is open, and its divinely enabled potential should shape the present. It is not just any future that carries such potential. The Apostles' Creed says that it is Jesus who will come to judge. Ultimately, the future will have a *Jesus shape*. All else is perverted and passing. For the believer, the Jesus shape of tomorrow is to be the embodied mind of Christ today (Phil. 2:5).

Says C. Norman Kraus: "What God has done and is doing in history is crucial for understanding what he will do in the future.... Therefore, when predictions about God's future actively contradict

---

[25]Justo González, *Out of Every Tribe & Nation* (Nashville: Abingdon Press, 1992), 90. He argues that the Bible does not speak of human beings in parts like body and soul. "A disembodied soul is not a human being, just as a dis-souled body is no longer a human being" (127). The Bible thinks of "salvation" in a whole manner with reference to real human history in its material, social, and spiritual dimensions.

his self-revelation in Christ, we can safely ignore them."[26] Theodore Jennings makes a similar point in relation to life on earth, now so threatened by human greed and hatred. "If there is to be any future at all it will be shaped like Jesus. For this planet there can be no future that does not begin with justice for the poor; there can be no future that does not lay aside the implements of violence; there can be no future without the end of avarice in generosity, the end of bitterness in forgiveness, the end of enmity in reconciliation."[27]

Elaborate speculations about end things (always claiming, of course, to be precise biblical teaching) usually manage unintentionally to undercut Christian mission by tending to place the Christian's hope in some future time and state. The concern for prediction often abandons potential embodiment and ministry in the troubled present. The Marxist critique of Christianity and all religion insists on just this point. Rather than bringing life abundantly within the harsh realities of this present life, religion is claimed to function for the masses as an escapist reliance on an abundance reserved only for the hereafter. On the contrary, the Christian call is to present integrity, to actual incarnation of the good news in this world, not to a current capitulation that becomes bad news for others.[28] Christians should understand their faith as a stimulus to pray *and* act accordingly. We Christians are to be "construction workers and not only interpreters of [God's] future."[29]

To be assumed in relation to each major Christian doctrine is the immediate relevance of eschatology. Those things anticipated

---

[26]C. Norman Kraus, *God Our Savior* (Scottdale, Pa.: Herald Press, 1991), 190.

[27]Theodore Jennings, *Loyalty To God* (Nashville: Abingdon Press, 1992), 160.

[28]Laurence Stookey speaks helpfully: "The future of God is not some escapist notion that allows us to make peace with unrighteousness on earth; instead it is the divine tug that motivates the reform of the present state of things" (*Eucharist: Christ's Feast With the Church*, Abingdon Press, 1993, 26).

[29]Jürgen Moltmann, *Religion, Revolution, and the Future* (New York: Charles Scribner's Sons, 1969), 34.

ultimately should have present impact on Christian believing and living. John Howard Yoder says that "there is no significance to human effort...unless life can be seen in terms of ultimate goals. The *eschaton*, the 'Last Thing,' the End-Event, imparts to life a meaningfulness which it would not otherwise have." Eschatology, then, is "a hope which, defying present frustration, defines a present position in terms of the yet unseen goals which give it meaning."[30] Whatever is *orthodox expectation* should also be *radical application*. The purpose of the biblical testimony to the future life "is not to describe in detail what will happen as if with scientific certainty, but to console, encourage, and engender hope in what God has provided in the future, and faithfulness in this world" (1 Cor. 15:58; 2 Pet. 3:11).[31] God will care quite adequately for the later on; in the meantime, God's children are to be instruments of the Spirit in divine history-making here below.

Living From and Toward a Vision

The biblical narrative of God's redemptive activity moves toward its climax, the final chapter of the story of God's relation to creation. Confidence in a sure, just, and merciful climax becomes vision and strength for present engagement of this world on behalf of that which soon will be and, in part, already is. Why could the prophet Jeremiah purchase land when he knew that shortly it would be overrun by brutal invaders (Jer. 32)? Because he had faith in the future of God, a sturdy faith that enabled bold, present action in defiance of all negative appearances and short-lived evil realities.

Christians are "looking at the image of the future given in the gospel, which inspires our journey through history. Eschatology is about the image shaped by the revelation of God in Christ, which tells us what God's purposes are and projects their ultimate real-

---

[30]John Howard Yoder, *The Original Revolution: Essays on Christian Pacifism* (Scottdale, Pa.: Herald Press, 1972), 56.

[31]Thomas Oden, *Life in the Spirit* (San Francisco: Harper, 1992), 373.

ization."[32] Not merely about "last things," eschatology is a way of viewing all Christian belief, life, and hope in light of the Kingdom come in Christ and coming in Christ. It is a trajectory launched in the past, in motion in the present, and sure to impact and shape the future as God originally intended. Therefore, salvation for Christians should be seen as more than long-term fire insurance! It is a commission and an enablement to be God's people in this world, new creations in Christ who are prepared to live redemptively *for* God's goals and *out of* a special vision of what has been, is, and finally will be.

Note the use of the *mañana* concept by Hispanic theologian Justo González. He reports that the dominant culture in North America has used this Spanish word to characterize Hispanics as listless and lazy people (why do today what can be put off until tomorrow?). But the word, González insists, means more than "tomorrow." It brings into sharp question what is unacceptable today and puts in alongside God's promise what is yet unfulfilled. There is the mañana vision of Scripture that sees God doing a new thing, so that the hope of tomorrow already is happening today! Mañana may not yet be, but at least "today can be lived out of the glory and the promise of mañana, thanks to the power of the Spirit."[33] Being the body of Christ requires an acquiring of life from the ruler of the coming order, thus living now in God's community as priests and kings (1 Pet. 2:9; Rev. 1:6; 5:10).

To live now, as new beings in Christ in the real history of our times, requires a careful understanding of the hopeful and dangerous dimensions of the present "millennium." Revelation 20 is the key here and is to be interpreted in the context of the whole Christian gospel, not in some narrow way that transforms one-time apocalyptic language into a conceptual key that controls the whole

---

[32]Clark Pinnock, in Pinnock and Delwin Brown, *Theological Crossfire* (Grand Rapids: Zondervan, 1990), 217-218.

[33]Justo González, *Mañana: Christian Theology from a Hispanic Perspective* (Nashville: Abingdon Press, 1990), 164.

sweep of the Bible's eschatological thought and intent. The Book of Revelation offers the appropriate key to its own interpretation. John sees an angelic representation of Christ as the one "dead and behold I am alive for ever and ever, and I have the keys of Death and Hades" (1:17f.). Death and resurrection have given Jesus Christ full control of the realm of rebellion, our present history. In his death and resurrection, God has acted to enable persons to be released *now* from the deceptive bondage of the Beast and False Prophet.

Robert Mulholland illustrates well the meaning of the ancient images with the use of a more modern one, a chess game. The Cross and Resurrection of Jesus...

> set the mating net; they are a mortal wound for the Dragon; they are the binding of the Dragon's activity within the context of God's victory. The Dragon's pieces (Beast and False Prophet) are locked into the victor's endgame (lake of fire), yet they continue to play out the losing game ("living").... Since the Millennium begins with God's setting the mating net in the death and resurrection of Christ, and closes with God's making the checkmate move that consummates the victory assured by the death and resurrection, then the Millennium must be the time of the endgame.[34]

Jesus said, "If I had not come and spoken to them, they would not have sin; but now they have no excuse for their sin" (Jn. 15:22). While the Dragon has been "bound," with the Beast and False Prophet being cast into the lake of fire and thus mortally disabled but not yet wholly inactive, people can and often still do choose to join the Dragon. But there is no excuse. There now is an alternative. "Christ disarmed the principalities and powers and made a public example of them, triumphing over them in the Cross" (Col.

---

[34]M. Robert Mulholland, Jr., *Holy Living in an Unholy World: Revelation* (Grand Rapids: Francis Asbury Press, 1990), 306-307.

2:15). John reports this saying of Jesus: "Now is the judgment of this world, now shall the ruler of this world be cast out" (Jn. 12:31; cf. 16:11). The pivotal events of the Cross and Resurrection inaugurated the millennium. This period is not a literal thousand years, but a major period, an era, the time in human history that begins with the death and resurrection of Christ and will end with the consummation of God's victory.

A primary biblical example of faithfully living from and toward such a divine vision is Abraham. Abraham is summoned by the God of promise and asked to leave his familiar and comfortable life and go in naked trust to some very distant and different place, a place wholly unknown to him (Gen. 12:1-3). Israel, when informed later by such memories of faith in God's promises of a future, was challenged to live from and toward a vision as certain as is God's own word (cf. Isa. 55:10-11). They could see by faith that the way it then was is not the way it always would be, and thus they could live accordingly in the meantime.

If Abraham is a primary biblical example of acting by faith on a vision of God's promise of a future, the overarching biblical metaphor is the Kingdom of God. This Kingdom serves as a vision of the fully realized reign of God. History is read by faithful visionaries as on its way to God's intended destination despite a maze of evil appearances and understandable lapses into hopelessness. Says Walter Brueggemann, "Because God oversees history, it is affirmed that present shapes of reality and power are all provisional, kept open for the other One, not yet here but very sure to come."[35] This is the future-oriented vision that releases the believer for present-oriented discipleship.

Christians, therefore, of all people must resist any absolutizing of present arrangements in society or the church. The "system" is never the solution. In fact, "the wind blows wherever it pleases. You hear its sound, but you cannot tell where it comes from or where it is going. So it is with everyone born of the Spirit" (Jn. 3:8).

---

[35]Walter Brueggemann, *Hope Within History*, 79.

Living in faith toward a vision of God's tomorrow allows hope to function outside the borders of every present circumstance that is resisting the tomorrow of God which one day will be.

Isaiah 55:1-5 is a prophetic vision of divine promise set in the despair of the Jews in exile in Babylon. Why should God's frustrated and fearful people settle for ingesting what cannot nourish for long? Why not live toward the vision of God's tomorrow? Instead of capitulating to passing problems, says the prophet:

> Come, all you who are thirsty, come to the waters; and you who have no money, come, buy and eat!... Why spend money on what is not bread, and your labor on what does not satisfy? (Isa. 55: 1-2)

And what would satisfy? Only an awareness that God "will make an everlasting covenant with you, my faithful love promised to David" (vs. 3). To live in hope requires that one know that God's people are still heir to the everlasting promise.

The three young Jewish men whose story is told in the Book of Daniel had a hope within their hearts that could see beyond Nebuchadnezzar's totalitarian system and arrogant demands. Sustained by this vision of hope in God, they would not submit to pressing temptations because they knew of a future yet to come, a future beyond the control of any earthly king. Rather than eating their fill at the king's table (Dan. 1), these men of sturdy faith chose to wait in hope for God's manna to arrive in the desert of their present days.

Faith in the ultimate victory of God's Kingdom is crucially important for Christian life in the meantime. This is true in at least five ways.[36] The believer, gripped by hope in Christ, knows: (1) That this world is temporary, that treasures should be laid up beyond (Matt. 6:20; 2 Cor. 4:16-18). Kingdom service now is

---

[36]Elaboration of these five points is found in Boyd Hunt, *Redeemed!: Eschatological Redemption and the Kingdom of God* (Nashville: Broadman & Holman Publishers, 1993), 246-247.

never too costly in worldly terms (none can outgive and be more gracious than God); (2) That today's decisions shape eternal destiny (1 Cor. 3:12-15); (3) That living toward God's future means resisting evil and fighting against injustice now, praying with Jesus that God's will be done *on earth* as it is in heaven (Matt. 6:10; (4) That a believer should not be paralyzed by fear of those who can only kill the body, but cannot interrupt the coming future (Matt. 10:28); and (5) That there never should be despair even in the worst of times. Whatever the persecution being experienced, it can be endured because of faith's certainty that the day is coming when "the earth will be filled with the knowledge of the glory of the Lord as the waters cover the sea" (Hab. 2:14).

The Church As Eschatological Event

A corporate eschatology lies at the heart of Scripture. God called a special people into being and gave the early promise to Abraham that this new nation would somehow be the means of blessing the entire world (Gen. 12:1-3). This people of Israel struggled and often failed in the turmoil of its own history, but God remained intent on restoring true community among humans and between creation and Creator. The New Testament sees in this light the body of believers in Jesus, the fulfillment of the ancient promise. It presents the church as an eschatological event, a creation of the Spirit, a new people of God founded on the fulfilling event of salvation—the living, serving, suffering, dying, and rising of Jesus Christ. The church has an eschatological mission, embodying and proclaiming the coming of God's Kingdom in its own life and in the yet-unfilled future. The church is not the Kingdom of God,[37] but it is to be the Kingdom's firstfruits, a provisional form of the Kingdom manifest already in human history and supposed to be on mission in the reality of common life now.

---

[37]See George Eldon Ladd, *The Presence of the Future* (Grand Rapids: Eerdmans, 1974), chap. 11, and John Bright, *The Kingdom of God* (Nashville: Abingdon Press, 1953), chap. 8.

Christian theology today should champion the gospel's potential for impacting the *present* time of believers. Rather than being shackled by the past or immobilized in any arid anticipation of the second coming of Christ, it should be a theology of the future that has historic roots and focuses on present realization. The incarnational God cares about concrete existence now, placing "political" responsibility on Christians. Theology should address the big public issues of our time, offering a unique hope and an alternative for change. The Kingdom is not merely or primarily about the future in any way that writes off the present as hopeless in God's eyes. The church is to be the future revealed in Christ and now really present in human history, the body in which the Word of God is preached, honored, and lived faithfully in a Christ community. The good news of the Kingdom of God, already come in Jesus and still coming in the Spirit, "can create, will create, perhaps even now is creating a movement of new vitalities coursing through the varicose veins of a church with tired blood."[38] The faithful church is the future Kingdom of God already operative under the limiting conditions of this present and sinful age.

The church is called to be the Body of Christ expressing now within its own life the characteristics of the coming Kingdom of God—peace, love, joy, freedom, equality, and unity. The church is "like an arrow sent out into the world to point to the future."[39] It is a new community of hope founded by the impact of the future of God in the history of the cross and resurrection of Jesus. It is on the way. It has not yet reached the goal of hope, but it knows the way and is deliberately moving that way under the guidance of the Spirit. The church "exists to exhibit through its life in the world a living hope *for* the world."[40] The church is intended to be a com-

---

[38]Carl Braaten, *Eschatology and Ethics* (Minneapolis: Augsburg Publishing House, 1974), 84.

[39]Jürgen Moltmann, *Theology of Hope*, 328.

[40]Carl Braaten, *The Future of God: The Revolutionary Dynamics of Hope* (New York: Harper & Row, 1969), 111, 117.

munity where people of faith experience continuous collisions with the future, where the coming of God is recognized, celebrated, and then embodied in witness for the sake of a world groping for any credible glimpse of God's future.

The church is to be a sabbath people conducting periodic sabbath services that demonstrate and nurture hope. Israel's expectation of the future, in which "the whole earth will be full of God's glory" (Isa. 6), was to be experienced in the weekly sabbath observance. The rhythm of the sabbath would interrupt the flow of ordinary time with the rest of God, a rest which is the goal of creation and will be the end of human history. Likewise, the Sunday worship of Christians should be an eschatological interlude, a resting in God, a celebration of Christ's resurrection, an in-streaming of the power of God's Kingdom yet to come in its fullness, but already present to make Kingdom life possible.

Jesus' concern with social justice and human need also falls within the historic Jewish tradition, serving as a corrective "against the temptation to be carried away by dreams of an apocalyptic glory," and reminding Christians that "we are to live the life of faith under the conditions of this world."[41] Jesus brought salvation down to earth. Christian faith is an incarnation faith. Note these prophetic insights of Michael Kinnamon:

> In a world seemingly bent on self-destruction, in a world where empathy seems so often confined to members of like-minded enclaves, in a world that appears to live more by fear than by hope, the ecumenical vision of Christ's one body, living as sign and foretaste of God's *shalom*, is not an optional commitment, not a luxury that is conveniently demoted on our ecclesiastical lists of priorities, not something best left to experts on the nuances of theological debate. It is an

---

[41]Otto A. Piper, "Church and Judaism in Holy History," *Theology Today* 18(1961), 68.

inescapable and indispensable part of what it means to be the church God wills.[42]

Basic to the church's essence and mission is the historic reality of Christ's resurrection. The biblical focus is on the real world and not merely on the subjective worlds of private individuals. The church for centuries has had to deal with philosophic perspectives which have sought to draw it away from the this-worldly reality prominent in the Hebrew tradition. Early it was the Hellenistic tradition. More recently it has been the Enlightenment. The characteristic Enlightenment emphasis on the omni-competence of human reason and autonomy led to the development in the eighteenth century of an intensely skeptical attitude toward the resurrection of Jesus as concrete event in real human history. Truth, it was argued, is not something to be accepted on the basis of any external authority. Truth is what is discerned, not imposed, something verified well beyond its status as tradition. Since resurrection from the dead is not a regular and observable aspect of modern-day experience, why trust New Testament reports?

In his *Life of Jesus* (1835), David Friedrich Strauss, on the basis of a clear Enlightenment worldview, declared his intention to explain "the origin of faith in the resurrection of Jesus without any corresponding miraculous fact." He located the origin of belief in the resurrection at the subjective level. It was merely an outgrowth of the cultural conditioning of the "premodern" outlook of the Gospel writers. The resurrection of Jesus, traditionally seen as the originating basis of Christian faith, was now viewed as its product. Rudolf Bultmann agreed in the twentieth century. Reflecting his "existentialist" assumptions, he taught that the resurrection was something experienced at the subjective level by the first disciples, not something which took place in the public arena of history. Jesus had been raised, not from a

---

[42]Michael Kinnamon, *Truth and Community: Diversity and Its Limits in the Ecumenical Movement* (Grand Rapids: Eerdmans, 1988), 118.

grave, but from his own teachings into the Christian proclamation of the Christ.

By the 1950s, however, Karl Barth was taking sharp exception to such views of Strauss and Bultmann.[43] Then in the 1960s Wolfhart Pannenberg restored a full-blown assertion that the resurrection of Jesus is not only central to Christian faith, but was an historical event open to critical inquiry separate from the subjective experience of those first disciples. In fact, the end of history, yet to come, has been disclosed in advance in the person and work of Christ. The resurrection of Jesus anticipates the general resurrection to come at the end of time and brings forward into history both that resurrection, the full and final revelation of God's power and intent, and the church as an historical agent of what is yet to come. No wonder the Book of Hebrews says that "since we have so great a cloud of witnesses surrounding us, let us also lay aside every encumbrance, and the sin which so easily entangles us, and let us run with endurance the race that is set before us, fixing our eyes on Jesus, the author and perfecter of faith (Heb. 12:1-2).

The church of God is the resurrection people of God's risen Messiah, inspired by the resurrection of Jesus and now anticipating its own. John Howard Yoder has called for the church to understand herself and her role while in this world and on the way to another.

> We are not marching to Zion because we think that by our own momentum we can get there. But that is still where we are going. We are marching to Zion because, when God lets down from heaven the new Jerusalem prepared for us, we want to be the kind of people and the kind of community that will not feel strange there.[44]

---

[43]Karl Barth, *Church Dogmatics* (1953), vol. 4, part 1.

[44]John Howard Yoder, ed. Michael Cartwright, *The Royal Priesthood* (Grand Rapids: Eerdmans, 1994), 207.

The church is not the Kingdom of God, but in present history it is to be a participant in Kingdom realities, a sign of the coming Kingdom, a "between the times" agent of the Kingdom. While not yet the ideal, the church is called to begin representing the ideal as it receives the promise of the coming fulfillment of the Kingdom and learns to live out of the assurance of that final victory. Like her Lord, the church is to be *incarnational*, being truly *in* but clearly not *of* the world (Jn. 17:13-15). The church is to be purified by the Spirit so that it can play a prophetic function in present society.[45] Accordingly, it is a grave error to think of the church in terms of withdrawal from the world. The church must not abandon its "worldly" mission because it sees itself as weak, or fears persecution, or chooses not to risk contamination by a dirty world. To the contrary, the church's mission is to be an eschatological community both because it witnesses to God's future victory and because it is to display the actual life of the eschatological Kingdom in the present evil age. The very existence of the church is intended to be a witness to the world of the triumph of God's Kingdom accomplished in Jesus and initially being embodied in the church.

One good definition of the church can be constructed from unusual uses of the verb *to be*. The church is that body of believers in Jesus Christ who are dedicated to being a body of Kingdom people, an advancing actualization of the *is-ness* of the *shall-be*. The Kingdom of God is *already* and is *not yet*. It is that for which the church now lives and for which it yet waits. It is the Christian task and hope. It is an accomplishment, but even more a divine gift. Believers work. They wait. They live between the times, find themselves caught up in a tension between the age to come and the present evil age. Such is the nature of the history that follows the coming of Christ and precedes his coming again.

---

[45] An excellent study of how the church is to be prophetic is Howard Snyder, *The Community of the King* (Downers Grove, IL.: InterVarsity Press, 1977), 106-116.

Will Our Faith Have Children?

Is there really a viable future in light of the precarious status of our nuclear age and the perennial faithlessness of the church itself? Will God's grace make possible a surviving of this world in spite of our own human selfishness and recklessness? Will our faith have children? Can others come to believe even when the church fails to be the Kingdom witness that is its mission? Surely any viable future will come only by the mercy of God (cf. 1 Cor. 4:7).

The Hebrew Scriptures feature the concern for securing an heir, for receiving a seed that will insure future generations. The Abraham-Sarah story in Genesis highlights this theme and the New Testament holds it high for Christian consideration:

> By faith Abraham, even though he was past age—and Sarah herself was barren—was enabled to become a father because he considered him [God] faithful who had made the promise. And so from this one man, and he as good as dead, came descendants as numerous as the stars in the sky and as countless as the sand on the seashore. (Heb. 11:11-12)

The believers in God's promises and future, the true children of Abraham, once found themselves in exile with no apparent way out. No enduring Jewish institutions were left; there was no real hope in the rise of a new generation of the faithful. But again there came the wonderful metaphor of miracle offspring. The presently barren indeed *will have children*. The lowly exiles were told to

> Enlarge the place of your tent, and let the curtains of your habitations be stretched out; hold not back, lengthen your cords and strengthen your stakes. For you will spread abroad to the right and to the left, and your descendants will possess the nations and will people the desolate cities. (Isa. 54:1-3)

Here is a vividly pictured promise that there would be a future, one enabled only by God regardless of all contrary human circumstances.

The point is that God is prepared to work a newness when all appears lost, to create a future when none seems possible. Build new bedrooms for the coming children! Let loose of the paralysis of present arrangements that are so bleak and believe in the surprising fruit conceived only by the Spirit of God. Joseph later would realize one day that an unexplainable conception within Mary was indeed the Spirit's work. Matthew and Luke are the only New Testament writers who report the virginal conception of Jesus. Their primary emphasis appears to be stress on this conception as an eschatological event. The point of this biblical story is that, from the very beginning of the earthly existence of Jesus, the Holy Spirit was the active agent in the dawning of a new age. The biblical narrative begins with the mystery of the origin of life in God and by God, and then proceeds to recount a series of events across the centuries that will culminate in the final judgment of the world and the salvation of the faithful children of God. What one day will be already is in Jesus. It was so from the moment and even by the means of his very conception. Herod soon tried unsuccessfully to make sure that the Jewish faith would have no children of promise. His best effort was hopeless. Beyond all Herods, there always is God! Beyond all present human barrenness, there is the richly conceiving God.

With the amazing birth and then the resurrection of Jesus in his mind, Paul spoke of Christians as those also born of the Spirit (Gal. 4:28-29). Christians know of their own lack of deserving and their inability to do such a thing themselves. Christian faith knows that, just like the past, the future is in the hands of the God now known in Jesus Christ. On the Fridays of crucifixion there is weeping, even despair. But surprise! Singing bursts forth on all Sundays of resurrection. God is not dead and the future is open to new possibilities. Time does move on—and the times are in God's hands.

We who believe in the sovereignty and goodness of God can have confidence in the ultimate future and are intended to be prepared by God's mercy to anticipate and work for that future in present history. The 1968 Uppsala Assembly of the World Council of Churches issued this call: "We ask you, trusting in God's renewing power, to join in these anticipations of God's Kingdom, showing now something of the newness which Christ will complete."[46] In fact, really being the church in the present probably is the church's primary task.[47] The church must be a visible sample of the kind of humanity that God intends. Successful evangelism rests in large part on the people of God overcoming economic, racial, and gender barriers to true human togetherness, an overcoming not possible except by the grace of God. When the observing world finds itself having to admit, "Behold how they love one another!", such faith and divine community will grow. There will be a future where no future seemed possible.

---

[46]The Message of the Assembly, quoted from K. Slack, Uppsala Report (SCM Press, 1968), v.

[47]See Stanley Hauerwas and William Willimon, *Resident Aliens* (Nashville: Abingdon Press, 1991). Recognizing that the church is caught in an "eschatological tension," John Bright seeks a New Testament plan for what the church should be doing. Finding no "program" of action prescribed, he concludes that this is the New Testament plan: "There shall no program be given you—except to be the church!" (*The Kingdom of God*, Abingdon Press, 1953, 253).

Matters Worth Exploring

1. How does the Hebrew heritage of the Christian faith inform how Christians should relate their faith to the world? Is there a conflict between serving in this evil world and waiting for the arrival of heaven?

2. Is there a distinctively "Christian humanism"? Can Christian believers really be *in* but not *of* this world?

3. As believers wait for God's age to come, how are they to be history-makers in the meantime?

4. Without a vision, people perish. What is the vision of Christians that is able to release them to live now with confidence and as God intends?

5. What is meant by the claim that the future will have a Jesus shape? What does this imply for a living out of "the mind of Christ" in the present?

6. What of helpfulness to present Kingdom ministry is provided by certain emphases of the African-American Christian tradition?

7. How does living in confident faith toward God's future assist the Christian in living faithfully and practically in the meantime?

8. How is the church of today supposed to be related to the Kingdom of God that will appear in its fullness in some tomorrow?

Chapter 7

ADVENT, EASTER, PENTECOST, AND THE END

❧

*"And surely I [Jesus] will be with you always,
to the very end of the age." (Matt. 28:20)*

❧

*God has broken into history—the new age has begun. We wait
for the consummation of history and hope for the glory
of God. We are neither optimistic or pessimistic
about the world, but wait in hope,
serving the Lord.*[1]

❧

The path from the cradle of Jesus to the consummation of the ages is a long and eventful one. It involves the complex inter-relationship of Advent, Easter, Pentecost, and the final coming of Jesus. Along this path there is pain and doubt, faith and assurance, forgiveness and responsibility, anticipation and always the companionship of the Spirit of the Christ. There also is the "dark side" of the first Advent of Jesus, followed first by the incredible brightness of Easter and then by the crucial divine presence of Pentecost, all resulting in the challenge for disciples to live in

---

[1]Clark Pinnock, *Flame of Love: A Theology of the Holy Spirit* (InterVarsity Press, 1996), 147.

God's now in light of God's yesterdays and in hope of God's yet-coming tomorrow.

We begin to trace this vital but volatile path from the empty grave of Jesus to the coming new creation with a lesson from the ancient Jews when they were stranded and nearly strangled in foreign exile (Psalm 137). How can God's people be truly hopeful when experiencing the depths of trouble? Having recalled this classic Hebrew struggle of faith, their hope languishing in near despair, there then comes the long road traveled by Mary and Joseph to Bethlehem where Jesus finally was born. Later, after the "black" Friday which saw Jesus hanging on a Roman cross, the amazing Easter Sunday actually came, to be followed soon by the dramatic Pentecost events. Empty cross and empty tomb combined with the flame of the ongoing divine presence to mean a full future!

The resurrection of Jesus is the main reason that we ever learned of him at all. For Christians, eschatology, like all else of the faith, begins on that pivotal Sunday morning. At Easter "the end appeared ahead of time. It appeared proleptically. Thus, the resurrection of Jesus Christ is the foundation upon which we must build our constructive thoughts regarding the future."[2] The Hebrew heritage of rugged hope and then the Easter and Pentecost events joined to launch the Christian faith and to preserve the living memory of a living Jesus. Jesus is risen from the dead—and the Spirit of Christ remains always to empower and guide!

The resurrection of Jesus is the pivotal eschatological event that makes possible a radical style of new life "in him." Because he lives again, we too can live as never before. The classic statement is Galatians 2:20: "I have been crucified with Christ and I no longer live, but Christ lives in me. The life I live in the body, I live by faith in the Son of God, who loved me and gave himself for me." There will be an eschaton, something final, to consummate the lives of the faithful and all of historical existence as we now

---

[2]Ted Peters, *God—The World's Future: Systematic Theology for a Postmodern Era* (Minneapolis: Fortress Press, 1993), 306.

know it. Jesus once came and is coming again! The key concern of Christians, however, should not be about the exact how and when of the end, but about what is supposed to happen in the church (and in the world through the church) because of Jesus' Advent and between Easter, Pentecost, and Eschaton.

The Dark Side of Advent

Psalm 137 models well the Hebrew experience of hoping in God with considerable difficulty while they were in the midst of pain, dislocation, and uncertainty. This psalm is hard to classify by literary type since it begins as a communal complaint, continues like a hymn, and ends as a virtual curse. There are several "cursing" psalms that shock modern readers. Knowing the context out of which they came helps the reader at least to understand the bitterness and defiance they reflect. Psalm 137 is one which contains an explicit historical reference. We know, therefore, that it arose from the Jewish community exiled in Babylon after Jerusalem's brutal destruction in 587 B.C.E. In this forced foreign exile was a Jewish faith community (1) now clinging to a fragile memory of a glorious past with God and (2) hoping passionately that God somehow—and soon—would enable a Jewish homecoming in Jerusalem and bring deserved judgment on those who ruined God's own city and now threatened the very survival of God's chosen people. This psalm is a "lament." It cries over the earlier destruction of Jerusalem and the present situation of the homesick and faith-strained exiles. "By the rivers of Babylon—there we sat down and there we wept when we remembered Zion" (Ps. 137:1).

The later use of this psalm in Jewish worship and home instruction transmitted to each new generation of Jews the yearning that belongs to every dislocated Jew. The great danger for exiled Jews (in Babylon and elsewhere later) was that their faith, once torn from historic and geographic moorings, would be drowned in the sea of a foreign culture and alien belief system. Could Yahweh be worshipped in a strange land where other gods seemed to be in complete control? It was a bewildering and frightening question. In fact, Psalm 137 reflects a time of many deep questions for those trying to be faithful in a "secular" setting.

The sense of irony is great. Psalm 137 follows immediately after two psalms which celebrate God's gift of the land to the covenant people. Then comes the big reversal, the stunning shock of the divine gift stolen and spoiled. Hard questions have to be faced in such severe circumstances. Will God forever allow the ruining of his own gift, the unjust suffering of his own people? How and when will God finally bring his people home? How can those seeking to still believe in God's future manage to be faithful in the meantime? In that awkward meantime, "how could we sing the Lord's song in a foreign land?" (vs. 4). How should God's people expect that God will act toward those who encouraged the awful destruction of Jerusalem, yelling, "Tear it down! Tear it down! Down to its foundations!" (vs. 7)? What if the exiled Jews should just forget the past and carve out a new future in the prospering land of Babylon? One clear answer to this last question is offered. The only real hope lies in remembering stubbornly and in cherishing the memory of Jerusalem "above my highest joy" (vs. 6). To forget is to be lost, to have no hope, to have no identity except what the Babylonians choose to give.

For Christians, there is an obvious problem that surfaces in the text. The psalm ends with a vindictive hope that brutal destruction will come on the enemies of the Jews (presumably God's enemies also), particularly on those who were responsible for Jerusalem's destruction. "Happy shall they be who pay you back what you have done to us!" (vs. 8). This prayer of defiant hope is addressed to God—"Remember, O Lord" (vs. 7). The Jews may not be called to take any action themselves against the "daughter of Babylon" (vs. 8). God can be trusted to judge—and fairly. God surely will not stay in the background as hero of a dead tradition, but must soon come to the fore, bringing justice in his hand. The ancient Jews had no highly developed belief in justice being done after this life, thus they thought of it being done soon and very much in this world. While any call for vengeance raises troubling moral questions today, it does remind us that the stark claims of the holy God may at times override what seems proper to us humans. Venom in the face of injustice is all too human; but the yearning for justice is admirable, especially when it is left in God's hands (God's ways are beyond ours—Isa. 55:8-9). When leaving the future to God, energy remains for God's people to nurture their prime memories of God's past actions and their sustaining hopes for what God yet will do.

Beyond the moral issue of vengeance, there also is in this psalm the additional problem of the "scandalous particularity of Jerusalem."[3] Is not one place potentially as "holy" as another? Is the future of the faithful necessarily linked to this one "holy" city? For the psalmist, Jerusalem represented the assured place of God's presence. Loyalty to Jerusalem was loyalty to God. The harsh statements about Jewish enemies are rooted in the religious frame-work of the psalmist—including concepts of a chosen nation, a ter-ritory possessed by divine right, and a holy city of God's special abode. These made possible belief in holy war, a divine crusade against all violators of God's place, people, and will. Thus, "happy shall they be who take your little ones [Babylon and its partners in destruction] and dash them against the rock!" (vs. 9). Made possi-ble also is the more modern Zionism which claims a Jewish "divine right" to the land of Israel and the "dispensationalism" of many Christians today (see chapter four) that sees God about to fulfill ancient promises by the return of Jews to Israel.

This psalmist "is claimed by God with a claim that will not let him go, yet he understands and responds to that claim from a pre-Christian perspective and in a not-yet-Christian spirit."[4] He

---

[3]Walter Brueggemann, *The Message of the Psalms* (Minneapolis: Augsburg Press, 1984), 74.

[4]John Bright, *The Authority of the Old Testament* (Nashville: Abingdon Press, 1967), 238.

yearns for the good news of God's intervention, but envisions inadequately the way of God's intervening. The ultimate presence of God, the place where justice finally will be done, where the price of evil finally will be paid, is not back in a restored holy city, but on an ugly cross outside its gates. The full presence of God in human history would not be in a rebuilt temple, but in a miracle child, Jesus, "Emmanuel" (God with us). The price to be paid for violating God's will and way eventually would be paid, not by the enemies of the Jews, but by a Jew, Jesus, in fact, by God himself in the sacrifice of his Son Jesus. God finally would absorb *into himself* the pain of the Jewish exiles! The eventual coming of the needed salvation is prepared by God, provided by God, and is with God wherever God is.

Jesus, a later Jew also living under foreign domination, rejected the call to vengeance and taught forgiving love—even for one's enemies (cf. Matt. 5:39, 41, 44). He made clear that God's central purpose is not to glorify Israel, including a smashing of its foes. While Christ clearly judges the psalmist's hateful response to enemies of God and God's people, he nonetheless affirms the passionate commitment that generated it. For the psalmist was a man "of zeal against the forces of sin, indifference, secularism, and pagan ideology that would destroy the church [Jewish community] and send it into exile."[5]

Christian believers, with deep roots in the Hebrew tradition, are to be "in the world but not of it." They are to endure, hope, wait, be in and of Jesus Christ. The challenge is to "have this mind among yourselves, which is yours in Christ Jesus, who, though he was in the form of God, did not count equality with God a thing to be grasped, but emptied himself, taking the form of a servant.... Our commonwealth is in heaven, and from it we await a Savior, the Lord Jesus Christ, who will change our lowly body to be like his glorious body, by the power which enables him even to subject all things to himself" (Philippians 2:5-11; 3:20-21).

---

[5]Ibid., 241.

Psalm 137 asks about the present capacity of believers to endure, maintain identity in a "foreign" land, and embrace a divine calling with seductive allurements all around. Can Christians at the end of the twentieth century identify with these weeping Jews of old? Admittedly, "it is hard for complacent bourgeois folk who have suffered little to understand the tenacity of affronted memory among the brutalized."[6] We must seek to remember with the Jews that the present arrangements in the world, while not right or acceptable, are not final. The practice of hope is to be kept alive, even when against great odds. To maintain faith requires a countercultural vision and commitment of the faithful who refuse to forget or blend into the mainstream of the unfaithful. Faith knows that one day there *will* be a homecoming to peace, justice, and freedom, a "new Jerusalem" coming down out of heaven (Rev. 21:2).

The ancient Jews were forced by their captors to sing their sacred songs in a strange setting in order to have highlighted their apparent helplessness (Ps. 137:1-3). This awkward irony was repeated in the German death camps of the 1940s, a deliberate humiliation intended to rob Jews of their identity by belittling their memories and dashing their hope. But many who really believed would not have their point of reference stolen easily. Their vision of Jerusalem was more precious than life: "The body they may kill, God's truth abideth still." Life and destiny finally are not controlled by any Babylon, ancient or modern. Stand firm and wait for the coming of God. Already God has come in Jesus, and God will do so yet again.

For Christians who follow a liturgical calendar of the faith, Advent begins the church year. Initially (and we wish it were otherwise), Advent is not about receiving a divine gift, but about wishing, longing for any sign of the divine presence. It is not first about the arrival of God in Bethlehem, but about the sometimes difficult waiting for God finally to arrive. Reads one Jew's message found in the rubble of the Warsaw Ghetto after the fall of Nazi Germany:

---

[6]Brueggemann, op. cit., 77.

"I believe in the sun even when it is not shining; I believe in love even when feeling it not; I believe in God even when He is silent." According to the testimony of Psalm 135:5, "I wait for the Lord, my soul waits, and in his word I hope."

Advent is to Christmas like Good Friday is to Easter, the necessary cross before the glorious resurrection, the hard preparation before the final coming of the birth. Advent is not first about Christmas, but about the frightening shadows before we are sure that there actually will be thrilling light. It focuses first, not on the glory of the destination in Bethlehem, but on the long journey through exile, persecution, unfaithfulness, and doubt. Mary, in late pregnancy, traveled a long and hard road to get to Bethlehem, not at all sure how things would turn out. Divine grace may be free, but it is hardly cheap. Hoping in God's promised future often has to be an exercise in sturdy faith. We who hope to experience God's coming must be ready, keep waiting, keep traveling, keep hoping and believing—no matter what. Will God ever come? Where is God? When will God's salvation finally get here? What is the best way to wait? How should people of faith deal with the dark days just before the dawn? All of these are key Advent questions. The Hebrew Scriptures are full of them. People mature in faith know them well.

Can it happen again like in days of old? Isaiah 64:3 relates the hoped-for coming of God to the remembered comings of God in the past: "When you [God] did awesome deeds that we did not expect, you came down, the mountains quaked at your presence." The verb "come down" echoes the formative memory of Israel's earlier exodus from Egypt (Ex. 3:8) and the quaking mountain of the covenant experience at Mt. Sinai (Ex. 19:16-18). "When you did" is a reflective reference to the "mighty acts of old." Here are allusions to the focal Israeli memories of Exodus and Covenant. Once, long ago, God had brought liberation and made a covenant, defeated evil, and enabled real community. In large part, the faithful in later generations hoped in the midst of their difficult presents because they remembered a foundational past and believed in the God whose future is sure and never far away. Regardless of negative circumstances, Advent is always the hope that Israel's salvation memory will be *reenacted* in our present time. The constant danger among believers is that they will *forget*—and thus have no basis for hope or a part in its eventual fulfillment.

Then it happens. After several verses of admitting to sin and lamenting God's silence, there comes in Isaiah 64:8 the disjunctive "yet" (nevertheless!). It almost leaps off the page. "Yet, O Lord, you are our Father: we are the clay, and you are our potter; we are all the work of your hand." Yes, we have fallen short, become disfigured clay. We now are undeserving, overanxious and faithless raw material. Nevertheless, the good news is that God still loves, remains, comes, and reshapes as the patient potter of precious, even if perverted clay. So, here is the early Advent message: wait, hope, submit, and hope still more. Do not forget. Believe in the sun even when your eyes do not now see it shining. Have faith in God's future even when its coming seems greatly delayed and now to be doubted. Accept by faith that the God who has and will come again does so in God's unique way and on a schedule not tracked by human computers or programmed by self-styled prophets of the end time.

Actually, for Christians there are at least three Advents. Christ has come in the life of Jesus, in the Pentecost of the Spirit, and in the anticipated return at the end of time. Even after Christmas there is waiting to be done. The "dark side" of Advent is a recurring reality. The life of faith is a journey in the interim between divine comings. The interim always is a time of transition marked by uncertainties and ambiguity. We are instructed to pray for the divine gifts that are sufficient for the in-between times (1 Cor. 1:3-9). Our prayer is to be, "O God, show us the future in the distress of our todays!" We wish we were home; but often we find ourselves only on the way. When we are almost at the end of our collective or individual ropes, our hope is for the advent of the God who remembers us, even in our forgetfulness of God, for the coming of the God who graciously redeems and re-forms us as we are willing to receive and become agents of divine grace.

Yes, shadows are all around. That is nothing new. But look! The light of God's coming even now is breaking just over our horizons! God comes! Therefore, true community is possible after all. God comes! Therefore, justice can be more than merely the paternalistic language of the powerful. God comes! Therefore, joy becomes more than a cliché and Christmas more than an economic binge.

There is a strange Advent twist. While focused on the coming of Christ to earth, it also is we needy humans who are invited to come. "Come and see what God has done: he is awesome in his deeds among mortals" (Ps. 66:5). As we come in response to God's coming, there is this promise from Jesus as he went away from us: "And surely I will be with you always, to the very end of the age" (Matt. 28:20). God has come, and always will be coming to the grateful and faithful ones. Potentially, it is like Christmas every day of every year. There is good reason to pray continuously:

Come, O come, Emmanuel!
Renew our memories of what You already have done in past comings.
Be our Potter, reshaping our lives according to your image.
Lessen our anxieties by increasing our faith.
Brace us with wisdom and strength for the awkward interims we now face.
Make your fragile children into a covenant community of your obvious grace.
Enable we who believe to become light for the darkness of others.
For we pray in the name of the One who graced Bethlehem on a dark night so long ago,
And soon will bring justice and mercy at the end of the age. Amen!

God's Then Enables God's Now

Some years after the filled cradle in Bethlehem came the drama of the empty grave in nearby Jerusalem. Could it be possible? When the worst had been done to God's best by humiliating and publicly murdering Jesus, his very *tomb* became a new *womb*. Death flowered into even more beautiful life! With this flowering, the first disciples were overcome with a sense of surprise, awe, and wonder. From this flowering came three crucial implications that form the theological ground on which Christians are to live in every present and on which they are to walk confidently into the future. The resurrection of Jesus forms the ground of Christian faith by: (1) clarifying that Jesus really is Lord of all; (2) dramatizing that God alone has the last word in our historical process; and (3) focusing for believers their present mission. Believers engage the present with really good news because they know what has been and what will be, and what they should be doing to be faithful in the meantime.

This womb, from which emerges the anticipated tomorrow of God that already is present in Jesus, seems never free of the tombs of doubt and persecution. The Christian life, as pictured especially by the Gospel of Mark, knows something of the hiddenness of God and even the absence of Jesus. Everyone "will be salted with fire" (Mk. 9:49). Believers often know suffering because they are "in a world at the juncture of the ages, where Satan's opposition is strong but in its terminal stage."[7] For Mark, Jesus is the suffering Son of Man who came to serve and give his life a ransom for many (Mk. 10:45). True Christian discipleship lies in a similar losing of oneself for the sake of the gospel of Jesus (Mk. 8:34-35; 9:33-37). The eschatological dimension of Mark's Gospel is prominent. The Kingdom of God is "at hand" (1:15). The resurrection of Jesus is wonderfully real and time is probably short. The Kingdom will

---

[7]Stephen Barton, *The Spirituality of the Gospels* (Peabody, Mass.: Hendrickson Publishers, 1992), 46. Compare Mark 1:24.

come soon "with power" (9:1). In the meantime, disciples must be willing to leave everything and suffer for the sake of Jesus and the good news now come in Jesus and coming in its fullness and finality in the near future (10:28-30).

Jesus really is Lord, even now and despite whatever suffering comes along. His resurrection was a graphic way of repeating what God had said about Jesus at his baptism by John: "This is my beloved Son, with whom I am well pleased" (Matt. 3:17). Further, if Jesus had not been raised, the claims he had made—to be able to forgive sins, to be the Son of God, to be the one true path to God—would not have been worth believing any longer. The resurrection was a vindication of all that Jesus had said and done and a gripping glimmer of what yet will be in God's coming future.

As Lord, the resurrection of Jesus brought and still brings assurance that God alone has the last word regardless of the rampant evil of this world. Despite the disciples' dashed hopes, Jesus was indeed the one who would redeem. In the resurrection, we see...

> God's decisive victory not only over death but over all God's other enemies as well. In that one climactic event we see the certainty that someday, in the kingdom of God, there will be no more violence, war, jealousy, or death. No more displaced persons. No more kidnappings. No more murder. No more disease. No more holocausts. No more terrorism. No more nuclear weapons. These forces are still alive and at work in the world, but because of the victory that God won at Easter, their doom is certain. One day death will die (Rom. 6:9).[8]

With Jesus known to be Lord, and God known to have the last word, there comes to believers a freedom and courage to witness

---

[8]Stephen Davis, *Risen Indeed: Making Sense of the Resurrection* (Grand Rapids: Eerdmans, 1993), 200-201.

to this good news wherever they are. John Stott states well the intended implications *now* of Jesus returning *later*:

> This promise of his coming is not a piece of unpractical theologizing. On the contrary, Christ and his apostles never spoke of it to satisfy idle curiosity, but always to stimulate practical action. In particular, it is a further spur to our evangelism. For he himself forged a link between our proclamation and his return, and we remember his words that the Gospel must first be preached to all nations "and then the end will come" (Matt. 24:14). So the interim period between his two comings, between Christ's ascension and return, is by his own appointment to be filled with the mission of the people of God.[9]

Yes, the interim, our troubled todays, should be filled with redemptive living, even with mission—liberating laughter. Believers fully aware of the agony of Christ's cross and the wonder of Christ's empty grave should now be "laughing with the gospel." Knowing the power of sheer grace and being taught true wisdom by the Spirit (1 Cor. 2:6-13), there is no more need to be deceived by worldly pretensions to power. David Buttrick speaks of African-American congregations often acquainted with oppression by establishment powers or some radical fringe of society, congregations that nonetheless "can see through the pretensions of power and can know what's truly going on in the hiddenness of God's purpose."[10] There is a sense of "eschatological reversal" in the New Testament. Christians can begin to live freely by the patterns of God's coming Kingdom, celebrating with a grace-full glee. Laughter, even when one is being perse-

---

[9]John Stott, *The Lausanne Covenant—An Exposition and Commentary* (Wheaton, IL: Lausanne Committee for World Evangelization, 1975), 35.

[10]David Buttrick, "Laughing With the Gospel" in Barry Callen, ed., *Sharing Heaven's Music* (Nashville: Abingdon Press, 1995), 129.

cuted, is possible because of *known location*. Believers live on the resurrection side of the cross and thus are able to laugh at the doomed pretensions of the world. They are fortified with "the assurance of things hoped for, the conviction of things not seen" (Heb. 11:1).

The future of Jesus is also the future of believers. One day we who are in Christ will rise as Jesus once rose. Rather than any status-quo present being either absolutized in false security or abandoned in premature despair, hope in the coming future already should be a stimulus to reshaping the present. The intended new shape is to be molded by the mind of Christ (Phil. 2:1-11). The resurrection of Jesus is the beginning of the resurrection of the dead— which is the beginning of God's final triumph over all enemies, even death itself. The divine triumph over sinful forces is intended to be seen eschatologically. That is, the war between good and evil already is won in principle, but with real battles still going on and yet to be fought—although there is a liberating present awareness of future victory. This present awareness is enabled by the move of God from Easter to Pentecost.

A crucial transition occurs in the Apostles' Creed when historic memory moves to contemporary meaning. Having affirmed as sacred memory that Jesus was conceived, born, suffered, crucified, dead, buried, descended, risen, and ascended, the creed dramatically shifts to meaning in the present tense. This same Jesus now is "seated at the right hand of the Father" (1 Pet. 3:22). This being "seated" is the time of the church's life, bracketed by the past events of the Christ on earth and the anticipation of Christ's coming again "to judge the living and the dead." Between formative past and culminating future is the *present of the Spirit*, the reigning and ruling, enlivening and gifting of the Spirit of Christ. In the gift of the Holy Spirit, explains Jürgen Moltmann, word and sacrament, ministries and divine gifts "become comprehensible as the revelations and powers of Christ and his future. As the emblematic revelations of Christ, they are the messianic mediations of salvation. As glorifications of Christ they are actions of hope pointing towards the kingdom."[11]

Paul raised the pivotal questions in Romans 8:33-35, concluding that no one and nothing can separate believers from the powerful love of Christ, the One who now sits at the right hand of God and ministers through the Spirit. Ephesians 1:20-21 likewise affirms that Christ currently has complete authority. First Peter 3:22, having noted that Christ now is at the right hand of God, gives assurance that any persecution can be endured if one is steadfast in faith.

It was common in the biblical world for sitting to be the body language of authority.[12] For Jesus to be "sitting" suggests not his relaxation, but his aggressive activity in exercising authority by the very power of God. Here is belief that sustains the faithful between the resurrection and final return of Jesus. This Jesus is the Lord of the between time. Indeed, "it is by fixing our attention on the one who is the true authority for life and history that we learn to turn away from a life of compulsion (Col. 3:5), division (3:8), and deceit (3:9), and turn instead to a life formed by forgiveness, peace, and gratitude (3:12-17)."[13] Life formed in this new way, on the pattern of Christ, is the work of Christ's Spirit. The Spirit is God now present lovingly and powerfully.

Genuine Christian living comes from knowing that, in the very time when any disciple lives, the biblical story of God-with-us is moving steadily forward, featuring Christ sitting at the Father's right hand on our behalf. The Christ of the New Testament church is not the absent Christ, once here in Jesus and now gone with Jesus. He "has never resigned his position as head of the

---

[11]Jürgen Moltmann, *The Church in the Power of the Spirit* (N.Y.: Harper & Row, 1977), 205-206.

[12]Note Ex. 18:13; 2 Kings 25:28; Dan. 7:9; Matt. 5:1; 13:1-2; 20:21; 23:2. A current example with similar meaning is referring to the one in charge of a group as the "chair" of the committee.

[13]Theodore Jennings, Jr., *Loyalty to God* (Nashville: Abingdon Press, 1992), 155.

church and vested the governmental authority in a self-perpetuating clerical caste.... He administers it himself through his Holy Spirit.... The basis of every man's [believer's] authority and responsibility is, therefore, not human appointment or official position, but the divine call, gifts, and qualifications that he [or she] possesses."[14] Life with Christ and for Christ's mission is enabled by life in Christ's Spirit.[15]

Jesus Christ, crucified and resurrected, is the center of the biblical revelation, the substance of the Christian good news. This glorious center, however, is not a static point on the long storyline of God's choice to be with us. Jesus is both historically definitive and dynamic. Jesus was and is. The gospel announces a present reality. The New Testament highlights Pentecost as the pivot between past, present, and future. There is continuity between the Jesus who once was in the flesh and salvation now disclosed and made possible by the living presence of the Spirit of Christ.

It would appear that Luke intentionally used parallel language in describing the Spirit's work in first preparing the human body of the Messiah, Jesus, and later Christ's new body, the church, to carry on the life of Christ. An angel told Mary: "The Holy Spirit will come upon you, and the power of the Most High will overshadow you" (Lk. 1:35). In Acts 1:8 Jesus is reported to have informed his disciples: "You will receive power when the Holy Spirit has come upon you." Obviously there is close association between the ministry of Jesus, which is the work of the Spirit (Lk. 3:22; 5:1, 18), and the ministry of the church in the life of the Spirit.

The collapsing of one socio-political status quo brought into being one of the more influential of all the rethinkings of New

---

[14]F. G. Smith, *The Last Reformation* (Anderson, Ind.: Gospel Trumpet Co., 1919), 135.

[15]The Spirit of Christ is the Spirit of *life*, a new order of creation in Christ (2 Cor. 5:17), the Spirit of *wisdom* which is the mind of Christ (1 Cor. 2:10-16), the Spirit of *power* with the death-overcoming resurrection potency of Christ (Eph. 1:19-20), and the Spirit of *love* and *peace*. See development of these in C. Norman Kraus, *God Our Savior* (Scottdale, Pa.: Herald Press, 1991), 154-157.

Testament teaching about the role of Christian faith in the midst of this fragile world. It is an example of narrative theology, a working out of key faith perspective as inspired commentary on the experience of present life—always in light of the biblical revelation. Augustine of Hippo (354-430) wrote the *City of God* in the midst of the rapid decay of the Roman Empire. He concluded that the complexity of the Christian life, especially its political aspects, lies in a tension between two cities, the city of the world then being observed crumbling and the city of God that surely would come very soon. Christian believers live in the intermediate period separating the incarnation of Christ and his final return in glory. The church is to be seen as the body (city) of Christ's pilgrims moving through the world's city, carrying present responsibility, but citizens of the Kingdom yet to come in its fullness. In every era of despair, Christians are to live in hope,[16] sustained by the promised "Comforter" or "Advocate" (Jn. 14:16, 26).

Christians wait eagerly and pray for the coming of God's Kingdom (Matt. 6:10), for "the resurrection of the body and the life everlasting" (Apostles' Creed), for "a new heaven and a new earth" (Rev. 21:1). Believers long for the triumph of God over all that corrupts creation and resists the will of God. The biblical revelation, detailing a long pattern of God's redemptive activity on behalf of a fallen world, begins by recounting the initial creation and moves finally toward that creation's last moment. That final moment will be a resolution of the struggle between good and evil, the complete coming of the divine Kingdom, a radical renewal of creation by the grace and power of God. In the meantime, the time between now and that final moment, it is crucial to understand something about God and how God as the Spirit chooses to relate to the fallen creation.

---

[16]The circumstance faced by Augustine so long ago seems so contemporary! The "modern" world is crumbling, its self-centered and grasping values discredited even by many people who still seek frantically to live by and profit from them. Robust faith is required in a setting of widespread desperation and frequent despair.

"God is limited," explains Elton Trueblood, "but limited in a special way.... He is limited by the conditions of goodness." Assuming that God has a good purpose in creation and providence, "God's purpose would be defeated if goodness were compelled." Therefore, "if the possibility of goodness involves choice, it also involves the possibility of evil; and, if the possibility is genuine, it will sometimes be realized."[17] Evil is the high price paid for moral freedom. God's Self-limitation in relation to evil derives not from the nature of reality (as though evil had equal status with God, an unbiblical dualism), but from the nature of goodness which is the nature of God seen throughout the biblical revelation. The God of loving grace[18] grants freedom, risks rebellion, chooses vulnerability to the emergence of evil. Such is the way of real love.

There is in the biblical revelation a way to begin addressing the problem of evil. That way holds together the love of God, the power of God, and the reality of evil. This way does not solve the difficult problem by bringing into question any one of these basic facts of present existence. The adequate way is understanding the faith in narrative terms so that evil is given its deserved due in the tension-filled and Bible-illumined drama of real historical existence. Assyria, Exile, Holocaust, Vietnam, and AIDS happen, and the painful questions they raise must be heard. The hearing, however, need not be deafened by a theological vacuum.

In the beginning of history, reports the biblical revelation, the love of God expressed itself as God's voluntary vulnerability to the potential for evil. This divine risk was taken for the sake of human freedom, required by the nature of love and authentic covenant relationship. In the central chapter of the biblical story, when the actual presence of sin came to require divine confrontation, the power of God is revealed as other than the mere ability of God to

---

[17]D. Elton Trueblood, op. cit., 249-250.

[18]See Barry Callen, *God As Loving Grace* (Evangel Press, 1996), especially pages 256-268 where the problem of evil is discussed at length.

exercise brute force to accomplish the divine intention. The resurrection of Jesus proved to be stronger than the misdirected muscle of those responsible for his cross. In reality, God is the One hanging horribly for all to see. This hanging, apparent divine weakness, turned out to be, not God's tragic inability or absence, but God's lovingly distinctive and saving presence.

Such divine sovereignty being expressed through vulnerable servanthood, so the biblical narrative relates, relentlessly, though not coercively, pursues its redemptive goal along the tortured trail of human history, from the first sin all the way to the end of time. God is patient, often pained, but never defeated. The overarching fact is that one day every knee shall bow in recognition of the One who has the last word (Phil. 2:10). History moves from divine beginning to divine ending. An evil-filled tension lies between. Sometimes the pain of the present is best endured by looking ahead and reading again about the assured ending.[19]

The final chapter of the biblical story "points toward the consummation of the divine intention, the fulfillment of God's promise, the maturation of the Not Yet developing in the womb of the Already...."[20] The not-yet will be the "day of the Lord," a day of the dramatic end of present existence (2 Pet. 3:12). The garment of God's creation will be changed, but God will remain the same forever (Heb. 1:10-12).

God is known in Christ as the "God of hope" (Rom. 15:13). We who now glimpse through a darkened glass believe in a time when we shall see clearly the substance of that hope (1 Cor. 13:12). In the meantime, believers have at least general awareness of what God now is doing and finally will do, an awareness enabled especially by the divine disclosure in Jesus Christ (Eph. 1:9-10) and by the ministry of the Holy Spirit. In Christ this world is seen as the

---

[19]See Gabriel Fackre, "Almighty God and the Problem of Evil," *Pacific Theological Review* 15 (Fall 1980), 11-16.

[20]Gabriel Fackre, *Ecumenical Faith in Evangelical Perspective* (Grand Rapids: Eerdmans, 1993), 115.

theater of God's action, the place where the divine story of redemption is unfolding toward a sure and victorious future. Christian life now is lived between the times of the Savior's incarnate life, the Kingdom inaugurated, and the Savior's return, the Kingdom consummated (2 Thess. 2; Rev. 1:1-8).[21] Therefore, the perennial Christian prayer is "*Maranatha*—our Lord, come!" (1 Cor. 16:22; Rev. 22:20).

As the ancient Apostles' Creed begins, "I believe in God, the Father Almighty." The precise meaning of the identity of God as "Father" and as "Almighty" comes to be known only by awareness of the life and work of God's Son, Jesus Christ. In turn, the meaning of that life and the fruit of that work are mediated to and brought alive in today's believers only through the ongoing work of the Spirit of God. By God staying with us (the Spirit) and providing for all our needs, we can launch out on divine mission. We can serve in liberating faith because the Spirit takes the benefit of Christ's reconciling work and brings pardon *for* the believer and then power *in* the believer. The Spirit of God is "the presence of that Jesus who was crucified and raised, and who constitutes the realization of the promises of God. Thus, the presence of the past of Jesus and the presence of the future of God characterize the action of the Spirit."[22]

One day there will be a consummation, a final climaxing of the biblical story of salvation history. The primary biblical concern, however, is hardly to satisfy human curiosity about this most welcome future. It is rather to highlight that God's reign and future intent *already* have broken into human history in Jesus Christ and

---

[21]The main theme of the Second Assembly of the World Council of Churches (Evanston, Ill., 1954), was "Christ the Hope of the World." This focus represented increasing awareness that the nature of Christian life and action is determined in part by an understanding of humanity's final destiny. Life in the coming Kingdom is available now as foretaste. Such foretaste is the distinctive dynamic of Christian earthly existence and the hope of the world.

[22]Theodore Jennings, Jr., *Loyalty To God: The Apostles' Creed in Life and Liturgy* (Nashville: Abingdon Press, 1992), 180-181.

in the continuing work of the Spirit of Christ. The present of faithful disciples is to be lived in light of God's future. Those who believe that this future already is here in Jesus Christ receive by grace and then are to share "eternal life."

A Theology of Hope

In the Gospel of John the phrase "eternal life" means much more than an unending existence. "Eternal" in the New Testament often means "pertaining to an age," or life with the quality that reflects God's age to come later in its fullness. In part this future of God is available for humans to experience now. John's great thought is that eternal life already is the possession of those who come to Christ and find in him new birth by the Spirit. Jesus came that abundant life might be available in the present (10:10). God gave the Son, a Self-giving out of profound love, so that everyone who believes might have this life eternal (3:16). The good news of Easter is that in Christ we too may be raised to newness of life, now, in accord with and in the service of that age yet to come.

The Greek *aiônios* often is translated as *eternal* or *everlasting*. Its most significant New Testament use is as an adjective defining the new life granted by God to the disciples of Jesus. Here the word is a "word of eternity in contrast with time, of deity in contrast with humanity," thus meaning that the eternal life in view in the New Testament "is nothing less than the life of God himself."[23] It suggests more than the wonder of coming perfections; it speaks of the ethical demands of present discipleship responsibilities. Eternal life is the gift of God to those who believe (Jn. 3:16). It is the way of holiness (Rom. 6:22). It comes to those who show patience in well-doing (Rom. 2:7). It cannot come to anyone who continues to devalue and misuse a brother or sister (1 Jn. 3:15). It does come to those who keep themselves faithfully in the love and service of God (Jude 21-23).

---

[23]William Barclay, *More New Testament Words* (N. Y.: Harper & Brothers, 1958), 28.

The story of Christian believers today is to be an unfolding drama of the fallen creation now on its way, by God's grace, to regaining the true holiness of God's intention. The church is to be a carrier of "eternal life," embodying the reality seen in and inaugurated by the first coming of Christ. Says Paul, God in Christ "has made known to us the mystery of his will" (Eph. 1:9). This mystery is an assured vision of the Christ-shaped future rooted in the gospel of the Jesus already come among us. It brings to believers the needed direction and inspiration for their journey through history. Repentant sinners become new creatures, newly enlivened by the very life of God, and divine agents as their personal life stories are caught up in and reshaped by the life-giving and hope-generating truth of the biblical story of God in Christ.

That which yet will be opens the door of hope and power in relation to what might come to be, even now in our troubled times. Paul makes clear that such sanctification of the present is the work of the Spirit. The divine goal is the enablement of ethical character and action patterned after the likeness of Christ (1 Thess. 2:13; 4:3ff). Paul is elaborating the full implications of life in the new age, the age that already is inaugurated by Christ and now is being activated by the Spirit in the lives of the believing church. Delwin Brown says it well: "If we are to be faithful to our confidence in a God who through us is able to do more than we ask, more even than we can imagine, then we must emphatically reject any effort to put a limit on the kind of personal and social transformation that might be accomplished in history, even in our own time."[24] Stanley Grenz elaborates further on such Christian hope and task: "Because of their awareness of the significance of the present in the light of the future, those who acknowledge the lordship of Christ seek throughout this epoch (time between the *already* of Christ's first coming and the *not yet* of the full realization of God's future) to proclaim in word

---

[24]Ibid., 236.

and action, by the power of the Holy Spirit, the good news about the reign of God."[25]

Jürgen Moltmann, Wolfhart Pannenberg, and other contemporary theologians of hope rightly maintain that Christian hope is not an abstract utopia of no relevance to the troubled present. To the contrary, it is a passion for God's future that has become wonderfully possible thanks to the resurrection of Jesus Christ. This Spirit-fired passion is biblically founded, eschatologically oriented, and politically responsible. Pannenberg has been particularly concerned with the disunity of the church since it undermines the credibility of the church in its mission to the secular world. The church, as an eschatological body, already is to be exhibiting characteristics of God's coming Kingdom. It should be a unifying sign of the coming Kingdom, and thus a source of hope to a badly divided world.

The biblical revelation leads from the vision of the resurrected Christ to an enduring hope that inspires and enables *present mission*. At the heart of this vision, hope, mission, inspiration, and enablement is the Spirit of God, the Sustainer, the One who stays close to believers in the interim time. This crucial interim, the current era of the church, lies between the comings of Christ and is the time of living out the mission of Christ. Now is the Age of the Spirit.

As seen in the early chapters of Acts, the function of the Spirit is to make it possible for the believing community to live already, at least in part, in the not yet of the full reign of God. That reign, already inaugurated in our midst, calls for self-less loving and giving, which is why it is so difficult for the rich to enter the Kingdom (Matt. 19:24). When one's investments are in the present order, usually there is little commitment to being a pilgrim journeying eagerly toward full realization of a new order of things. When investments are in the age to come, there is freedom to impact the present by a pilgrim existence that contrasts with and

---

[25]Stanley Grenz, *The Millennial Maze* (InterVarsity Press, 1992), 200.

speaks prophetically to the world. The church is to be a journeying band of "resident aliens."[26]

The events of that first Christian Pentecost are a central part of the drama of the incarnation. In fact, the whole story of Jesus is the historic baseline, the "and it came to pass" of God's promises through the prophets (Heb. 1:1-2). But the fullness of the good news about the coming of Christ is that the incarnational work of God extends from Jesus to this very moment. The announcement that now brings great joy is about a continuing narrative of what God did and *is doing*. The full gospel is the good news that in Christ the "power of God for salvation" (Rom. 1:16) can become present reality for all who will receive. The relevance of the historic gospel is that it can and should be received and represented *now*.[27]

The first disciples of Jesus were so transformed by the life, death, and then dramatic resurrection of Jesus that they acquired a vibrant hope of his soon return. They believed in the nearness of the *parousia*, the full and final presence of the Risen Lord. They viewed this coming again as the next and culminating act of God in the grand scheme of human redemption and restoration. Knowing that what

---

[26]See Stanley Hauerwas and William Willimon, *Resident Aliens* (Nashville: Abingdon Press, 1989). According to Lesslie Newbigin, "the most important contribution which the church can make to a new social order is to be itself a new social order" (as quoted in *Christianity Today*, December 9, 1996, 27).

[27]The Anabaptist or Believers' Church tradition judges that true reformation of the church must include holiness. Christian faith is not merely what church members believe. It is who they now are and how they now live, especially as a faith community in contrast to the world. See Alan Kreider, *Journey Towards Holiness* (Scottdale, Pa.: Herald Press, 1987). John Wesley showed an increasingly close affinity with this tradition later in his life (see Howard Snyder, *The Radical Wesley*, InterVarsity, 1980). Snyder identifies four broad correlations between Wesley's understanding of the Christian life and what is characteristic of what he calls "charismatic" movements: (1) the stress on God's grace in the life of the church; (2) the significant role of the Holy Spirit in theology; (3) the emphasis on the church as community; and (4) the tension between the vision of the church and its institutional expressions (see Howard Snyder, with Daniel Runyon, *The Divided Flame: Wesleyans and the Charismatic Renewal*, Grand Rapids: Zondervan, 1986, 54-64).

God had done and would do in Christ was the center and meaning of all history, they found themselves living daily in the light of eternity, as though each day were their only day (Rom. 13:11-14). Discipleship became the process of living moment by moment in faithful expectation, being *now* what *soon will be* in its fullness and finality.

Downpayment on the Promise

Divine enablement is required for living the divine life in every present. That is why Jesus instructed his disciples to begin their witnessing and serving lives by waiting (Acts 1:4). Pentecost would be a central foundation for true Christian living. The church is to live in hope for the future as it continues to remember the crucified and resurrected Christ, all by the power of the Spirit of God. Summarizes Jürgen Moltmann:

> The present power of this remembrance and this hope is called "the power of the Spirit," for it is not of their own strength, reason, and will that people believe in Jesus as the Christ and hope for the future as God's future.... Faith in Christ and hope for the kingdom are due to the presence of God in the Spirit.[28]

Paul refers to the Spirit of God as the "first fruits," or "downpayment" of the final resurrection (Rom. 8:23; 2 Cor. 1:22; 5:5; Eph. 1:13-14). Into our present has broken God's future! What then of the resurrection of Jesus Christ? It was more than an isolated event in which one individual overcame death. It was "the death of the old aeon and the birth of the new aeon. Hence to be in Christ or in the Spirit (which we have seen to be synonymous) is to be in the age to come and to participate in its power."[29] The Spirit allows *final* things to have *present* impact.

---

[28]Jürgen Moltmann, *The Church in the Power of the Spirit* (N. Y.: Harper & Row, 1977), 197.

[29]H. Ray Dunning, *Grace, Faith & Holiness: A Wesleyan Systematic Theology* (Kansas City: Beacon Hill Press of Kansas City, 1988), 476.

In the yet imperfect present, Christians know both the reality of Jesus' resurrection and have God's gracious gift of the Holy Spirit. Christian eschatology is a Pentecost reality. Conversion is an event of the life-giving Spirit (2 Cor. 3:6) that brings within the believer a living water in the desert of sin, a flow of God's life that springs up into eternal life (Jn. 4:10, 14; 7:37-39). To be baptized in the Spirit "links us to the Lord's journey and anoints us for his ministry.... The promised Spirit of the end times is being poured out, and people are being introduced to the age of messianic salvation."[30]

Paul uses the word *arrabôn* three times, always in the same connection. He reports that God has given us his Spirit "as a first installment" (2 Cor. 1:22) or "as a guarantee" (2 Cor. 5:5) and that the Holy Spirit is the "pledge of our inheritance" (Eph. 1:14). In classical Greek the word *arrabôn* means the caution money that a purchaser had to deposit and later forfeit if the purchase was not fully carried out. God's gift of the Holy Spirit, then, is the disciple's divine guarantee, an advance foretaste of the life which the believer some day will live when the coming inheritance is fully consummated. The being of God has been put on the line voluntarily as a sure promise that it will be so! The joy that comes now is the pledge of the coming perfect joy to be known later in heaven. Although we now see only through a frosted glass, we at least are beginning to see and some day we who are faithful will know fully, just as we now are known by God (1 Cor. 13:12).

The present experience of the Spirit of God features the resurrection power of Jesus, the risen Christ. Jesus' first disciples, once aware of his resurrection, knew that it was really just the beginning. However rich their Jewish heritage and however dramatic the saving events of God in Christ, God also was propelling them into the future. They were learning that "to be a Christian was [is] to be a risk-taker. Every day they could expect that God's Spirit

---

[30]Clark Pinnock, *Flame of Love: A Theology of the Holy Spirit* (InterVarsity Press, 1996), 162-163.

would do creative things in making Jesus' presence real."[31] Suddenly a once frightened Peter could not be shut up in his public proclamation of the Risen Christ (Acts 2-4). To live in Christ is to live by God's loving grace, through the Spirit of God, as an extension of the emerging post-resurrection life of Jesus. To do so together as the body of Christ is to be the church, the community of the Spirit now on mission in this world.

What happened at Pentecost provided "the connecting link between past and present."[32] The continuity between the historical presence of Jesus and our present salvation and call to ministry was disclosed in the living presence of the Spirit of Christ. The Kingdom of God announced and embodied by Jesus is not forced to await some future millennium. There is the potential of meaningful Kingdom fulfillment in the present, made possible by the outpouring of the Spirit on waiting disciples. We who choose to wait on the coming God have the promise that we *will receive* (Acts 1:8). Being filled with power from on high is a significant part of the Christian good news! God came in Christ—and still comes in the Spirit!

Christians can wait in hope and live distinctive lives of sacrificial service because they have God's promise and the Spirit, the downpayment on that promise's final fulfillment. In Romans 8 Paul says that believers groan in travail with the whole creation, waiting for the day when the creation will be freed from its bondage. Meanwhile, we have the first fruits of the Spirit. The work of the Spirit includes equipping disciples of the Christ with "the powers of the age to come" (Heb. 6:5). We who believe and choose to be open to the Spirit's work can dare to hope because the triumph of goodness, grace, love, and justice does not depend ultimately on us, but on the power and work of the Spirit.

---

[31] Alan Kreider, *Journey Towards Holiness: A Way of Living for God's Nation* (Scottdale, Pa.: Herald Press, 1987), 204.

[32] C. Norman Kraus, *The Community of the Spirit* (Scottdale, Pa.: Herald Press, 1993), 13.

Those who believe and seek the gift of being Spirit-filled dare to be self-giving and can be united in all their weakness and human diversity. Jesus prayed for a unique unity among all disciples (Jn. 17) and Paul insisted that "in Christ Jesus" there no longer should be the destructive human divisions typically based on race, gender, and nationality (Gal. 3:26-28). This possibility of the accomplishment of such extraordinary new community exists only because of the empowering and blending benefits of the Spirit's life within and among the faithful. Testified one hymn writer who had learned that the sanctifying presence of a holy God brings the present potential of a unified fellowship among believers:

> How sweet this bond of perfectness,
> The wondrous love of Jesus!
> A pure foretaste of heaven's bliss,
> O fellowship so precious!
>
> Beloved, how this perfect love,
> Unites us all in Jesus!
> One heart, and soul, and mind,
> We prove, the union heaven gave us.[33]

Having made the harsh but justified judgment that much of what passes for traditional Christian theology is in reality "the result of the alliance between the church and the power structures of society," Justo González went on to speak for an ethnic round-table of Christians representing the world's oppressed. They believe in the church because they believe in God's future. They hope, "not because we trust our own programs of reformation, and even less because we trust its structures and committees, but because we trust in the Holy Spirit."[34]

---

[33]Daniel Warner and Barney Warren, "The Bond of Perfectness," as in *Worship the Lord: Hymnal of the Church of God* (Anderson, Ind.: Warner Press, 1989), 330, vs. 1 and chorus.

[34]Justo González, *Out of Every Tribe & Nation* (Nashville: Abingdon Press, 1992), 115.

Despite the challenges and possibilities, even we who believe in the Christ and seek to live in the Spirit have a faith that is fragile and performance well below perfection. The Spirit is the full eschatological gift in the present, but the Spirit's current presence is only the first portion of what eventually will be the full harvest of God's grace. We who believe still gaze expectantly forward because of what already has been fulfilled for us and in us and because we know that what God intends is yet far from realized. Having ingested a small bite of God's goodness, we naturally long for the full and promised heavenly banquet (Ps. 23:5). Here is a truly appropriate Christian prayer:

> My heart cries out, living flame of love, ever burn on the altar of my heart. Welcome, Holy Spirit! Come and renew creation. Breathe on these dead bones, *fill us with hope*, lead us into God's embrace. You are at work everywhere, even where unnamed and unnoticed, preparing for new creation and the marriage supper of the Lamb. Therefore we adore you, Lord and giver of life; come to us and set us free. Be no more a stranger or a lost relation, but fill us up with your love.[35]

Knowing in detail about that eventual future is beyond us now. What is not beyond us is the knowledge that the future will be the Christ-future, the culmination of the present work of the Spirit. Since Jesus Christ was the full image of the invisible God (Col. 1:15) active among us, we already know at least right images of the Christ-future. To an explanation of these we now turn.

---

[35]Clark Pinnock, *Flame of Love: A Theology of the Holy Spirit* (InterVarsity Press, 1996), 247. Emphasis added.

Matters Worth Exploring

1. If the first coming of Jesus was cause for "joy to the world," what is meant by a "dark side" of his advent?

2. The Jews, when exiled in ancient Babylon, dreamed of returning to Jerusalem by a divinely provided vindication over their enemies. Is that hope still valid in the sense of its being related to the literal city of Jerusalem in modern Israel?

3. What is the meaning of the "eternal life" now granted to believers in Jesus? What are its present implications?

4. Christian eschatology is said to be a "Pentecost reality." What does this mean?

5. The Spirit of God is said to be the believer's "first install-ment." What already has come as present reality and what is yet ahead?

6. In wanting to be effectively faithful in this present world, should Christians place their hope in their present ministry programs and their church structures and efforts at renewal? What is the alternative?

7. Do you really believe that God's Spirit is the one who renews creation, fills believers with real hope, and is even now preparing the final marriage supper of the Lamb?

8. Are you ready to join in the prayer that welcomes the Holy Spirit to the altar of your own heart?

Chapter 8

IMAGES OF CHRISTIAN HOPE

❦

*"Then I saw a new heaven and a new earth; for the
first heaven and the first earth had passed away, and
the sea was no more." (Rev. 21:1)*

❦

*We are living in a world in which, for all its sin and sadness, Christ
has left one vacant tomb in the wide graveyard of the earth.*[1]
*The consummation of the Kingdom, although breaking into history, will
itself be beyond history, for it will introduce a redeemed order whose
actual character transcends both historical experience
and realistic imagination.*[2]

❦

Chapters six and seven make the point that Christian hope
must not be isolated from human history. Final things have present
meaning and responsibilities for every Christian who is willing to
be faithful. This chapter goes on to explore the related assumption
that Christian hope, necessarily relevant to current history, also
extends to far more than its current relevance. Being faithful *now*
is the path of discipleship that leads toward God's ultimate *then*.

---

[1] A. M. Hunter, *Interpreting Paul's Gospel* (London: SCM, 1954), 126.

[2] George Eldon Ladd, *The Presence of the Future* (Grand Rapids:
Eerdmans, 1974), 337.

One symbol rich in meaning for the whole Judeo-Christian tradition is the menorah. It is an eight-branched candelabra with one branch lighted on each day of an annual Jewish festival. The history behind this celebration of lights, Hanukkah, is the rededication of the Jerusalem Temple in 164 before Christ. A Syrian-Greek occupation had threatened the very existence of Jewish faith, inspiring the surprisingly successful Maccabean revolution that restored worship in a cleansed Temple. If the Syrian-Greeks had prevailed, the very soil out of which Christianity soon would emerge would have been poisoned almost beyond recovery. But God stood with his people, fashioning a future out of near disaster. According to a 13th-century German song of Hanukkah:

Rock of ages, let our song
Praise Thy saving power:
Thou, amidst the raging foes
Wast our shelt'ring tower.
Furious they assailed us,
But Thine arm availed us,
And Thy word
Broke their sword
When our own strength failed us.

Use of the word "images" is significant as one considers final things. The nature of biblical language about the future and our limited awareness as finite human beings join to caution Christians against brash literalisms and arrogant assumptions about the extent of detailed knowledge of the future. We know that the future is God's and that it will have a Christ-shape. We know that there will be accountability and that faithfulness now has long-term implications later.

Beyond such basic realities of Christian expectation, it is necessary to rely on images given by a biblical revelation not interested in satisfying our curiosity or distracting disciples from present responsibilities. There certainly are images of tomorrow available, images that bring believers important perspective and assurance. While the glass through which we now gaze is frosted, there is light enough to reveal the general shapes of things to come. As believers peer through the frosted glass, it is crucial initially to recall that the *past* shapes the *last*.

The Past, Last, and Present

What shape does the Christian hope take if not well informed by confident chronologies of future events and millennial models that feature dreams of social utopia and/or nationalistic fulfillment on earth? Put most simply, the thrust of the biblical revelation is that the Christian hope centers in the eventual and complete victory of the creative, Self-expending, community-forming love of God. This includes a confident expectation of "the triumph of the love of God over all hate, of the justice of God over all injustice, of God's freedom over all bondage, of community with God over all separation, of life with God over the power of death."[3] Beyond these marvelous and foundational affirmations, there is little consensus in the Christian community about the particulars of times and events that will close this age and usher in the one where God will be all in all. There are, however, a series of central images and guiding principles of God's intended future that are believed by most Christians—whatever they do or do not believe in addition.

Some writers have identified helpfully at least guiding principles for interpreting the Christian hope. Karl Rahner is one such writer.[4] Another is Daniel Migliore who suggests five such principles worth noting. (1) The language of Christian hope is language stretched to the limits, language rich in symbol and image. (2) Christian hope is centered on the glory of the Triune God that is

---

[3]Daniel Migliore, *Faith Seeking Understanding* (Grand Rapids: Eerdmans, 1991), 238.

[4]Karl Rahner, "The Hermeneutics of Eschatological Assertions," in *Theological Investigations*, vol. 4 (N. Y.: Seabury Press, 1974), 323-346. Rahner's theses are summarized approvingly by H. Ray Dunning, *Grace, Faith & Holiness* (Beacon Hill Press of Kansas City, 1988), 574-577.

revealed above all in the resurrection of the crucified Jesus, the pivotal event that contains the promise of new life for all creation. (3) Christian eschatological symbols should be interpreted so that they point toward fulfillment and wholeness in all dimensions of life. (4) These symbols, rightly understood, relativize all historical and cultural achievements of humanity. (5) Christian hope and its rich imagery are immensely evocative and should give birth not to patient passivity, but to creative, Spirit-inspired human activity on behalf of Kingdom goals in the present.[5]

What clearly is appropriate is human modesty in any presumed knowledge of the precise nature and timing of all that yet will be. Even Jesus confessed humility about such things (Matt. 24:36; Mk. 13:23; Acts 1:6-7). The eschatological language of hope and expectation, of symbol and image, should not be limited prematurely and singularly to a literalized relation to the political events of a given time—so tempting and so often tried over the centuries, usually to little avail except to create considerable confusion. "Last things," like the first things of the creation, are not accessible to us in the sense of scientific detail and political prediction.

What we do have are biblical pictures that convey "an authoritative testimony of faith to the great destination of the universe, which has its goal in God.... At the end of the world, as at the beginning, there is not nothingness, but God."[6] The biblical narrative makes clear that history is linear rather than cyclical. It is moving meaningfully toward a sure point of consummation. Believers are to be present signs of such future hope. The hope is in the One who is able to do far more than we can ask or imagine (Eph. 3:20). In pleadings here against claiming knowledge of detailed maps of the future, the intent is not to deny biblical authority, only to interpret carefully what the Bible promises in

---

[5]Migliore, op. cit., 240-242.
[6]Hans Küng, *Credo: The Apostles' Creed Explained for Today* (N. Y.: Doubleday, 1993), 166.

the Bible's own context rather than in an easy arrogance that assumes that our own context is what the Bible really had in mind. Such care in interpretation is not to deny the certainty of the Lord's eventual return, for instance, but to admit human limitations and allow God to surprise us by patterns of fulfillment that likely will far surpass what we now conceive.

Here is what appears certain at a minimum. Whatever will be at the end of the ages will be continuous and in character with the center of the biblical revelation, God come and coming in Jesus Christ (see chapter five). In this sense, *last* things are to be understood in terms of *past* things. A key principle of eschatological interpretation is the analogy of faith. Believers learn of the future through thinking by analogies about what God has done in the past and is doing in the present divine-human relation. Thomas Oden explains: "Faith hopes for completion of what remains unfulfilled but anticipated in the history of redemption, for clarity in what remains stubbornly ambiguous, for victory over what still remains disputed, for reliable vision of what remains in time uncertain. The future is read in the light of God's self-disclosure in the past."[7]

Keeping in mind the kairotic past events of the biblical narrative, those pivot points at which the biblical story hinges, several pictures of the future are central for Christian faith. Four active verbs characterize the work of the now come and still coming Son as portrayed in the parable of the last judgment. "When the Son of Man *comes* in his glory, and all the angels with him, he will *sit* on his throne in heavenly glory. All the nations will be *gathered* before him, and he will *separate* the people one from another as a shepherd separates the sheep from the goats" (Matt. 25:31-32, italics added). Four central images of Christian expectation, then, are the anticipated realities of second coming, resurrection, separation (judgment), and no more sea (heaven).

---

[7]Thomas Oden, *Life in the Spirit* (San Francisco: Harper, 1992), 373.

A Second Coming

The promised return or second coming of Jesus (Jn. 14:2-3; Acts 1:10-11) will be the arrival (or full presence) of none other than the crucified and risen Christ. The indispensable clue to the nature and purpose of the second coming of Jesus is the nature and purpose of his first coming. What God will do eventually will be in character with what God already has done in Jesus Christ. Believers may know precious little about the future; but they do know that God is not capricious or arbitrary. Jesus Christ was and will be at the center, and he is the same "yesterday, today, and forever" (Heb. 13:8). In expectation, the church prays: "Come, Lord Jesus" (Rev. 22:20). This is a hope anchored in knowledge since the One still to come already has come once and thus is well known in his nature and intent.

The divine reign inaugurated centuries ago certainly will be consummated in its fullness and finality. The concluding act of the biblically revealed drama of redemption will be played out for all humans to see. It will be a real, historical, momentous event or series of events. Again, whatever will happen in the future will be in full character with what already has happened in Jesus Christ. The story of God with all of creation, from its beginning to its end, holds together. The end is only the flowering of the center, Jesus Christ. In fact, fulfillment of the original vision of the creation (Isa. 65:17) brings the biblical story full circle. What began with creation ends with new creation. The Creator is the same in both instances.

The second coming of the Christ will mark the beginning of the end of God's plan of redemption and the process of historical time as now known. Jesus promised that he would come again (Matt. 24:30). The expectation of this return was central to the faith of early Christians (Acts 1:11). The coming again will be unexpected as in the days of Noah (Matt. 24:37). In sharp contrast to the humble circumstances of the first advent in Bethlehem, the second advent will be one of great power and glory (Mk. 13:26) that involves the triumphant Christ, the Lord of all, sitting on a throne, judging all the nations (Matt. 25:31-46). According to the Nicene Creed dating from A. D. 381, Jesus "shall come again in glory to judge the living and the dead." Apart from all speculations that insist on knowledge of the future in addition to such coming and judging, this straightforward affirmation has been the consensus belief of Christians across the centuries.

When will the second coming happen? What is the exact status of the dead in the meantime? We do not know and probably should not spend time speculating (Mk. 13:32-33). This anticipation of the coming of the Christ, whatever its timing, is to focus Christian hope, energize Christian life, and make the many associated questions of relatively little consequence. There is wisdom in the common comment, "Whatever will be will be." The "whatever" is defined basically by the "who" and the "why" of the future. The bottom line of such a comment should not be, "So let's forget the whole thing," but rather, "So let's relax from needless anxiety and get on with the Lord's present business since we are confident that the future is the future of our beloved Lord Jesus."

While the second coming will be dramatic and definitive, there is to be no denial that the Spirit of Christ has been with us always (Matt. 28:20). The hope of the second coming only affirms that at some point the Christ will be with us fully and finally. In fact, the New Testament places emphasis on the "coming" rather than the "second." It will be a coming of the One already present, a complete presence now known only in part and glimpsed as an image through a frosted glass. All power already belongs to Christ (Matt. 28:18; Col. 2:10), but the victory already won is yet to be disclosed beyond the region of faith (Acts 7:56; Heb. 11:1; 13, 27).

Biblically speaking, Christ's coming again will have at least four characteristics. It will be visible, sudden, cosmic, and glorious. Every eye will see him (Rev. 1:7). It will be like lightning (Matt. 24:27) or a thief in the night (Matt. 24:43; 1 Thess. 5:2; 2

Pet. 3:10). It will include earthquakes, resurrected bodies, and a new earth. In contrast to the first coming of Jesus in poverty and humility (Phil. 2:5-8), at his second coming "every knee will bow to him and every tongue confess him Lord" (Phil. 2:10-11).

With the second coming there also will be other dramatic happenings, other future images of Christian anticipation. These are indicated by additional pictures of the eschaton that follow immediately as aspects and consequences of the ultimate coming of God in Christ.

A General Resurrection

The New Testament presents the resurrection of Jesus as extremely important for Christian faith. There are two basic reasons. One is Christological since the resurrection provided key insights into the identity and significance of Jesus. The other is one of hope since the resurrection of Jesus declared that the believer one day will share in Christ's resurrection. Jesus' resurrection, therefore, is both the ground and the anticipation of the future resurrection of believers. Reads the chorus of a beloved Christian song: "Because He lives, I can face tomorrow, Because He lives all fear is gone; Because I know He holds the future, And life is worth the living, just because He lives."[8]

The historical resurrection of Jesus, already past, is linked biblically to a general resurrection of all people in the future. This will be at Jesus' second coming which will initiate the end of human history (1 Cor. 15:16). The Jesus resurrection event of the first century is the "first fruits" of the eventual resurrection of believers (1 Cor. 15: 20-23). Little is known in detail, except that "when he is revealed, we will be like him, for we will see him as he is" (1 Jn. 3:20) and "he will transform the body of our humiliation that it may be conformed to the body of his glory" (Phil. 3:21). The Apostles' Creed ties "life everlasting" to the biblical concept

---

[8]Gloria and William Gaither, "Because He Lives" in *Worship the Lord* (Anderson, Ind.: Warner Press, 1989), 209.

of resurrection of the "body" (1 Cor. 15:44), not to the "immortality of the soul" idea of Platonic philosophy.[9]

Christian hope trusts in God's creative and recreative power rather than in any intrinsic property of human nature. "Soul" (*nephesh*) is viewed biblically as the life principle of a unified person, not a separate something conceivable apart from bodily existence. Gabriel Fackre is right: "Christian faith has too profound and critical an understanding of human spirit to consider it the 'divine' segment of the self worthy of immortality, and too high a view of the body to disdain and separate it from our final destiny."[10] Paul was confident that the risen faithful will be like their Risen Lord in that their risen bodies will be transformed to be like his, no longer subject to illness and death (1 Cor. 15:50-58). This is an image of the essence of coming reality, not a scientific description, the kind of detailed analysis that modern rationalists tend to prefer.

There are at least three important reasons for believing that the Christian hope for life beyond death lies in the resurrection of the body rather than in an inherent immortality of the soul. These reasons are:

(1) The good news of the apostles was not that Jesus was an immortal soul, but that God has raised Him from the dead; (2) the Bible in general has little to say about the soul as an immortal entity, speaking usually instead of "soul" as roughly equivalent to livingness; and (3) resurrection in the biblical proclamation is a resurrec-

---

[9]See Oscar Cullmann, *Immortality of the Soul or Resurrection of the Dead?* (N. Y.: Macmillan, 1958). Modern biblical scholarship has challenged the classical Greek dualism of the body and spirit, arguing instead that such dualism is foreign to the primary understanding of the Bible about the nature of human beings. Contrary to the Greek philosophic tradition, so influential on Christian theology and popular piety, the body probably is not viewed best as the mortal shell of the immortal soul.

[10]Gabriel Fackre, *The Christian Story*, rev. ed. (Grand Rapids: Eerdmans, 1978, 1984), 245.

tion of the body, and thus implies yet another affirmation of the goodness of the material order in a way that "immortality of the soul" simply does not and cannot.[11]

Christian hope for meaningful life beyond physical death comes from the biblical revelation, not from rational theory;[12] it comes from belief in the resurrection of Christ, not from a philosophic assumption about the inherent immortality of the soul. Christian hope centers in the power and faithfulness of God to bring life out of death. Resurrection stresses that final victory, like the initial origin of all things, will be by a creative act of God's grace. This, of course, is not to ignore the continuity of the experience that there will be then with the "eternal life" that is to be now, an experience that survives death (relationally speaking). Death cannot separate the believer from the life and love of God (Rom. 8:38-39; 1 Cor. 15:53). The woman or man who chooses to live in Christ and die in Christ will find that not even the dark valley of death can manage to swallow or distort that sacred relationship (Ps. 23).

When Christians affirm belief in the "resurrection of the body," they are announcing confidence that the corruptibility evident everywhere in our world will not be the final word. God's intent is to grant new life to the whole person, not merely to perpetuate life in a disembodied soul. Of course, noting the example of the body of the resurrected Jesus, we have more questions than answers about the nature of our future bodies. Even so, "the sym-

---

[11]Michael Lodahl, *The Story of God: Wesleyan Theology & Biblical Narrative* (Kansas City: Beacon Hill Press of Kansas City, 1994), 225.

[12]One such pattern of interpretation with significant influence in recent decades is the "process" perspective based in large part on the philosophy of Alfred North Whitehead. Recognizing that process theologians are not in full agreement with each other, Charles Hartshorne is hardly alone in viewing death as the "absolutely final event in the life of an individual." He rejects the notions of bodily resurrection and an immortal soul, thinking rather of eternal life as "God's perfect knowledge and memory of us throughout the entire chain of events that constitutes creation" (Harold Hewitt, Jr., in D. Musser and J. Price, eds., *A New Handbook of Christian Theology*, Abingdon Press, 1992, 119).

bol stands as a bold and even defiant affirmation of God's total, inclusive, holistic redemption."[13] Some form of bodily existence is in biblical view. Further, and contrary to modern individualism, the Christian hope also includes a transformed world, a new heaven and earth (Rev. 21:1).

Christ's resurrection in the past and ours yet to come constitute a hope by which believers can live and a light by which they can see adequately for the discipleship demands of the present. The phrase "resurrection of the body" in the ancient creeds (Apostles' and Nicene) "expresses the whole genius of the Christian faith."[14] It has to do with the mystery that, while yet unrealized, is nonetheless an "assurance of things hoped for" (Heb. 11:1) based on the Jesus-past already known. The apostolic witness points directly at Jesus. He arose again by the power of God, actually and fully, with a new and real, though different body. He is "the first-born from the dead" (Col. 1:18). We who belong to Christ will be next (1 Cor. 15:23). "Thanks be to God who has given us the victory through our Lord Jesus Christ!" (1 Cor. 15:57). The presently significant good news is that this resurrection victory that lies ahead already is at work in those who are in Christ (Eph. 1:19b-20). Looking forward in faith leads to living now by faith in the potential of resurrection existence.

All persons will participate in the resurrection yet to come (Rom. 14:10), the one and only resurrection (Jn. 5:28-29; Rev. 20:11-15). Some millennial schemes assume two separate resurrections still to come, one for the faithful and one for unbelievers. Such a tenuous biblical interpretation is encouraged by a preconceived system of events assumed by these interpreters, a system not clearly assumed by the Bible itself. The New Testament joins the occurrence of the last judgment with the return of Christ (Matt. 16:27; Jn. 5:28-29; Rom. 2:15-16; 2 Tim. 4:12, etc.). Only

---

[13]Migliore, op. cit., 244.

[14]Reinhold Niebuhr, *Beyond Tragedy* (N. Y.: Charles Scribner's Sons, 1937), 289-290.

in Revelation 20:11-15, as interpreted by premillennialists, is a millennium period placed between the second coming and the last judgment.

A Separation: Hell

For some people the coming resurrection will not be good news. What lies beyond death is more than some soft and friendly light or the welcome relief of endless nothingness.[15] The climactic meaningfulness of the biblical revelation is captured in its final scenes. Asserts the Apostles' Creed, God "will come again to judge the living and the dead." All that ever has been will then be seen clearly for what it really was. Judgment and justice will join the chorus of resurrection joy.

If the doctrine of resurrection teaches that people really matter to God, so that existence is divinely willed even after death, the doctrine of judgment teaches that their significance is accompanied by their accountability (Dan. 12:2). The certainty of a coming judgment is reassuring as well as being a solemn prospect. It is reassuring in that it offers the hope of justice in a world gone so wrong. A final day of reckoning is morally inevitable in a purposeful universe where responsible persons are governed by a righteous and merciful God. History's injustices finally will be righted! The first will be last and the last will be first (Matt. 10:30; 20:16). Human beings are not asked whether they wish to be born; but they are expected to live responsibly between birth and death, after which there is no further opportunity to choose. We humans come to our final accounting in light of our actual life choices (Heb. 10:26-31). Human life is like the

---

[15]In recent years it has become fashionable to report death as either (1) a pleasant "out-of-the-body" experience of light, warmth, and acceptance for all or (2) an achieving of welcome non-existence, the final escape from evil and the cycle of supposed reincarnations (the influence of Eastern faiths in "New Age" forms). The point, however, is to be biblically faithful and not religiously fashionable.

falling of a tree: "in the place where it falls, there will it lie (Eccles. 11:3).[16]

Death, while fixing one's destiny, is not the last word. It is not the eternal victory over life. Death's "sting" has been removed by the resurrection of Jesus (1 Cor. 15:55). All people will be raised from the dead (Acts 24:15) by another creative act of God, and then comes an accountability that will include divine-human separation for some. Today is the day of salvation (Heb. 4:7). After death comes judgment (Heb. 9:27), and judgment means separation between believers and unbelievers (Lk. 16:19-31). God's coming judgment on the faithless will be grounded in their attitude toward Jesus (Matt. 25:41-46), not on God's reluctance to save (2 Pet. 3:9). The divine purpose does not include the damnation of anyone, except as they freely choose separation from God (1 Tim. 2:4).[17] There will be divine victory over all evil and a final separation of good from evil. In this present life the weeds and the wheat grow together (parable of Jesus, Matt. 13). That will change. Those who finally reject the work of the Holy Spirit will find no shalom "either in this age or in the age to come" (Matt. 12:32; cf. Lk. 18:30; Gal. 1:4; Col. 1:26).

---

[16]Also see Lk. 16:19-31; 2 Pet. 2:4, 9; and Jude 7-13, all of which assume that human destiny is fixed at death. Even so, the Roman Catholic Church identifies a "purgatory," a place of further opportunity for those who die in good relationship with the church but whose souls are not pure enough to enter heaven initially. Support for this identification is found in 2 Maccabees 12:39-45; Micah 7:8; Zech. 9:11; Matt. 12:32; 1 Cor. 3:13-15, 15:29. For a good discussion of purgatory, "soul sleep," and the "intermediate state" in general, see Stanley Grenz, *Theology for the Community of God*, Nashville: Broadman & Holman, 1994, 766-778.

[17]Rather than hell being total separation from God's presence, Boyd Hunt (op. cit., 339) argues that it is exposure to God's presence in judgment, an exposure without Christ as mediator and without the benefit of God's mercy and blessing. Hell is the spurning of God's ever-present love and mercy. This is hell as torment, the self-damning of spurned mercy and love. God, then, should not be thought of as always designing new ways to make the doomed more miserable— the medieval torture-chamber view of hell that caused Clark Pinnock to protest that such a hell "makes God into a bloodthirsty monster who maintains an everlasting Auschwitz for victims whom he does not even allow to die (quoted by Hunt, 338).

By truly loving every person and according them genuine dignity, divine love considers human decisions significant. People choose. One day they will give an account of their choices and be separated accordingly. God remembers. All that is and ever has been resides in divine memory and will participate in the culmination of the biblical story of redemption. One day death will lose its ugly grip. All things will be judged at the time of the last things (Jn. 5:28-29; 1 Cor. 15). While judgment is sure, there is special hope in the knowledge that we will be judged by the same One who can empathize with our human condition and understand the obstacles that make even our believing lives so imperfect. The fact that judgment belongs to God as revealed in Jesus Christ is reassuring indeed. Human judgments so often are arbitrary and self-serving. They tyrannize and destroy. But God, as known in Christ, is amazingly Self-giving (the Cross), and God's judgments are altogether righteous (Rom. 2:1-11).

What, then, is the final destiny of good and evil? Is hell real and forever? Christians have seen three different scenarios in biblical teaching, differing patterns of envisioning what eventually will be at and beyond future judgment. The issues are large and the biblical information is sparse, at least at the detail level.

Scenario One. The most common scenario of future judgment and the destiny of the faithless is that at the great judgment there will be a sharp separation of all people into two groups, with each group then existing for eternity in different "places." The righteous ones will live joyously in heaven and the wicked terribly in hell, some to know eternal life and others eternal punishment (Matt. 25:31-46; Rev. 14:10-11). Right will be forever vindicated and God's justice forever satisfied. Hell is at least to be against God and thus in a state of being without God. Hell receives those who imagine themselves good; Jesus receives those who know themselves sinners, but who have chosen to rely on God's saving grace.

Michelangelo's famous painting on the wall of the Sistine Chapel, for instance, depicts Christ, the stern judge, gesturing rejection to the damned. A common grouping of images in medieval churches was of angels carrying the righteous away to heaven while devils drag the wicked into the hell of everlasting damnation. In the middle of all this carrying and dragging sits Christ on the judgment seat with a two-edged sword between his lips. The Judge issues only two verdicts, eternal life or eternal death.

Even if this medieval courtroom way of portraying the last judgment is unbalanced in its singular harshness, God, while being revealed biblically as love and mercy, also is said to be a "consuming fire" (Heb. 12:28-29). In fact, consuming fire is a vivid New Testament image of judgment. More than any other person in the Bible, Jesus is reported to have spoken about "hell" (*gehenna*). The reference is to the "Valley of Hinnom" located just south of Mount Zion in Jerusalem (Neh. 11:30). It once was associated with idolatrous rites such as child sacrifice, a passing of children through the fires of Moloch (Jer. 7:31; 2 Kings 23:10; 2 Chron. 28:3; 33:6). In Jesus' time the city garbage and discarded corpses of the familyless burned there daily. Jesus saw this awful place as a symbol of the coming judgment to be experienced by those who, in their sin and rebellion against God, refuse God's gracious forgiveness (Mark 9:43, 45, 47; Matt. 5:22; 8:12; 13:42; 25:30, 46). The fire of hell is a frightful image of the ongoing anguish of those who are forever aware that they invested their lives in what was temporal and perishable rather than in what was imperishable and eternal (Matt. 6:19-20; Lk. 12:16-21).

Two variations of this first scenario of the coming separation of good and evil differ concerning whether or not God pre-ordains the constituency of each group. John Calvin assumed the view that all people deserve damnation because of sin, but, out of sheer and wholly unmerited mercy, God has chosen some for salvation. These chosen are called and finally saved, while all others are rightfully and eternally lost. Such a double predestination view pictures God's sovereignty fully prevailing as some people are chosen (grace) and some are not (justice).[18] Other interpreters, like John Wesley, place more weight on the role of human freedom that is understood to have been granted by God. God thus enables all people to choose relationship with the divine through Christ, desiring that all be saved and predestining no one otherwise. In the final judgment, God will act in line with previous human and not divine choice. Those who so choose "perish because they refused to love the truth and so be saved" (2 Thess. 2:10). Humans choose now; later God will separate accordingly. This is neither an infringement on the divine majesty or the human achieving of salvation by any other means than divine grace.[19]

A particular theological problem haunts this first and most common scenario, whether of the Calvin or Wesley variation. The concept of a punitive hell that exists as a place of punishment forever (Matt. 25:41, 46) seems to some interpreters as not compatible with the justice and mercy of God and, therefore, an unsatisfactory answer to certain key theological questions. How can one reconcile the sovereignty of a truly good and powerful God with the assumption that evil (the opposite of God) will persist forever as a heavily populated hell? Will the antithesis of God never go away? Will divine retribution never rise to restoration so that the ultimate intent of God that all be saved finally will be realized? Is not the judgment of God a loving one that, as in the cross of Christ, moves toward human salvation even in the face of human rejec-

---

[18]Explains H. Henry Meeter: "When once you have adopted the view that God shall be God in the full sweep of his many relationships to his creatures, you will arrive at predestination as a very logical conclusion. All limitations of God's decree regarding man restrict God's supremacy and infringe upon his majesty" (*The Basic Ideas of Calvinism*, 6th ed., Baker Book House, 1990, 21).

[19]Key to John Wesley's view is his concept of "prevenient grace" made available to all people. See Barry Callen, *God As Loving Grace* (Nappanee, IN: Evangel Press, 1996), 128-130 and 146-148. See also the chapter "Spirit and Universality" in Clark Pinnock, *Flame of Love* (1996).

tion? Is it not unfair that sin committed and not repented of in the few short years of a human lifetime should result in an unending punishment? Such hard questions are heard often.

Is hell, real as it is, to be the last word in the grand biblical story of human redemption by God? While scenario one speaks rightly of the sure judgment of sin, it may or may not hold in adequate tension other motifs of the Christian message. The forward movement of the biblical revelation is toward the fulfillment of divine purpose, not its everlasting frustration for most of the creation.[20] Concerning hell, then, I join Adrio König in observing that the following should be said first. "We cannot speak of hell as we speak of heaven, as if it were one of the streams rising from a common source and flowing down opposite sides of a mountain. The sentence of final damnation is not a realization of the *eschaton* or *telos*, God's original purpose in creation. Hell is indeed an end, but only an end without an accomplished goal, i. e., an end which has miscarried."[21]

Scenario Two. Does the promise that God finally will be all in all imply the eventual elimination of even hell? Rather than the unrighteous forever suffering outside the blessed community of God, is it not reasonable to assume that God eventually will eliminate hell and all consigned there? Seeking to answer such questions, a second scenario has arisen among Christians as a variation of the first. Called *annihilationism*, it anticipates the eventual destruction of evil instead of its persisting existence as unending punishment. The old heaven and earth finally will be destroyed by fire and new ones will be cre-

---

[20]Some biblical scholars, however, view more broadly the purpose of God, seeing the divine purpose being both the antecedent will to save all and the consequent will to deal justly with choices freely made by humans. The promise of an everlasting hell, therefore, is not an expression of the failure of God's purpose, but of its fullest completion.

[21]Adrio König, *The Eclipse of Christian Eschatology* (Grand Rapids: Eerdmans, 1989), 221.

ated where only righteousness dwells (2 Pet. 3:7, 11-13). The wicked will be destroyed (Matt. 10:28; 2 Thess. 1:9).[22] Death and hell are pictured biblically as themselves being thrown into the lake of fire (Rev. 20:14), possibly implying the ultimate annihilation of all evil, including hell and all of its inhabitants. Annihilationists argue that the idea of eternal and conscious punishment is an intrusion into Christian theology of the Greek idea of the soul's immortality. By contrast, the biblical view is a conditional immortality. We humans receive immortality from God only through participation in the coming resurrection.

Once resurrected and judged, the question is whether those judged negatively by God will survive at all. While theologians like Thomas Finger are clear that "we cannot rule out the possibility of eternal conscious torment," they note the promised complete triumph of heaven. Therefore, it is "less likely that hell will be an eternal, consciously experienced process existing alongside it…. Some sort of gradual, at least partially experienced annihilation seems the most likely fate of the condemned."[23] "Eternal" is a word whose New Testament

---

[22]Clark Pinnock, e. g., came to the position of annihilationism because he found the idea of an unending hell of torment "both morally intolerable and fortunately biblically unnecessary." He insists: "It just does not make any sense to say that a God of love will torture people forever for sins done in the context of a finite life. It implies a vindictiveness in God that I cannot imagine in the Father of our Lord Jesus Christ…. Hell is indeed a place of destruction rather than torture" (in Pinnock and Delwin Brown, *Theological Crossfire*, Zondervan, 1990, 226, 230). Jerry Walls, following John Wesley, argues to the contrary that, when human freedom and radical evil are taken into account, divine goodness and an eternal hell are not necessarily incompatible morally (*Hell: The Logic of Damnation*, University of Notre Dame Press, 1992, chapter four). Kenneth Grider agrees. Both universalism and annihilationism sacrifice the holiness of God to divine love. While God is love, "He is more basically a God of holiness," meaning that God acts justly as well as lovingly. "When infinite holiness is sinned against and grace is refused, justice decrees punishment that is eternal (*A Wesleyan-Holiness Theology*, Beacon Hill Press of Kansas City, 1994, 546).

[23]Thomas Finger, *Christian Theology*, vol. 1 (Scottdale, Pa.: Herald Press, 1985), 161. For a refutation of annihilationism, see David Wells, "Everlasting Punishment," *Christianity Today* (March 20, 1987), 41-42.

meaning is not wholly clear. Stephen Travis argues that it may mean "the permanence of the *result* of judgment rather than the continuation of the act of punishment itself."[24] Thus, eternal punishment may mean only that God's final judgment cannot be reversed. Even so, the New Testament appears to assume that hell is as eternal as heaven (Matt. 25:46) and writers like C. S. Lewis insist on the power of habit to fix character in permanent rebellion against God's righteousness.[25] Having reviewed carefully the biblical texts used to support annihilationism, Millard Erickson's conclusion stands as an important caution: "We conclude that the theory of annihilationism in its various forms, as appealing as it may seem as a solution to some theological problems, cannot be sustained, philosophically, biblically, or theologically."[26]

Scenario Three. Any eventual divine destruction of evil, as suggested by an annihilationist view, while highlighting the final triumph of God, would do so at great cost to God's known intention that no one perish (2 Pet. 3:9). So a third scenario is argued by some, one called *universalism*. This position looks to biblical statements that the eschaton will be a reconciliation and restoration of all things in Christ (Rom. 5:18; Eph. 1:10; Col. 1:19-20; 1 Cor. 15:22-28). It sees in such verses a case for the ultimate salvation of all people, the

---

[24]Stephen Travis, *I Believe in the Second Coming of Jesus* (Grand Rapids: Eerdmans, 1982), 199.

[25]C. S. Lewis, *The Great Divorce* (N. Y.: Macmillan, 1946). Note also W. Ralph Thompson who identifies the series of biblical texts used by annihilationists and critiques their usual use in support of this position (in Charles Carter, gen. ed., *A Contemporary Wesleyan Theology*, vol. 2, Francis Asbury Press, 1983, 1106-1109).

[26]Millard Erickson, *How Shall They Be Saved?: The Destiny of Those Who Do Not Hear of Jesus* (Grand Rapids: Baker Books, 1996), 232.

final triumph of the power of redeeming love beyond any and all judgment.[27]

The position that hell is imposed only for a limited time goes back to several of the early church fathers. Origen (185-254 A. D.), for instance, held that even Satan himself one day would be welcomed into everlasting bliss since God's reconciling power eventually wins over all creaturely resistance. Not until 543 A. D., at a synod in Constantinople held in opposition to Origen, was the punishment of hell defined by the church as being of eternal duration.

According to this line of argument, Jesus taught his disciples to love even the enemy and forgive repeatedly. Therefore, a similar attitude in the heart of God suggests the eventual potential for universal salvation based on the repeated forgiving of God. The typical objection to universalism is that it is an overly sentimental, a "soft love" view that champions "cheap grace," a view that "does not measure the depths of sin in the human heart and the accountability to God for this lethal resistance."[28] Would not a tenuous hope that God is too kind to punish the ungodly become a deadly opiate for the consciences of millions? Many exponents of universalism, however, argue vigorously to the contrary. Note Jürgen Moltmann:

> The all-reconciling love is not what Bonhoeffer called "cheap grace." It is grace through and through, and grace is always and only free and for nothing. But it is

---

[27]The argument is made by universalists that aionios ("eternal") means the character and not the duration of punishment in key passages like Matt. 25:46. For the testimony of a biblical scholar who is a universalist, see *William Barclay: A Spiritual Autobiography* (Grand Rapids: Eerdmans, 1975). This popular biblical commentator states: "I am a convinced universalist. I believe that in the end all men will be gathered into the love of God." Not dismissing the heavy penalty of sin, Barclay says that "the choice is whether we accept God's offer and invitation willingly, or take the long and terrible way round through ages of purification" (58).

[28]Gabriel Fackre, *The Christian Story* (Grand Rapids: Eerdmans, 1984 ed.), 238.

born out of the profound suffering of God and is the costliest thing that God can give: himself in his Son, who has become our Brother, and who draws us through our hells. It is costliest grace.[29]

The case typically made by Christian universalists rests more on the presumed logic of love than on explicit biblical teaching. The position of the Wesleyan theological tradition, stressing the importance of *human response* to divine grace, does not embrace universalism, inviting as it is.

All three of these scenarios of the final destiny of good and evil can present some biblical support, with most going to the first.[30] Biblical metaphors of the ultimate future abound and, as with all aspects of eschatological expectation, modesty regarding detail is an appropriate human virtue. Humility here is furthered by awareness that all three scenarios, each insisting on biblical origin, have been influenced by various settings in which the church has done its thinking on the subject. Enlightenment views of human nature and destiny have contributed to universalist thinking. Earlier views of penal justice for criminals obviously impacted the traditional views of heaven and hell. Cultural views should not dictate the meaning of the biblical revelation, of course, but clearly they do influence our various understandings of it.

Some things do appear certain. There will be judgment and humans will be held accountable. The intent of God is that all people finally will be saved. Justice and love are coordinate divine realities and God truly is sovereign, even over evil and death. Exactly how all of these truths finally relate and resolve themselves is beyond our present knowledge. As Gabriel Fackre wisely concludes about universalism, for instance: "We cannot declare

---

[29]Jürgen Moltmann, *The Coming of God: Christian Eschatology* (Minneapolis: Fortress Press, 1996), 254.

[30]See William Crockett, ed., *Four Views on Hell* (Grand Rapids: Zondervan, 1996).

that God will save everyone, as the universalist does who claims to know too much about the final will and way of God. The home-coming of all is an article of *hope*, not an article of faith."[31] Without question, God will be all in all. But this does not neces-sarily mean that divine grace and divine love will be manifest in the same way for every person. In fact, for those who reject and deny their Lord, God's love will be destructive and chastening. For those who accept and rejoice in the Saviour, God's love will be restorative.

It is an error to think of hell as the sovereign territory of Satan that lies beyond the pale of God's love. Those who resisted divine love and spent their lives running from God do not finally get their wish by escaping the reach of that love. They are like Jerusalem. Jesus wept as he viewed her, a beloved city, on its way to tragedy nonetheless. Hell, rather than freedom from God's seeking and even suffering love, is the ongoing experience of isolation from the blessing of that love. Hell is not the ending of God's love, but the experiencing of its chosen dark side. While God remains present and loving, his love now cries instead of celebrates. But for those who gratefully receive Jesus, who is the light of the world, there is only joy at going-home time. Holiness in this life is crucial so that the eventual brightness of the light of God's love will illumine and not sear. Disciples are to become like God, holy as God is holy, in part so that when they reach heaven they will recognize where they are and really be at home.

The possibility of hell can arise from a vigorous understand-ing of the God who is loving grace. Donald Bloesch rightly affirms

---

[31] "I Believe in the Resurrection of the Body," *Interpretation* (January, 1992), 48. Karl Barth agrees, suggesting that we who believe in the astonishing gift of saving love in Jesus Christ hope and pray that there may be a final redemp-tion greater than now looks justified (*The Humanity of God*, John Knox Press, 1960, 61-62). Jerry Walls concludes, however, that "the traditional doctrine of hell should not be abandoned unless the case against it is clear and compelling, both scripturally and philosophically.... I [Walls] have tried to show that that case is yet to be made" (*Hell: The Logic of Damnation*, 158-159).

that "both heaven and hell are products of God's love as well as of his holiness."[32] Insists Stanley Grenz:

> We dare not confuse God's love with sentimentality. As the great Lover, God is also the avenging protector of the love relationship. Consequently, God's love has a dark side. Those who spurn or seek to destroy the holy love relationship God desires to enjoy with creation experience the divine love as protective jealously or wrath. Because God is eternal, our experience of God's love—whether as fellowship or as wrath—is also eternal. Just as the righteous enjoy unending community with God, so also those who set themselves in opposition to God's love experience his holy love eternally. For them, however, this experience is hell.[33]

With John Wesley, it probably is wisest to stay clear of both universalism and determinism (predestination). Christians can at least hope that, in light of 1 Timothy 2:4, an all-conquering divine love will prevail even beyond the fires of judgment. "Here is," says Fackre, "a modest Christian hope. . .leaving all to God's final will, yet shaped by the promise and power of a God who will be all in all." Christian faith, without ignoring the severe penalty for sin, hopes "that eternal death means the burning love of an eternal God cleansing the dross as only eternity can do, a lasting but not everlasting death."[34] If, however, such a hope turns out to be only wishful thinking, then our human sympathies for the people forever lost will have to be set aside and our human logic rest with this question: "Will not the Judge of all the earth do right?" (Gen. 18:25).

---

[32]Donald Bloesch, *Essentials of Evangelical Theology*, Vol. 2 (San Francisco: Harper & Row, 1979), 225.

[33]Stanley Grenz, *Theology for the Community of God* (Nashville: Broadman & Holman, 1994), 836.

[34]Gabriel Fackre, *The Christian Story* (1984 ed.), 240-241.

An Absence of the Sea: Heaven

The opposite of the frightening possibility of permanent separation from God is the joyous possibility of being forever "present with the Lord" (2 Cor. 5:8). The Christian concept of heaven is first one of wonderful presence. "Heaven" is an English word derived from the Anglo-Saxon *hebban* (to heave). It is the end result of a life of faith that is heaved upward into the very presence of God. Heaven is the "place" of God's welcoming and rewarding presence, the intended home of God's beloved. It is the fulfillment of Jesus' promise to disciples: "I am going there to prepare a place for you" (Jn. 14:2).

How might we image this wonderful place called heaven? We must rely on an image since this reality is beyond present experience or direct revelation. The people of ancient Israel were shepherds, farmers, and later city dwellers, but rarely were they sailors on the sea. They had a fascination with observations about the sea that made it a significant religious symbol for them. On the positive side, the sea suggested the unfathomable immensity of the being of God and of God's measureless love. As a Christian hymn says, "There's a wideness in God's mercy, like the wideness of the sea; there's a kindness in His justice, which is more than liberty."[35] The vastness of the watery expanse reminds one of God's eternity, and the gentle ripples the peace of God. But there also is a negative side. Terror often lurks in the deep. Evil forces inhabit the mysterious pathways of the sea.

The early baptismal liturgies of Christianity used images of watery demons now conquered by God's grace. The believer, submitting to immersion into the symbolic darkness of death, is raised from the waters, saved from the sea, resurrected with Christ to newness of life. Hope is expressed by stories of the sea being conquered. God divides the sea, breaks the heads of dragons, crushes

---

[35] "There's a Wideness in God's Mercy," in *Worship the Lord* (Anderson, Ind.: Warner Press, 1989), 107.

Leviathan (Ps. 74). At creation God triumphed as the Spirit breathed over the chaotic waters and brought order and life. The flood of God's judgment finally subsided so that life could resume on dry land outside the ark. The sea was parted so that slaves in Egypt might reach a promised land. Jesus calmed the fury of a foaming sea, saving his terrified disciples. Even the biblical vision of that which yet will be is put in a nautical metaphor. One day there will be a new order, heaven, a permanent place with *no more sea*, only a gentle river of the water of life flowing through the perfect city (Rev. 21). Here is a way of picturing heaven through a metaphor with vivid meaning to the ancient Israelite.

Other metaphors for heaven may speak more immediately to the transitoriness, rootlessness, even homelessness of people in fast-paced modern societies. Busy people, rather than fearing the sea, now fly over oceans without bothering even to look down (or cruise across, eating and playing all the way). A more effective metaphor now may be *the end of homelessness*. Jesus promised that he has gone to prepare *a place* (Jn. 14:2-3), a place where one truly belongs, has identity, where relationships again are whole since all who are there are in full and fulfilling relationship with God. The church, even now, is to be a sign of grace to the world, a pre-heaven fellowship of acceptance and love, a real *home place* for the lost and place-less. Christians, as pilgrim people in societies of listless wanderers, look forward to a place "whose architect and builder is God" (Heb. 11:10). They are to be faithful in the meantime, allowing God to make them such a place for others, even now.

Heaven will be an eternal life with God, free of the terrors and tears of the present sin-soaked existence. It will be fully restored relationships, unbroken communion in concert with all others who rejoice in God forever. Instead of isolated selves happy in their unending closets of private praise, the biblical images of heaven (e.g., new Jerusalem, great banquet) are communal, even as God exists as loving community ("trinity" teaching). Heaven will be the Kingdom of God, the "Kingdom of ultimate salvation, of the fulfillment of justice and perfect freedom, the Kingdom of unambiguous truth, of universal peace, of infinite love and overflowing joy, indeed eternal life."[36]

The biblical view of heaven is more dynamic and current than merely being a perfect "place" out there in the ultimate future. It is where God is fully obeyed (Ps. 103:19-20; Matt. 6:10). It is the eschatological realization of the presence and power of God. It is a consummation of the salvation process in which the penalty, power, and even presence of sin are eliminated. It is the realization of God's reign when the divine will is done on earth as it is in heaven (Lord's Prayer). Rather than believers going up to heaven, a legitimate and final hope, the immediate biblical concern is that heaven will come down to earth so that "the earth will be filled with the knowledge of the glory of Yahweh, as the waters cover the sea" (Hab. 2:14; Isa. 11:9).

Therefore, explored in the next and final chapter is the now ongoing process of the people of God journeying through this world's wilderness toward the fullness of what yet will be. The journey for the church means being a "holy nation" (1 Pet. 2:9) whose citizens carry a "new passport—that of the holy nation which God is forming."[37] While on their way to heaven, God's people are to function redemptively as a heavenly people with a heavenly purpose in this present world.

---

[36]Hans Küng, *Credo: The Apostles' Creed Explained for Today* (N. Y.: Doubleday, 1993), 183-184.

[37]Alan Kreider, *Journey Towards Holiness* (Scottdale, Pa.: Herald Press, 1987), 48.

Matters Worth Exploring

1. Why does this chapter speak of "images" of Christian hope? Are there limits to human knowledge of God's future? Is there danger that Christian disciples will get so curious about the coming future that they will lose the central focus on their call from God related to life now?

2. How is the Jewish festival of Hanukkah an apt image for symbolizing hope in the midst of apparent disaster?

3. How many "comings" of Jesus are there? How is the Spirit of Christ who came at Pentecost crucial for disciples who want to be God's faithful people before the final coming?

4. Why is the resurrection of Jesus after his crucifixion so important for Christian faith? Will our "bodies" also be resurrected some day just like his was?

5. Is hell the permanent state of all those who are faithless and refuse God's love? Is it a place entirely separate from the presence of God? Do Christians have sure answers to such questions?

6. Why are some biblical interpreters tempted to believe that all of creation, including all people, finally will be restored to right relationship with God? How might such an expectation be hurtful to our view of the seriousness of sin and the urgency of evangelism? Is such an expectation the natural outgrowth of belief in the great love of God?

7. Describe what heaven will be like. Do you find yourself necessarily reaching for images of heaven that are drawn from your own experience?

8. In what way should the church be the "heavenly people" already present on earth?

Chapter 9

THY TENTS SHALL BE OUR HOME

⁂

The Lord is good to those who wait for him, to the soul that seeks him. It is good that one should wait quietly for the salvation of the Lord. (Lam. 3:25-26) Do not lag in zeal, be ardent in spirit, serve the Lord. Rejoice in hope, be patient in suffering, persevere in prayer. Contribute to the needs of the saints; extend hospitality to strangers. (Rom. 12:11-13)

⁂

Holy Spirit, come and dwell within me. Touch me with the joy of Your presence and fill me with the power of Your love. For now is the time of celebration; the revealing of Your way of being. Amen.[1]

⁂

The ancient Hebrews did not begin their national story with the stability of the Temple in Jerusalem, but with the mobility of tents in the desert. They were not residing with a domesticated god "like the nations," but following faithfully after the God who was moving through human history with redemptive purpose. That purpose still proceeds, and God's faithful followers are to be moving with it toward what one day will be its final destiny. Christian believers are to be mobile, tenting with God in this passing world, looking toward a promised future and being faithful in the meantime.

---

[1]Prayer from Schuyler Rhodes, *Words to the Silence: A Book of Uncommon Prayer* (Prescott, AR: Educational Ministries, Inc., 1994).

The proper image for living the Christian life today is still that of believing people joining the divine journey.[2] This is the model of the life of faith that comes from the Hebrew Scriptures. Abraham walked with God by faith. The Jews were liberated from Egyptian bondage and then journeyed together in the wilderness in dependence on the provision and guidance of God. Life is a pilgrimage. A proper relationship with God is the essence of the walk of faith. Jürgen Moltmann speaks this way of his own understanding of the Christian life, now liberated by God, but still very much on the way. "My image is the Exodus of the people, and I await theological Red Sea miracles."[3] We journey on toward the final fulfillment of God's promise, toward the anticipated new creation, the anticipated Canaan land of God.

The Epistle to the Hebrews proclaims Jesus as the pioneer who already has arrived at the goal and now acts as the "perfecter of our faith" (Heb. 12:2) while his disciples journey on. Christians are pilgrims on an adventure of faith. It is a new exodus-wilderness-Canaan journey with God. Believers are on-the-way people, rescued by grace from all Egypts of oppression and sin, marching through the wilderness of this present world, always inspired and comforted by the promise of the coming Canaan of final rest in God's perfect and perpetual presence. This hope for and early foretaste of the coming Canaan of final consummation braces the resolve of the wilderness people to be faithful in the meantime.

The Bible, the history book of God's promises to believers and the deposit of God's expectations of those believers, is to be seen as the divine communication that reveals to us "the coming God."[4] Waiting for the fullness of that coming, however, is not

---

[2] See, for instance, Barry Callen, *Journeying Together: A Documentary History of the Church of God (Anderson)* (Anderson, Ind.: Leadership Council and Warner Press, 1996).

[3] Jürgen Moltmann, *The Coming of God: Christian Eschatology* (Minneapolis: Fortress Press, 1996), xiv.

[4] Jürgen Moltmann, *The Experiment in Hope* (Philadelphia: Fortress Press, 1975), 45.

easy. The classic expression of the difficulty was expressed by Augustine (354-430 A.D.) in the face of the collapse of the Roman Empire. His famous book *City of God* pictures the dilemma of Christians who find themselves living simultaneously in two "cities," the one of God and the one of this present evil world. The church is in exile in the "city of the world," being very much in it and seeking to be very much not of it. What characterizes each city is the direction of love, whether it is toward the things of this passing world (the earthly city) or toward God and God's future (the heavenly city). The journey through time is inevitable, but the nature of the journey, the direction of affection and expectation, is a choice.

Augustine lived many centuries ago when the cohesive structure of civilization as he knew it was crumbling. At the end of the twentieth century the circumstance he knew seems to be reoccurring—or even worse. Never before has humanity been so poised and so able to unleash destructive power. In a few hours earth now can be made literally uninhabitable. Never before has human greed, over-population, ethnic hatred, and deliberate poisoning activity threatened to bring a physical collapse of the whole environment that supports life itself. In this especially troubled setting, Christians are called to journey on, shaped by key memories and a dream, a heavenly vision that is intended to make a real difference in who they are and what they do on the way. The light of the future of God shines on faithful believers and is intended to alter the manner of their living in the troubled present. Those "empowered to see the Light and walk in the Light traverse the shadowy valley in hope."[5]

Journeying in faith includes being faithful in the meantime. Those on their way to God's future are to be setting up signs along the road that show to others the manner of the Kingdom of God and the way toward its final realization. Martin Buber speaks of the

---

[5]Gabriel Fackre, *The Christian Story*, rev. ed. (Grand Rapids: Eerdmans, 1978, 1984), 247.

"narrow bridge," a precarious pathway along which humanity moves in its ever-passing presents. The way is dark, lacks external securities, but is illumined from moment to moment by gracious lightening flashes of God's enlightening presence. Christians are themselves to be flashes of God's gracious lightening helping to illuminate the darkness of every present for every groping person. Authentic celebration is one important form of such illumination.

Celebrating In Advance

Christian believers are to celebrate in every present the glory of that which is yet to be. In Jesus, the eschaton (end and fulfill-ment of all things) already has begun to occur. In Him the begin-ning of the end began long ago. His resurrection is the first fruit of the final resurrection. The gift of Christ's Spirit is a foretaste of the glory soon to come. The peace God places in the hearts of humble believers by the ministry of the Spirit foreshadows a larger shalom to be part of the coming shalom of the Kingdom of God. As God's people in the world, the church is to be a sign of the divine Kingdom already becoming present. In spite of its imperfections, the church is to point beyond itself to the vision which it seeks to embody and the coming future it is called to anticipate.

The act of celebration rejoices in something good that was and exudes hope in what should and can yet be. It is a delightful dance pointing backward and forward simultaneously. Celebrating the presence of hope brings strength and identity to the present. True celebration is more than only itself since it is spawned in some wonderful past and points ahead with invigorating confi-dence. In a Christian context, this pointing beyond, the proleptic aspect of Christian existence, is nowhere better exhibited than in the church's liturgical actions. Such actions are times of celebra-tion that mark the church as a distinctive social body with differ-ent standards, divine foundations, and a compelling hope that per-meates its present life. The fullness of Christian hope is dramatized in the remembering, celebrating, and witnessing that are inherent especially in Christian baptism and the Lord's supper. These sacred celebration practices have often helped to maintain in Christian consciousness the vision of both last things and present responsibilities, all based on the prior action of God[6] and oriented to *what now should be* in light of *what soon will be*. They pattern and help enable the distinctive life that should characterize the community of believers in the meantime, that is, before the return of Christ to end the present era.

1. Baptism. Baptism gives vivid expression to a new believer's having been convicted of sin, turned in penitence from sin to new life in Christ, and thus become a member of God's people on journey and mission. Baptism into Christ is the conscious choice of the new believer to be in solidarity with Christ in God's redemptive plan and with Christ's new people in their redemptive reach to a lost world. It signifies membership in the one church that is committed to defying the destructive barriers that sin has erected between human beings. It is public initiation into God's people and into a life of radical discipleship that is defined and enabled by Christ's life, death, and resurrection. Baptism is a ceremonial celebration of the burial and resurrection of our Lord, dramatizing the believer's following Christ in such death and resurrection (Gal. 2:20; Col. 2:12; Rom. 6:2, 4) for one's own sake and for that of the world.

The eschatological significance of Christian baptism is crucial. The practice appears dramatically in the New Testament, signifying identification with the coming Kingdom of God and abandonment of all reliance on traditional religious identity for salvation (Matt. 3:9; Lk. 3:8). It demonstrates that believers *now* are heirs of the Kingdom by divine grace (1 Cor. 6:9-11; Jn. 3:3-5). Baptismal candidates do more than witness to an inner spiritual experience, although they surely are doing that. They also commit to life in the body of Christ, Kingdom life possible only through

---

[6]See Geoffrey Wainwright, *Eucharist and Eschatology* (London: Epworth Press, 1971).

249

the power of the Spirit. In that transforming process new believers thrive and truly celebrate the already come and still coming Kingdom of God. Baptism, therefore, signifies that a Christian has received and is becoming a willing instrument of the Spirit of God as the "first fruits" (Rom. 8:23) of the grand harvest still ahead.

Baptism involves the believer in the drama of the shifting of the aeons, symbolized well by the process of total immersion (submerged into death and resurrected to new life). All prior definitions of human identity are thus transcended. Paul writes that, if anyone is baptized into Christ, the whole world is new and the standards of the previous world have ceased to count in the proper estimate of a person (2 Cor. 5:16-17). As an advance sign of the Kingdom coming, among the baptized the barriers of human discrimination are to come down (Gal. 3:28) in the face of a new humanity (Eph. 2) and a new creation (2 Cor. 5).

This is celebration time! The reign of Christ, before it becomes fully evident one day, is joyously recognized to have begun already on the day of an individual's baptism. Accepting Christian baptism should be a joyful public event that acts out in dramatic symbol the commitment of a grateful new believer to be faithful by being a living sign of God's coming future in the meantime of the years yet at hand.

2. Lord's Supper. The Lord's supper is a Christian practice with deep Hebrew roots. The annual Passover celebration recalled ancient Israel's protection from death on the way to its liberation from slavery. Jesus, a faithful Jew fulfilling this divinely initiated Hebrew tradition, adapted this perennial festival of grateful memory and invested it with the fresh meaning of his own coming death and a sure hope for all who would be liberated by it to a new future with God.

This sacred supper, by the Lord's own direction, is to be viewed as a Christian celebration of thanksgiving for the foundational fulfillment of God's plan of redemption. We see in this celebration all the elements of any story—setting, theme, plot, and resolution. The setting is human history, the theme the rescue of humankind from self-destruction, the plot God's redemptive entry into human history, especially in the costly work of Jesus Christ, and the resolution, the final judgment and consummation of the Kingdom of God. Stated otherwise:

Setting   Thanksgiving to the Father (creation)
              Give thanks to God for bread (1 Cor. 11:24)
Theme   Memorial of the Son (redemption)
              This is Jesus' body given for us (1 Cor. 11:24)
Plot   Communion of the Faithful (church)
              We are one body as we partake together
              (1 Cor. 10:16-17)
Resolution   Meal of the Kingdom (eschatology)
              Do this until he comes again (1 Cor. 11:26)

First Corinthians 11:20-34 highlights three dimensions of the Lord's supper that transform and redirect past realities and future expectations into present mission. Beyond remembering a given past and anticipating a glorious future, participation with Jesus at this table highlights a present responsibility. The meal of Christ is at once a sanctifying, a social, and a seditious sacrament.[7] By the power of the age to come, faithful participation in the Lord's supper remembers (re-members), alters destructive relationships by "discerning the body of Christ," and rejects the prevailing values of the world in favor of those of the coming Kingdom.[8] This sacred meal is a living sign of the coming Kingdom of God, a declaration of believers that by faith they are leaving behind the old world in joyful and grateful anticipation of

---

[7]The word "sacrament" is not used here to mean that God's saving grace is available to anyone because of mere participation in the Lord's supper or any other church practice. What is available is a nurturing and sustaining grace for each participating believer who is genuinely thankful and committed.

[8]M. Robert Mulholland, Jr., "Discerning the Body," in *Weavings: A Journal of the Christian Spiritual Life* (May/June, 1993), 20-26.

the new and that they are prepared by the power of the Spirit to begin living the radical life of the coming new creation, in part by being faithful in the meantime.

The supper is a love-feast of community celebration (Acts 2:42, 46) staged in light of the eschatological banquet prophesied by Isaiah (25:6-8) and already begun in Jesus (Acts 10:40-41; Lk. 24:30-31; Jn. 21:9-14). The sacrificial Christ who is made known to us in the breaking of the bread and sharing of the cup is the very One who one day soon will be the host at the great feast of the Lamb! The Lamb now on the altar is alone worthy "to receive power and wealth and wisdom and might and honor and glory and blessing!" (Rev. 5:12). This very Lamb, eventually to be recognized as such by all people, already is to be the church's Lord. Only obedience to this present lordship enables the church to model in its own life the future of the divine Kingdom that Jesus came to proclaim and one day soon will return to fulfill.

In the periodic taking of the bread and cup, disciples not only celebrate a memorial of Jesus' death; they proclaim by an advance celebration their wonderful awareness of the coming of the anticipated future consummation of the reign of God: "For as often as you eat this bread and drink the cup, you proclaim the Lord's death *until he comes*" (1 Cor. 11:26). The church lives between Pentecost and Parousia. These pivotal "P's," of the Spirit's coming to the church and of the Christ eventually coming again to receive the faithful church unto himself, form the brackets of the church's present life and mission. The church is invited to celebrate in symbol and embody in life the reign of God already come, coming now, and soon to come in its fullness at the end of time.[9] Disciples of the Christ celebrate as they journey, serving faithfully as symbols of new creation on their way to their destiny with God.

---

[9]John Howard Yoder, for instance, speaks of the Lord's supper as "an act of economic ethics." The eucharistic meal, what we Christians are to do together, was "their ordinary partaking together of food for the body" (*The Royal Priesthood*, Eerdmans, 1994, 365).

All of this celebrating, embodying, and anticipating is enabled by the work of the Spirit, the God of loving grace who is sanctifying and sustaining those who believe and are being faithful. Worship is at the center of the church's life. In worship, especially in the Lord's supper, "the Christian community anticipates and symbolically celebrates the praise of God's glory that will be consummated in the eschatological renewal of all creation in the new Jerusalem."[10] Note a similar point made about the "Eucharist"[11] in response to chapter twenty of the Book of Revelation:

> To participate in the Eucharist is to experience the reality of the first resurrection and to affirm and actualize the priesthood of the church and its reigning with Christ. The Eucharist is the triumphal coronation liturgy of New Jerusalem. But the church must also realize that this is a priesthood that is carried out in the midst of a world that constantly pressures the church to worship the Beast and its image and to receive its mark.[12]

To resist such constant pressure to false worship, the church is called to remember and periodically celebrate the divine source of its special life and to model this new life to the world. In the interim before Christ returns and the present age of the Spirit climaxes, the church is to celebrate and serve faithfully out of its memory and in its anticipation. Death remains the enemy because it still appears to be the ultimate threat to a celebration of life. Even so, with a bracing faith in God's coming future of life eternal, already being celebrated and lived out in the present, the faithful church is helped more

---

[10]Wolfhart Pannenberg, *Christian Spirituality* (Westminster Press, 1983), 36.

[11]The word "Eucharist" means a celebration of thanksgiving and is used by some Christian traditions as the word for the Lord's supper.

[12]M. Robert Mulholland, Jr., *Holy Living in an Unholy World: Revelation* (Grand Rapids: Francis Asbury Press, 1990), 311.

clearly to "identify by contrast all that menaces and limits life and so to oppose it in the name of the eschatological life and liveliness for which we hope and which even now we begin to celebrate."[13] The unlimited and unimpeded celebrating that one day will go on without end around the throne of the triumphant Christ is to begin now around Christ's table and throughout Christ's world.

Accountability and Mission

The Apostles' Creed affirms the New Testament teaching that Jesus will come again to judge. For the Christian this is reason to hope, not fear. Looking to the Hebrew Scriptures, the fundamental meaning of a "judge" is salvation and deliverance. People like Deborah and Samson were not called judges of Israel primarily because they handed out rewards and punishments in a court of law. What they did in judging Israel was rescue God's people from bondage to oppressive powers, reintroducing justice, reconciliation, and peace. A byproduct of rescuing the repentant, of course, is condemning the guilty; but condemnation is secondary to the central biblical theme of liberation.

By delivering the weak and oppressed, the judge stands in opposition to those who are unjust in their use of power. There will be a day when all things will be made right (Rev. 11:15). In the meantime, as God's faithful transients in this present world, those already forgiven by Judge Jesus are to be judging like Jesus in mercy and liberating love. Believers will be judged in the future according to how they judged in the present (Mark 8:38). The Christ who taught a new way of life (e. g., in the Sermon on the Mount) finally will judge on the basis of a review of that expected way of life. Believers are freed by the Spirit to judge justly in every now, at risk to themselves, because they have faith in the coming resurrection that will overcome death, including their own. Such good news about the future inspires the often troubled journey of

---

[13]Theodore Jennings, *Loyalty To God* (Nashville: Abingdon Press, 1992), 224.

believers through this world, allowing those who are in Christ to be good news to many others who, in the absence of such belief, have lost all hope.

One day all people will give a final account. We all will be judged on our response to the love of God in Jesus Christ. Are we in faithful and thus saving relationship with Christ? Have we chosen to be responsible in the ways that a saving relationship would imply (Matt. 12:36; 2 Cor. 5:10)? Have we been faithful in the meantime, judging in mercy and justice as we traveled the rocky roads of this world? While salvation is by grace through faith and is not earned by any works of our own, genuine salvation nonetheless is intended to issue in lives of love, justice, and reconciliation, all fruit of the Spirit and evidences of the reality of restored relationship with God. Judgment on this basis is both a present reality (Jn. 3:18; Rom. 1:18-32) and an unavoidable fact of the last day (Rev. 20:11-15). We who are made new in Jesus Christ by faith are expected to be faithful to the implications of that newness until he comes.

The final judgment will establish as enduring reality the nature of the relationship with Christ that was chosen in this life. Although no person was born by his or her own choice, the nature of human destiny is only by choice (Heb. 10:26-31). Death apparently ends the choosing process (Gen. 27:2-10; Eccles. 11:3; Jn. 9:4). At death "the burden of freedom is lifted; the wealth of freedom spent."[14] The sober reality is all too clear. Our individual life stories in this present world are significant and have permanent implications in the final unfolding of the divine story.[15]

---

[14]Thomas Oden, *Life in the Spirit* (San Francisco: Harper, 1992), 379.

[15]This stance, one might argue, does not take into adequate account those many people who have never heard of Christ in this life, or at least were never faced with a credible witness that allowed reasonable opportunity for a response of saving faith. See the section "Pluralism and Particularity" in chapter one of Barry Callen, *God As Loving Grace* (Evangel Press, 1996). The phrase "He descended into Hades" in the Apostles' Creed apparently refers to the concern of many early church leaders about the destiny of those who never hear the good news in Christ. Christ's saving work may reach beyond death in such special cases. See 1 Pet. 3:19-20, 4:6; Eph. 4:8-9; Rom. 10:7.

This permanence of the consequences of human choice for or against reconciliation with God may be put this way: "If the concept of the reign of God suggests that there are real potentials within history that we have not yet dreamed of, the concept of eternal life affirms the everlasting importance of that history and our lives within it, individually and corporately. The details of our lives—what we bind in history and loose in history, what we heal and what we destroy—abide forever in the God who is the heart of the universe."[16] So a Christian's eschatological vision, while looking beyond human history, does so in a way that dignifies rather than nullifies the current significance of that history. The intent of biblical prophecy is to "energize around the vision of a new possibility."[17] That possibility is *now* as well as *then*. It is accountability and mission in addition to being hope in everlasting life with God.

Jürgen Moltmann shows the way to relate properly the vision of a promised future and Christian mission for the present. While a prisoner of war in a British camp until 1948, Moltmann observed that prisoners with hope were best suited for survival. Later, he came to an important conclusion. Eschatological expectation "produces here a horizon of ethical intuitions which, in turn, gives meaning to the concrete historical initiatives."[18] He thus set out to realize the Christian hope in the service of present world transformation. Christians are to be faithful in the meantime, making a difference in the world's *now* by the power of God's *hereafter*. Proper Christian theology thrusts believers toward the praxis of Christian discipleship in a needy world. "The promise of divine righteousness in the event of the justification of the godless," he concluded, "leads immediately to the hunger for divine right in the godless world, and thus to the struggle for public, bodily obedience. The

---

[16]Delwin Brown, in Clark Pinnock and Brown, *Theological Crossfire* (Grand Rapids: Zondervan Publishing, 1990), 241.

[17]As quoted in Myron Augsburger, *The Peace Maker* (Nashville: Abingdon Press, 1987), 13.

[18]Jürgen Moltmann, in *Theology Today* 25:3 (October, 1968), 370.

promise of the resurrection of the dead leads at once to love for the true life of the whole imperiled and impaired creation."[19]

The promise of the sure fulfillment of what God has begun creates hope that makes believers restless in the present, dissatisfied with the evil status quo, determined to be God's sacrificial instruments for change. There is important ethical significance in Moltmann's manner of viewing Christian eschatology. In summary:

> What we dream shapes what we do; hence, the importance of eschatological recovery for social change. The *confidence* that the End will truly consummate the purposes of God, as anticipated by Exodus and Easter, energizes the believing community to set up signs on the way to that kingdom and city. Hope mobilizes, while despair paralyzes. The *content* of that End—glorified bodies, the "holy city with the radiance of some priceless jewel" (Rev. 21:10), crystal waters, and flourishing forests—renders unacceptable emaciated bodies, cities of the homeless and hapless, poisonous rivers, and decimated forests. Eschatology makes us pilgrims and strangers in the wilderness short of the New Creation and disturbers of the facile peace of the way things are.[20]

One New Testament writer speaks in truly radical terms of the destruction of this present world (2 Peter 3:10ff). The question he then poses is what sort of people we should be in light of this certain prospect (2 Peter 3:11, 14). In the midst of descriptions in the Book of Revelation of the new heaven and earth are sprinkled warnings about proper life before the end comes (Rev. 21:8, 27; 22:3, 11, 14-15). This final book of the New Testament lays bare for persecuted Christians "the meaning of the present in the con-

---

[19]Jürgen Moltmann, *Theology of Hope* (London: SCM Press, 1967), 225.

[20]As quoted by Gabriel Fackre, "I Believe in the Resurrection of the Body," *Interpretation* (January, 1992), 46.

text of history's march to its consummation."[21] The meaning is dominated by hope, but a hope yet facing more of a difficult journey this side of the final victory of the Lamb of God. The Christian life is the dangerous life of a pilgrim in an alien world. Jesus said that his disciples would experience persecution in this world (Jn. 16:33). Kingdom victories are assured, but they will be at real cost since "the sign of the cross hangs over every kingdom victory. Yet God is not mocked! The ultimate triumph is Christ's."[22] So Christians journey on as celebrating pilgrims who have a sure guide, real purpose, and a definite destiny.

In the Wilderness with God

Since the earliest generations of Christians, it has been necessary to learn to deal with the delay of Christ's coming again. The problem of delay clearly had a long history in the Hebrew tradition. In the book of Habakkuk, for instance, a prophet surveys the evil and violence that marked his times and asks why God is so slow to correct the situation: "O Lord, how long shall I cry for help, and you will not listen?... Why do you make me see wrongdoing and look at trouble?" (Hab. 1:2-3). The divine answer received was: "There is still a vision for the appointed time; it speaks of the end, and does not lie. If it seems to tarry, wait for it; it will surely come, it will not delay.... The righteous live by their faith" (Hab. 2:3-4).

In the early Christian church, the seeming delay of the anticipated soon return of Jesus focused on the fear that believers who died prior to the return would miss out on the chance to experience the new era. Paul addressed this in 1 Thessalonians 4:13-18. But there seems to have developed early even more radical questions about the delayed return of the resurrected Christ. So we find this

---

[21]William Dumbrell, *The Search for Order: Biblical Eschatology in Focus* (Grand Rapids: Baker Books, 1994), 331.

[22]Boyd Hunt, *Redeemed! Eschatological Redemption and the Kingdom of God* (Nashville: Broadman & Holman, 1993), 152.

in 2 Peter 3:3-4: "In the last days scoffers will come, scoffing and indulging their own lusts and saying, 'Where is the promise of his coming? For ever since our ancestors died, all things continue as they were from the beginning of creation'." Peter argues in response (3:8-13) that God's apparent slowness actually represents a merciful extension of the time during which believers can witness to the good news of Christ's first coming and sinners can repent. During the extension, while traveling through the wilderness of this world, it remains the steadfast hope of believers that the dusty trail will one day turn into gold (Rev. 21:18). Meanwhile, brothers and sisters in the faith journey together toward a Kingdom whose Prince has come ahead in the current ministry of the Spirit and has promised to be a constant escort on the way (Matt. 18:20; 28:20).

Beyond the issue of *delay* is the other troubling concern, the crucial issue of *shift*. The United States at the end of the twentieth century is no longer a nation formed in, nurtured by, or even extensively permeated with the Judeo-Christian tradition. Just a generation or two ago the Christian faith tended to be the only real religious option readily available to most Americans. The society's rhetoric, values, and laws drew heavily on this tradition. But now a major shift has come. Now "few parents, college students, or auto mechanics...believe that one becomes Christian today by simply breathing the air and drinking the water in the generous, hospitable environment of Christendom America.... It is no longer 'our world'—if it ever was."[23]

The demise of a sturdy and singular Christian culture in the United States is not, however, a wholly bad thing. Removing the artificial supports to Christian faith leads increasingly into the wilderness with God—precisely where those early children of Israel found themselves as they moved from slavery to the promised land. Being in the wilderness is hardly comfortable, but it does help a people to know who they really are and on what they

---

[23]Stanley Hauerwas, William Willimon, *Resident Aliens* (Nashville: Abingdon Press, 1989), 16-17.

really should and can depend. The end of a culture on which Christians can rely to prop them up and help mold their young is an opportunity for the church to find again its own soul.

Free of the temptation to accommodate to a surrounding and supporting ethos, no longer able to rest on the general culture for approval and support, North American and European Christians now "are at last free to be faithful in a way that makes being a Christian today an exciting adventure."[24] To gain the attention of Generation X (Baby Busters), the church will have to present a credible alternative to the world, actually and visibly embodying what it hopes the young will take seriously in the church's words of witness. Successful evangelism will take more than innovative marketing of the church's religious wares. The authors of *Reckless Hope*, for instance, explain well how basic biblical concepts like creation (for a generation concerned about the earth's environment), covenant (for a generation that has grown up with broken promises), and community (for a generation hungry for true family) have power to speak today—especially if the speaker is a credible model of these biblical concepts.[25] If the world today is a wilderness, then the church is to be a living oasis traveling refreshingly in its midst.

One should not romanticize the wilderness adventure. The very idea of "wilderness" suggests the mysterious and unknown. There is great distance, danger, dryness, and risk of despair. Thomas Merton once pondered prayerfully the awkward experience of being in the wilderness with God:

> My Lord God, I have no idea where I am going. I do not see the road ahead of me. I cannot know for certain where it will end.... I believe that the desire to please you does in fact please you. And I hope I have that desire in all that I am doing.... And I know that if I do

---

[24]Ibid., 18.

[25]Todd Hahn and David Verhaagen, *Reckless Hope* (Grand Rapids: Baker Books, 1996), 113-123.

this you will lead me by the right road though I may know nothing about it. Therefore will I trust you always though I may seem to be lost and in the shadow of death. I will not fear, for you are ever with me, and you will never leave me to face my perils alone.[26]

Wilderness is named "Antichrist" in the New Testament. There is frightening anti-gospel opposition out there in the untamed wildness of the world. It was clear to the New Testament writers that Antichrist was no distant figure who would appear only once at some isolated end time. John describes this opposer to the Christ in no uncertain terms (1 Jn. 2:18-22; 4:3; 2 Jn. 7) and warns the congregation of his time to be on guard. Paul alerted the Thessalonians about the enemy (2 Thess. 2) who already was at hand. Two important matters appear clear from these texts. The Antichrist is a *present* and a *plural* reality.[27] In all times and circumstances, the church is called to "test the spirits to see if they are of God, since so many deceivers and false prophets exist in the world" (1 Jn. 4:1-3; 2 Jn. 7). That was the case in the first generations of Christians and in all others ever since.

A prominent problem characteristic of the present generation, at least in the developed Western world, is seen in a college student who walked across campus wearing a big button that read: "Since I gave up hope, I feel much better." Our time of "downsizing" has taken hope down with it for many people. Suicide is not typically the result, just a quiet resignation that things are not good and probably will not get better. People are left to traveling an empty wilderness with no sure guide and no particular goal. They are not going anywhere, just surviving the perils of each day. In order to avoid becoming part of this problem themselves, Christian

---

[26]Thomas Merton, from *Thoughts in Solitude* (N. Y.: Farrar, Straus, and Giroux, 1958).

[27]Adrio König, *The Eclipse of Christ in Eschatology* (Grand Rapids: Eerdmans, 1989), 175.

believers always must hope that their own minds are being renewed and their persons and corporate life as the church are being shaped in ways that will allow them to know and do the will of God (cf. Rom. 12:2). So Christians sing and pray:

The future lies unseen ahead, It holds I know not what;
But still I know I need not dread, For Jesus fails me not.

The glory of eternal dawn, Shines from His smiling face;
So trusting Him, I follow on, With heart made strong by grace.[28]

Such praying reaches upward in the present time of unfinished journeying or continuing interim. Using the typology of Exodus, the interim between the *passion* of Jesus in ancient Jerusalem and the *parousia* of the Risen Lord yet to be seen by all the world, between the Egypt of oppression and the Canaan of promise, is the wilderness wandering for believers. To those who live in this middle period, "the ends of the ages have come" (1 Cor. 10:11). Satan is "the god of this world" (2 Cor. 4:4); nonetheless, one of the elements in present Christian experience is a taste of "the powers of the age to come" (Heb. 6:5). The hopeless can find hope when this taste becomes obvious to the public through the faithfulness of believers.

Here is the really good news. There is help for the journey! God not only gives bread from heaven and water from the rock, but, as Isaac Watts' familiar lines put it:

The hill of Zion yields
A thousand sacred sweets
Before we reach the heavenly fields
Or walk the golden streets.[29]

---

[28]Lyrics of the Charles Naylor hymn, "I'll Follow With Rejoicing" (vss. 1, 4) as in *Worship the Lord* (Anderson, Ind.: Warner Press, 1989), 436.

[29]As quoted by Dale Moody, *The Word of Truth* (Grand Rapids: Eerdmans, 1981), 521.

The image of a mirage is helpful as Christians seek to be faithful in the meantime (although all images have their limitations). A mirage, as opposed to an hallucination, has a definite relationship to reality. The reality may not be on the immediate horizon as it often seems and as we who gaze longingly hope. Even so, the shape of the mirage relates to coming reality. Christians journey through the present wilderness and may not reach the vaguely visible goal as soon as they think they should. But as the image of Jesus Christ stays before the longing eyes of faith, those eyes know the history of Jesus and by faith the general nature of his coming reality. They know shape and quality if not the exact location and timing of the destiny of faithful believers. The shape of life that is to be lived in the meantime is a servant stance in this world. Having confidence in the coming resurrection of the dead and the life everlasting, it is more possible in the meantime to face with defiance, joy, and confidence the forces that now breed injustice, oppression, and death. We who are drawn on by the never-fading image of the already come and yet coming Christ discover the courage to die for the sake of life. Indeed, we "will not be allured by the promise of life after death as though this meant the denial of life before death."[30]

End of the Story

True believers are those who have learned history's real direction and its Lord and have chosen to be servants of the Christ, servants who are faithful in the wilderness of time until time is no more. Then one day, some day soon, comes the culmination. From beginning to end, with Jesus Christ always the center of history's meaning and hope, God stands steady and supreme. The grand story of redemption, stretching across millennia, eventually will be brought to its end. God once declared through Isaiah: "Behold, I will create new heavens and a new

---

[30]Theodore Jennings, *Loyalty To God* (Nashville: Abingdon Press, 1992), 224.

earth" (65:17). This promise became the basis of the following vision recorded in the Book of Revelation: "Then I saw a new heaven and a new earth, for the first heaven and the first earth had passed away" (21:1).

God is Prologue, Plot, and Epilogue to the whole biblical story of creation's origin and redemption. The beginnings of this story presume the creating, preserving, covenanting God who comes to the historical process rather than abandoning it in its now fallen state. The feature chapter of the story focuses on the reconciling and liberating work of Jesus of Nazareth in whom God suffers on behalf of the salvation of all creation. The continuing thrust of the story reveals the Spirit of God carrying forward that which God planned from eternity and provides in Christ. The dramatic birth of the church shifts the scene back and forth from the inner life of personal renewal of individual believers to the church's outer mission of peace, justice, and liberation. The new community of the Spirit, the church, is called to model for the world that which is yet to be. It is to strengthen believers for active participation with the victorious Christ in a breaking of the power of canceled sin. Such participation comes in the interim before all such evil will be divinely stopped and judged forever.

While the church is being faithful in the meantime, all of time moves toward the ultimate consummation, the end of the biblical story of God-with-us for our salvation. God is before all and after all, the Alpha and Omega. "Before the mountains were brought forth, or ever you had formed the earth and the world, from everlasting to everlasting you are God" (Ps. 90:2). God predates and postdates all else. God far exceeds the reach of all human reflection on the divine nature. Nonetheless, God is with us in Christ through the present ministry of the Spirit, and thus is truly known even in the midst of mystery.

Praise the Lord! Take courage! Life's sorrows can be endured. The church's mission can be accomplished. Ultimate divine meaning one day will overcome temporary human madness.

No sickness or sorrow need mar the happiness that lies ahead. Christian faith, nurtured by the biblical story of God-with-us, knows that some day "with time behind us, eternity before us, the angels and the redeemed of all ages around us—this will be heaven, our eternal home."[31] Therefore, believers are to stand firm, giving themselves fully to the current work of the Lord, always aware that their work is not in vain (1 Cor. 15:58). Since the church acts under the Lord's mandate (Matt. 28:19-20), the very gates of Hades cannot prevail against it (Matt. 16:18).

The detail of what lies ahead is not yet ours to know. Believers live in the dim light of the Already—Not Yet continuum, the dawning rather than the high noon of the Kingdom. But they know the Christ who is key to both past and future, and they know that the powers of darkness do not control the future. So they travel confidently on, making the tents of God their daily home. Christian eschatology, then, is God's call for all who are his faithful ones to engage the powers of evil still active in the present, assured of God's future no matter what happens.

Beloved church leader Louis (Pete) Meyer died of cancer in December, 1993. On Easter Sunday morning, 1993, he stood weakly in the pulpit of Park Place Church of God in Anderson, Indiana (his home congregation), having been asked to share his testimony of Christian hope, even as his body was dying of a humanly incurable disease. He shared the following with a trembling voice and quiet assurance:

> ...the real test is to leave the future in God's hands without demanding a detailed road map. That requires much more trust than many of us have. Therein is the lesson of Easter—the power of the resurrection.... There is hope. God can be trusted. There are no conditions, not even death, that can rob us or have the power

---

[31]F. G. Smith, 15th rev. ed., *What the Bible Teaches* (Anderson, Ind.: Gospel Trumpet Co., 1913, 1945), 360.

to divert us from the path to abundant life. May God make it so in your life.[32]

There is a God, a goal, the possibility for salvation, a right way to go, hope! Along life's roadways, believers, as God's loving agents of reconciliation, are privileged to leave signs pointing toward the New Jerusalem. All the while, whatever the pain or doubt, the Spirit enables the glad song of the saints of God:

> The future lies unseen ahead, It holds I know not what;
> But still I know I need not dread, For Jesus fails me not.

> The glory of eternal dawn, Shines from His smiling face;
> So trusting Him, I follow on, With heart made strong by grace.

> I'll follow Him with rejoicing, With rejoicing, rejoicing;
> I know He safely will lead me, To my eternal home.[33]

On the way to that home, always avoiding the tempting escapism that diverts from present Kingdom responsibility, Christians join with joy in affirming:

> Let us labor for the Master from the dawn till setting sun,
> Let us talk of all His wondrous love and care;
> Then when all of life is over and our work on earth is done,
> And the roll is called up yonder, I'll be there![34]

As Christians labor and talk for the Master here below, it always should be recalled that the wisdom and power that sustains the faithful church comes from God. Thus, as Martin Luther said long ago:

---

[32] "Pete Meyer's Testimony," in *Vital Christianity* (April, 1994), 21.

[33] "I'll Follow with Rejoicing," in *Worship the Lord* (Anderson, Ind.: Warner Press, 1989), 436, verses 1, 4, and chorus.

[34] "When the Role is Called Up Yonder," in *Worship the Lord* (Anderson, Ind.: Warner Press, 1989), 725, verse 3.

It is not we who can sustain the church, nor was it those who came before us, nor will it be those who come after us. It was, and is, and will be the one who says, "I am with you always, even to the end of time." As it says in Hebrews 13: "Jesus Christ, the same *yesterday, today,* and *forever.*" And in Revelation 1: "Who *was,* and *is,* and *is to come.*" Truly, he is that one, and no one else is, or ever can be.[35]

Psalm 122 is a Hebrew song of pilgrims ascending the hills to the Holy City, Jerusalem. Joy is the dominant emotion as the weary faithful return with gladness to "the place that the Lord your God will choose...as his habitation" (Deut. 12:5). It is the seat of God's justice (Ps. 122:5). The pilgrims pray for peace in this special place (122:6), knowing that the achieving of justice is essential for the presence of peace. They also know that there will be a wonderful end to the long road of life for those who have been faithful in the meantime, faithful to the ways of peace and the divine call to justice. As the beloved Fanny Crosby wrote:

> We are pilgrims looking home,
>   Sad and weary oft' we roam,
>   But we know 'twill all be well in the morning.
> When, our anchor safely cast,
>   Every stormy wave is past,
>   And we gather safe at last in the morning.[36]

In the meantime, in the pilgrim now of the hope for then, we who believe are to remain responsible, bolstered by a buoyant hope. We serve in faith and sing in joy as we are marching to Zion:

---

[35]Martin Luther, as quoted by Alister McGrath, *Spirituality in an Age of Change: Rediscovering the Spirit of the Reformers* (Grand Rapids: Zondervan, 1994), 196.

[36]Verse one of the song "In the Morning" as in *Free Methodist Hymnal* (Winona Lake, Ind.: Free Methodist Publishing House, 1950), 296.

Come, we that love the Lord, And let our joys be known,
Join in a song with sweet accord, Join in a song with
sweet accord,
   And thus surround the throne, And thus surround the
   throne.
We're marching to Zion, Beautiful, beautiful Zion,
   We're marching upward to Zion, The beautiful city of
God.[37]

All properly oriented and disciplined Christian eschatology
finally comes to expression in worship and life.[38] We conclude,
therefore, as Paul concluded in two of his writings. To the church
in Corinth he announced: "Since, then, we have such a hope, we
act with great boldness" (2 Cor. 3:12). In his letter to Rome, following a long and complex theological argument extending
through sixteen chapters, Paul comes to an outburst of affirmation,
joy, and blessing. The final lines share this doxology:

> Now to God who is able to strengthen you according to
> my gospel and the proclamation of Jesus Christ, accord-
> ing to the revelation of the mystery that was kept secret
> for long ages but now is disclosed, and through the
> prophetic writings is made known to all the Gentiles,
> according to the command of the eternal God, to bring
> about the obedience of faith—to the only wise God,
> through Jesus Christ, to whom be the glory forever!
> Amen (Rom. 16:25-27).

---

[37]Verse one and chorus of the song "We're Marching To Zion" by Isaac
Watts and Robert Lowry.
   [38]Geoffrey Wainwright entitles his whole systematic theology *Doxology:
The Praise of God in Worship, Doctrine and Life* (London: Epworth Press, 1980).

268

Matters Worth Exploring

1. Do you feel alone in some wild wilderness of life? Is God in this place with you? What difference does God's presence make in such a place?

2. Are we now living in a time when civilization seems to be crumbling around us? What attitude should Christian believers have about their responsibilities in such a difficult and dangerous time?

3. The "Baby Buster" (Generation X) youth culture of today's United States seems to be characterized by a sense of nothing in life but wilderness—life alone, changing, directionless, hopeless. How can the church minister effectively to such a generation, bringing real hope?

4. Does belief in life after death tempt Christians that you know (maybe even yourself) to deny *life before death*—that is, to keep them (you) from sacrificing worldly security and reputation to resist actively those people, institutions, and traditions that rain injustice and death down on others?

5. Are baptism and the Lord's supper just traditional rituals Christians sometimes do in the church, or are they somehow vital to who Christians are and yet will be as faithful believers?

6. What does it mean for the New Testament to teach that there is "Antichrist," a *plural* and *ever present* reality resisting God's work in the world?

7. Does your heart almost burst with joy as you anticipate the end of the biblical story when every knee shall bow in recognition of Jesus Christ and those who have been faithful in the meantime will enter into the rest and rewards of their dear Savior?

SELECT BIBLIOGRAPHY
Key Books on Christian Eschatology

In the footnotes of this book there appear many published sources in addition to those listed below. This select listing includes only books found most valuable by the author. The intention is to provide the reader with an awareness of key sources for the further study of Christian eschatology.

1. Armerding, Carl and Ward Gasque, eds. 1977. *Dreams, Visions and Oracles*. Baker Book House.
2. Beasley-Murray, George. 1993. *Jesus and the Last Days*. Hendrickson Publishers.
3. Berkhouwer, C. G. 1972. *The Return of Christ*. Eerdmans.
4. Braaten, Carl. 1969. *The Future of God: The Revolutionary Dynamics of Hope*. Harper & Row.
5. Braaten, Carl. 1974. *Eschatology and Ethics*. Augsburg Publishing House.
6. Braaten, Carl. 1977. *The Flaming Center: A Theology of Christian Mission*. Fortress Press.
7. Bright, John. 1953. *The Kingdom of God*. Abingdon Press.
8. Brown, Charles. 1927. *The Hope of His Coming*. Gospel Trumpet Company.
9. Brueggemann, Walter. 1987. *Hope Within History*. John Knox Press.
10. Clouse, Robert, ed. 1977. *The Meaning of the Millennium: Four Views*. InterVarsity Press.
11. Crockett, William, ed. 1996. *Four Views on Hell*. Zondervan.
12. Cullmann, Oscar. 1958. *Immortality of the Soul or Resurrection of the Dead?* Macmillan.

13. Cullmann, Oscar. 1962 rev. ed. *Christ and Time*. SCM Press.
14. Davis, Stephen. 1993. *Risen Indeed: Making Sense of the Resurrection*. Eerdmans.
15. Dodd, C. H. 1936. *The Apostolic Preaching and Its Development*. Hodder and   Stoughton.
16. Dodd, C. H. 1951. *The Coming Christ*. Cambridge University.
17. Dumbrell, William. 1994. *The Search for Order: Biblical Eschatology in Focus*. Baker Book House.
18. Dunning, H. Ray, ed. 1995. *The Second Coming*. Beacon Hill Press of Kansas City.
19. Erickson, Millard. 1977. *Contemporary Options in Eschatology*. Baker Book House.
20. Erickson, Millard. 1996. *How Shall They Be Saved?: The Destiny of Those Who Do Not Hear of Jesus*. Baker Books.
21. Fackre, Gabriel. 1984 ed. *The Christian Story*. Eerdmans.
22. Faupel, D. William. 1996. *The Everlasting Gospel: The Significance of Eschatology in the Development of Pentecostal Thought*. Sheffield Academic Press.
23. Gaulke, Max. 1959. *May Thy Kingdom Come—Now!* Warner Press.
24. Grenz, Stanley. 1992. *The Millennial Maze*. InterVarsity Press.
25. Grenz, Stanley. 1994. *Theology for the Community of God*. Broadman & Holman.
26. Hunt, Boyd. 1993. *Redeemed! Eschatological Redemption and the Kingdom of God*. Broadman & Holman.
27. Jennings, Theodore. 1992. *Loyalty to God: The Apostles' Creed in Life and Liturgy*. Abingdon Press.
28. Kik, J. Marcellus. 1971. *An Eschatology of Victory*. Presbyterian and Reformed.
29. König, Adrio. 1989. *The Eclipse of Christ in Eschatology*.

Eerdmans.
30. Kraus, C. Norman. 1993. *The Community of the Spirit.*
    Herald Press.
31. Kreider, Alan. 1987. *Journey Towards Holiness.* Herald
    Press.
32. Küng, Hans. 1993. *Credo: The Apostles' Creed Explained
    for Today.* Doubleday.
33. Ladd, George Eldon. 1974. *The Presence of the Future.*
    Eerdmans.
34. Ladd, George Eldon. 1993 (rev. ed.). *A Theology of the New
    Testament.* Eerdmans.
35. Land, Steven. 1993. *Pentecostal Spirituality: A Passion for
    the Kingdom.* Sheffield Academic Press.
36. Marshall, I. Howard. 1969. *Kept By the Power of God.*
    Bethany Fellowship.
37. Moltmann, Jürgen. 1967. *Theology of Hope.* SCM Press.
38. Moltmann, Jürgen. 1969. *Religion, Revolution, and the
    Future.* Charles Scribner's Sons.
39. Moltmann, Jürgen. 1975. *The Experiment in Hope.* Fortress
    Press.
40. Moltmann, Jürgen. 1977. *The Church in the Power of the
    Spirit.* Harper & Row.
41. Moltmann, Jürgen. 1993. *The Way of Jesus Christ.* Fortress
    Press.
42. Moltmann, Jürgen. 1996. *The Coming of God: Christian
    Eschatology.* Fortress Press.
43. Mulholland, M. Robert. 1990. *Holy Living in an Unholy
    World: Revelation.* Francis Asbury Press.
44. Niebuhr, H. Richard. 1951. *Christ and Culture.* Harper &
    Row.
45. Oden, Thomas. 1992. *Life in the Spirit.* Harper/Collins.
46. Pannenberg, Wolfhart. 1972. *The Apostles' Creed in the
    Light of Today's Questions.* Westminster Press.

47. Paulien, Jon. 1994. *What the Bible Says About the End-Time*. Review and Herald Publishing Association.
48. Scott, R.B.Y. 1944. *The Relevance of the Prophets*. Macmillan.
49. Snyder, Howard. 1977. *The Community of the King*. InterVarsity.
50. Summers, Ray. 1951. *Worthy Is the Lamb*. Broadman Press.
51. Tiede, David. 1990. *Jesus and the Future*. Cambridge University Press.
52. Travis, Stephen. 1982. *I Believe in the Second Coming of Jesus*. Eerdmans.
53. Wainwright, Geoffrey. 1971. *Eucharist and Eschatology*. Epworth Press.
54. Walls, Jerry. 1992. *Hell: The Logic of Damnation*. University of Notre Dame Press.
55. Wilder, A. N. 1950 (rev. ed.). *Eschatology and Ethics in the Teaching of Jesus*. Harper & Row.
56. Yoder, John Howard. (ed. Michael Cartwright). 1994. *The Royal Priesthood*. Eerdmans.
57. Yoder, John Howard. 2nd ed. 1994. *The Politics of Jesus*. Eerdmans.

INDEX OF SUBJECTS AND PERSONS

Abomination of Desolation, 142

Abraham, 54, 107, 175, 183, 246

Advent, First of Jesus, 187, 193-196

Adventist Tendency, 120

African-American Christianity, 168-169

Age to Come, 18

Allen, C. Leonard, 127

Alsted, Johann, 105

Amillennialism, 101, 108-112, 114

Amos (Hebrew Prophet), 22, 50

Anabaptist tradition, 24, 169, 210

Anderson University, 14, 42-43, 164

Annihilationism, 233-235

Antichrist, 27, 40, 44, 46, 95, 101, 105, 119, 145, 261

Apocalypse, 16, 24

Apocalyptic Literature, 76, 126, 133, 173

Apocalyptic Teachings of Jesus, 124

Apostles' Creed, 31, 85, 120, 170, 200, 203, 206, 220, 224, 227-228, 254-255

Apostolic Foundations, 18, 120, 125

Armageddon, 38, 45-46

Arminianism, 80

Augsburger, Myron, 256

Augustine, 105, 108, 110-112, 203, 247

Aulén, Gustav, 147

Baby Busters, 16, 260

Baptism, 240, 249-250

Barclay, William, 207, 236

Barth, Karl, 97, 110, 181, 238

Barton, Stephen, 197

Bavinck, Herman, 107

Beasley-Murray, George, 139, 141-142

Beast (of Revelation), 43, 54, 101, 119, 174, 253

Bediako, Kwame, 151

Believers' Church Tradition, 112, 117, 147, 149, 210

Bengel, Johann, 40

Berkhof, Hendrikus, 64

Berkhouwer, C. G., 52

Bible, And Holiness, 85

Bible, Authority of, 84, 87

Bible, Integrity of, 61, 76-77

Bible, Interpretation of, 25, 62-68, 84, 87

Blackwelder, Boyce, 111

Blaising, Craig, 63, 107, 144
Bloch, Ernst, 66, 97
Bloesch, Donald, 111, 114, 169, 238-239
Bonhoeffer, Dietrich, 15, 236
Book of Mormon, 96
Boyer, Paul, 23
Braaten, Carl, 20, 23, 92-93, 178
Branch Davidians, 62
Bright, John, 177, 185, 191
Brown, Dale, 85
Brown, Delwin, 9, 208, 256
Bruce, F. F., 86
Brueggemann, Walter, 160, 166, 168, 175, 191
Buber, Martin, 247-248
Bultmann, Rudolf, 73-74, 99, 136, 149, 180
Buttrick, David, 199
Byrum, Russell, 91, 113

Calendar, Human, 19, 40, 47, 50
Callen, Arlene, 3
Callen, Barry, 42-43, 56, 68, 74, 135, 168-169, 199, 204, 232, 246, 255
Calvin, John, 92, 110, 231-232
Calvinism, 78, 80
Canaan Land, 246, 262
Carver, Frank, 52
Celebration, 162, 179, 199, 248-254
Cheap Grace, 236
Childs, Brevard, 86-87, 145
Chiliasm, 100

Christian Humanism, 165
Christmas, 194-196
Christus Victor (Model of Atonement), 147-149
Church, 13, 56, 68, 86-87, 102, 105, 107-109, 139-140, 143-144, 152, 168, 177-182, 203, 209, 213, 241-242, 248, 264
Church of God Movement (Anderson), 41-44, 111, 113
Church of Jesus Christ of Latter-day Saints, 96
Churches of Christ, 113
Clarke, Adam, 103
Clouse, Robert, 45, 100
Cold War, 16
Collins, Kenneth, 117
Common Market, 38
Cone, James, 66, 168-169
Covenant, Conditional, 78
Crockett, William, 237
Crosby, Fanny, 116, 267
Crucifixion of Jesus, 23
Crusades, 104
Cullmann, Oscar, 72, 137, 225
Cyberspace, 37

Daniel, Book of, 40, 42, 54, 76, 93, 126, 176
Darby, John Nelson, 106, 143
Davis, Stephen, 198
Dayton, Donald, 44, 112
Day of the Lord, 51, 205
Dead Sea Scrolls, 46
Death, 33, 56, 167-169, 225-226,

228-229, 253, 255

Delay of Lord's Return, 35, 64-65, 114, 118, 125, 128-129, 195, 258-259

Demons, 157, 168

Discipleship, 12-13, 18-19, 48-51, 83, 92, 109, 117, 128, 140-141, 169, 197, 207, 211, 227

Dispensationalism, 13, 41, 45, 63, 82, 84, 87, 106-108, 137, 143-144, 146, 191

Divining the Future, 49

Dodd, C. H., 17, 72, 133, 136, 140

Doomsday Science, 46

Dragon (of Revelation), 174

Dumbrell, William, 258

Dunning, H. Ray, 52, 63, 72, 115, 117-118, 127, 140, 211, 219

Dyrness, William, 151

Easter, 187-188, 194, 198, 200, 207, 265

Ecological Apocalypse, 16

Edwards, Jonathan, 71, 102

Enlightenment Mentality, 68, 74-75, 85, 96, 104, 136, 180, 203, 237

Erickson, Millard, 111, 235

Escapism, 22, 38, 55, 69, 96, 98-99, 115, 133, 171

Eschatological "Enthusiasm," 55, 67

Eschatological Kerygma, 17

Eschatological Language, 64, 73-75

Eschatology, 9, 11-12, 21-24, 26, 53, 55, 69, 73-74, 82, 97, 117, 119, 124, 134, 137, 139, 156, 172-173, 177

Essenes, 126, 132

Esther, Book of, 93

Eternal Life, 13, 73, 131, 157, 168, 207, 226, 230, 242, 256

Eternal Security, 77-81

Ethnic Genocide, 16

Eucharist, 253

European Community (Common Market), 37, 118

Evans, James, Jr., 168

Evil, 204, 235, 265

Exodus, 149, 194, 246, 262

Fackre, Gabriel, 205, 225, 236-239, 247, 257

Faith, 34, 52, 149, 160, 175, 193, 195, 210, 221, 246

Faithfulness of God, 52-56, 77-81, 115, 135, 183, 226

Fall of Humanity, 15, 34, 54

Faupel, William, 44

Feminist Perspective, 169

Finger, Thomas, 159, 234

Fiorenza, Francis Schussler, 87

Flying Saucers, 45

Ford, Mary, 85

Foretellers, 49-50

Forthtellers, 50

Fuller, R. H., 136-137

Future Shock, 22

Gaither, Gloria, 224
Gaither, William, 224
Gaulke, Max, 47
Generation X, 16, 260
George, Timothy, 38
Gnostic Tendency, 120, 155, 169
González, Justo, 67, 150, 169, 173, 214
Gospel Trumpet, 43
Grace, 78, 103, 106, 108-110 232, 251
"Great Disappointment," 41, 47
Greek Philosophy, 158-160, 180, 234
Grenz, Stanley, 85, 111, 144, 156, 208-209, 229, 239
Grider, J. Kenneth, 107, 113, 234
Gulf War, 38, 46
Gutiérrez, Gustavo, 66

Hades, 174, 255, 265
Hahn, Roger, 118
Hahn, Todd, 260
Hanukkah, 218, 243
Hartshorne, Charles, 226
Hauerwas, Stanley, 185, 210, 259
Heaven, 34, 75, 96, 115, 152, 155, 230, 233-234, 238-239, 240-242, 265
Hebrews, Book of, 181
Hebrew Scriptures, 53, 82, 119, 149, 160, 169, 183
Hebrew Tradition, 155-160, 180, 189-190, 245
Hell, 34, 75, 132, 229, 233-234, 228-239

Henry, Matthew, 103
History, Essential Context, 155-186, 180
Hitler, 93
Holiness, 238
Holiness and Biblical Interpretation, 85
Holiness and Social Mission, 162, 165, 207, 210
Holy Spirit, 9, 13, 17-18, 25, 56, 67, 83-88, 102, 132, 139, 167, 184, 188, 200-202, 209, 211-215, 248, 264
Hope, 14, 16, 25, 34, 53, 66, 94, 96, 98, 100, 109, 116, 121, 137, 157, 161, 165-166, 168, 178, 193, 203, 205, 209, 226, 238, 248, 257, 261,
Hoskins, Steven, 68
Hughes, Richard, 113
Humanism, 163-164
Hunt, Boyd, 139, 176, 229, 258
Hunter, A. M., 217
Hussein, Saddam, 46

Images of Christian Hope, 217-243
Immortality, 120, 132, 155, 225-226, 234
Inquisition, 47
International Theological Commission (RCC), 11
Iran, 118
Iraq, 118
Irenaeus, 18

Islam, 40

Israel, 9, 41, 54, 56, 78, 86-87, 98, 102, 107, 119, 143, 146, 175, 192

Jennings, Theodore, 151, 171, 201, 206, 254, 263

Jeremiah, 166-167, 172

Jerusalem, Destruction, 65, 142, 145, 189-191

Jerusalem, New, 181, 193, 241, 253, 266

Jesus Christ, 9, 12-13, 15, 17-18, 23-25, 55, 81-83, 87, 92, 113, 123-153, 165, 167, 170-171, 184, 192, 202, 215, 222

Jews, 10, 65, 86, 93, 105-107, 123, 155-156, 158

Joachim of Fiore, 100-101

John, Gospel of, 138, 140, 207

John the Baptist, 55

Johnson, Stephen, 117

Jones, Kenneth, 111

Josephus, Flavius, 143

Journey, Image of Christian Life, 246-263

Judgment, 131-132, 143, 163, 170, 223, 228-229, 254-255

Julius Caesar, 44

Justice, 161, 168, 170-171, 177, 190-192, 196, 232, 267

Kennedy, John F., 66

Khamenei, Ayatollah, 46

Kik, J. Marcellus, 104

Kingdom of God, 20, 24-25, 27, 57, 81, 102, 109-110, 118, 123-124, 126-128, 134-140, 144, 149-150, 157, 170, 175, 177, 242

Kinnamon, Michael, 179-180

König, Adrio, 26, 82-83, 156, 233, 261

Koresh, David, 62

Kreider, Alan, 140, 210, 213, 242

Küng, Hans, 126, 220, 242

Kuwait, 46

Kraus, C. Norman, 68-69, 83, 86, 147, 170-171, 202, 213

Ladd, George Eldon, 51, 100, 135, 137-138, 145, 155, 177, 217

Language, Religious, 73-75, 218-219

Larkin, Clarence, 106

LaSor, William Sanford, 21, 76

Last Days, 17, 25, 52, 57, 111, 118-119, 137, 139, 146, 220

Last Judgment, Parable of, 221, 227-228, 231

Last Reformation, 44

Latter Rain, 44

Laughter, 199-200

Lewis, C. S., 235

Liberation of the Oppressed and Sinful, 11, 66-67, 110, 112, 147-148, 150-151, 160, 163, 167-168, 170, 254

Life After Death, 132

Lindsey, Hal, 37, 45, 48, 63, 98, 143

Linn, Otto, 43, 111
Lints, Richard, 87
Lodahl, Michael, 55, 67, 125, 226
Long, Thomas, 35, 38, 168
Lord's Prayer, 141, 242
Lord's Supper, 67
Love of God, 239-240
Luther, Martin, 95, 117, 266-267
Lyon, Robert, 68
McClendon, James,
McCutcheon, Lillie, 111
McGrath, Alister, 267
Maddox, Randy, 53, 137
Malachi, 53
Mañana Concept, 173
Manning, Brennan, 56-57
Mark, Gospel of, 197
Mark of the Beast, 27
Marsden, George, 101
Marshall, I. Howard, 80
Martyr, Justin, 159
Marx, Karl, 22, 96
Marxism, 97, 171
Mary, Pregnancy of, 128, 184, 194, 202
Massey, James Earl, 169
Matthew, Gospel of, 124-132
Meeter, H. Henry, 232
Menorah, 218
Merton, Thomas, 260-261
Messianic Age, 17-18
Meyer, Louis (Pete), 265-266
Migliore, Daniel, 98, 219-220, 227
Millennium, 23, 70-71, 93, 100, 102, 108, 114, 129, 144, 173-175, 213, 228
Millennial Models, 100-111
Miller, William, 40-41
Miller, William Charles, 63
Mirage, Image of, 263
Miranda, J. P., 168
Mission of God's People, 11, 13, 16
Mojtabai, A. G., 116
Moltmann, Jürgen, 9, 12, 23, 31-32, 65-66, 88, 94, 139, 155, 157, 171, 178, 200-201, 209, 211, 236-237, 246, 256-257
Montanism, 39, 95
Moody, Dale, 262
Mulholland, M. Robert, 174, 251, 253
Mussolini, Benito, 44

Napier, B. D., 51
Naylor, Charles, 262
Need To Be Ready, 130
Nero, Emperor, 40
New Age in Christ, 17, 81, 126, 131, 136, 139, 146, 187, 202
New Age movement, 228
New Creation in Christ, 148, 163, 208, 222, 252
New Heaven and Earth, 227, 263-264
New Israel, 17
Newbigin, Lesslie, 210
Nicene Creed (381 A.D.), 223, 227

Niebuhr, H. Richard, 66-67
Niebuhr, Reinhold, 157, 227
Nixon, Richard, 66
Noll, Mark, 38
Nostradamus, 47-48
Nuclear Weapons, 37, 39, 45-47, 97, 116, 198

Oden, Thomas, 19, 69, 134, 146, 172, 221, 255
Olivet Discourse of Jesus, 65, 125, 142
Once in Grace, Always in Grace, 77-81
Origen, 236

Pannenberg, Wolfhart, 9, 120-121, 181, 209, 253
Parousia, 73, 131, 136, 252, 262
Passover, 250
Parables of Jesus
    Master's Household,
    Talents,
    Wise and Foolish Maidens,
Paul, Teaching of, 107, 115-116, 125, 146-147, 268
Paulien, Jon, 41, 130
Pentecost, 13, 57, 73, 86, 92, 109, 139, 187, 200, 202, 210, 213, 243, 252
Pentecostalism, 43
Perseverance of the Saints, 13, 77-81, 89
Peters, Ted, 188
Phan, Peter, 11

Pharisees, 126-127, 132
Pickett, L. L., 71-72
Pietist Tradition, 24, 85
Pink, Arthur, 79
Pinnock, Clark, 9, 61, 70, 84, 173, 187, 212, 215, 229, 232, 234
Polycarp, 94
Pope of Rome, 39-40, 95
Postmillennialism, 71, 101-104, 112, 114
Post-Tribulation, 25
Predestination, 67, 78, 80, 231-232, 239
Prediction, 34, 37, 44-45, 48-50, 57, 76-77, 85, 87
Premillennialism, 13, 41, 44, 71, 101, 104-106, 111-113, 228
Presbyterian Church (U.S.A.), 10
Pre-Tribulation, 25
Prevenient Grace, 232
Prophecy, 32-33, 38, 42, 46, 48-52, 70, 72-73, 256
Prophetic Pilgrims, 58
Protestant Reformation, 40, 169
Providence,
Psalm 122, 267
Psalm 137, 189-193
Puritans, 102, 106
Purgatory, 13, 229

Questions In Eschatology, 11

Rahner, Karl, 219
Rapture, 23, 107
Raser, Harold, 71

Rauschenbusch, Walter, 103

Remembering, Basis of Hope, 194- 195

Repentance, 18, 135

Resurrection, General, 132, 139, 143, 181, 224-228

Resurrection of Jesus, 17, 23, 25-27, 55, 73, 94, 109, 124, 132, 139, 147-152, 161, 180-181, 188, 197-199, 211, 224

Resurrection of Lazarus, 140

Resurrection Life of Christians, 57, 119, 121, 138, 140, 207, 213, 249

Revelation, Book of, 24, 40, 42-43, 51-52, 54, 62, 70, 76, 93-94, 101, 114, 116, 126, 129, 133-134, 174, 257-258

Revelation, Nature of, 74

Rhodes, Schuyler, 245

Ritschl, Albrecht, 104, 136

Roman Catholic Church, 43, 47, 95, 229

Roman Empire, Fall of, 40, 44, 203, 247

Russia, 38-39, 118

Ryrie, Charles, 137

Sacrament, 251

Sadducees, 126, 132

Sale-Harrison, Leonard, 44

Salvation, 170, 173

Satan, 39, 46, 105, 108-109, 114, 129-130, 148, 167, 197, 236, 238, 262

Schleiermacher, Friedrich, 104

Schwarz, R. W., 42

Schweitzer, Albert, 124, 136

Schweizer, Eduard, 133

Scofield Reference Bible, 106, 143

Scott, R. B. Y., 49

Second Coming of Jesus, 11, 15, 18, 23, 25-26, 33, 35, 38, 40-41, 43-44, 47, 74, 81-82, 92, 96, 99, 103, 105, 109, 114, 129, 131, 178, 222-224

Sectism, 43

Secularism, 11, 23, 96, 114, 157, 164, 190, 192

Seven Seals, 62

Seventh-day Adventist Church, 41-42

Shalom, 179, 229, 248

Shank, Robert, 78-79

Sheol, 132

Shifting Systems of Expectation, 25, 91-122

Signs of the Times, 21, 46, 52, 72, 81, 118-119, 145, 147

Skepticism, 36

Smith, F. G., 111, 202, 265

Smith, Joseph, 96

Smith, Uriah, 42

Snyder, Howard, 157, 182, 210

Social Responsibility, 156

Son of Man (Jesus), 127

Soothsayer, 50

Soul, 120, 132, 155, 160-162, 170, 225-226, 234

Speaking in Tongues, 43
Speculation, 31-59, 115, 119
Stafford, Gilbert, 123
Stanley, John, 43, 111
Staples, Rob, 75
State of Israel, 27, 33, 38, 45, 82, 102, 106-108, 137, 143, 146, 191
Stewart, James, 124
Stookey, Laurence, 171
Strauss, David Friedrich, 180
Strong, Marie, 111
Stott, John, 199
Suffering Servant (Jesus), 127
Summers, Ray, 114
Sylvester II, Pope, 39

Theology of Hope, 9, 66, 209
Thorsen, Donald, 84
Tiede, David, 134-135
Tillich, Paul, 99-100, 149
Time, Nature of, 69-70, 157
Timing, Divine, 18-19
Titus (Roman), 142
Torah, 53, 132
Travis, Stephen, 115, 235
Tribulation, 23, 44, 98, 101, 116, 119, 142-143
Trueblood, David Elton, 20, 204
Tuttle, Robert, Jr., 163
Two-Peoples Theory, 107

UFOs (see flying saucers)
Universalism, 234-237, 239
Utopian Movements, 94-100

Verhaagen, David, 260
Virginal Conception of Jesus, 184
Vision, Living From and Toward, 172-177
Visser't Hooft, W. A., 33
Vulnerability, Divine, 204-205

Wainwright, Geoffery, 249, 268
Waiting, 128-130, 211
Walls, Jerry, 234, 238
Walvoord, John, 46
"War of the Worlds," 36
Warner, Daniel S., 41-43, 214
Warren, Barney, 141, 214
Watts, Issac, 103, 262, 268
Weaver, J. Denny, 112, 147, 149
Weiss, Johannes, 124, 136-137
Wells, David, 234
Wells, Herbert George, 36
Wesley, Charles, 88
Wesley, John, 13-14, 36-37, 40, 67, 103, 117, 137, 148, 163, 210, 232, 234, 239
Wesleyan/Holiness Tradition, 24, 43, 55, 64, 67, 74, 116, 237
Wesleyan Hermeneutic of Scripture, 84, 103
Whitehead, Alfred North, 226
Whitelaw, David, 68
Wilderness, 258-263
Willimon, William, 185, 210, 259
Wilson, Marvin, 75-76, 156, 161-162
Wood, Laurence, 84
World Trade Organization, 37

Worship As Eschatological Interlude, 179, 253
Wright, Wendy, 129

Yoder, John Howard, 124, 147,
172, 181, 252

Zealots, 126
Zion, 267-268
Zionism, 191
Zoba, Wendy Murray, 38

Callen draws on a wide range of scholarship from right to left in order to survey with care the options on each of the traditional eschatological topics. His own preferences are irenically stated and are guided by a concern for present Christian discipleship rooted in a Wesleyan emphasis on God's love for all people. Lay persons and ministers in many demoninations can be aided by this book as they seek to clarify their own Christian hope and to understand its meaning for their present lives. I respect and appreciate Dr. Callen's important work.

John B. Cobb, Jr. Professor of Theology Emeritus
Claremont School of Theology

Finally! Here is a responsible book in a most crucial area. Pastors and Christian educators increasingly are being called on to address difficult issues in concise and understandable ways. Many subjects surrounding "end times" are especially prominent as the new millennium approaches. Dr. Callen's Faithful in the Meantime fills the vacuum in a timely and competent way. It clarifies how a biblical understanding of "eschatology" informs Kingdom living for today's church. Every pastor's heart will be warmed and every library enriched. Especially because of the Study Guide that is available at no additional cost, this book is readily usable in local church settings.

Jeanette Flynn, Director, Church and Ministry Service,
Church of God (Anderson)

Professor Callen develops his discussion of eschatology in faithfulness to both Scripture and Wesleyan theology. He avoids the twin pitfalls that either abandon a realistic divine consummation of history or is preoccupied with speculation about end-time events that properly rejects Dispensationalism as antiethical to both the New Testament and Wesleyuan biblical and theological presuppositions.

H. Ray Dunning, Professor of Theology Emeritus
Trevecca Nazarene University

I find this work a fascinating and imaginative treatment of endtime issues, Barry Callen offers here a wide-ranging survey of the best of eschatological reflection across the wealth of Christian traditions, and also offers a sobering warning to the doomsayers and soothsayers, whose numbers will undoubtedly increase as we near the end of the millennium. He may not have given us the "last" word on "last things," but he surely has given us a promising and invigorating one!

Michael E. Lodahl, Professor of Theology
Northwest Nazarene College